The Labour Party
and British Society
1880–2005

"This highly readable history of Labour over the past century and a quarter provides a clear and stimulating interpretation of the roots of New Labour in a party which was always more committed to social reform than to socialism and which succeeded with the electorate only when it took seriously the general public's lack of interest in and suspicion of ideology. Labour was always a coalition of left and right, socialists and pragmatists, the former preferring the moral purity of perpetual opposition and the latter seeking the power of government to introduce necessary social reforms. Only twice before 1997 did Labour win a convincing victory at the polls, in 1945 and 1966. Too often when in office it tore itself apart with arguments about personalities and policies as Labour ministers confronted the intractable problems of actually governing the country.

Throughout this admirable study the importance of individuals is recognised but the constraints within which they worked are stressed. Not only did policy need to be tempered to the economic climate (and Labour ministries were singularly unlucky with this) but programmes had to be rethought in response to the changing nature of society and to meet the expectations of the public.

The mood of post-war Britain was captured by Atlee in 1945 and he succeeded until the basic reforms on which there was general agreement had been accomplished; but after 1964 Wilson's attempts to build on the themes of modernisation and technology did not convince his party of the need to abandon old shibboleths and bases of support. The Thatcher reforms of the 1980s and prolonged years of opposition finally gave Tony Blair in 1997 the unprecedented opportunity to respond in unusually favourable economic circumstances to those social changes which had been transforming British society since the 1960s – the decline of manual labour, the increasing irrelevance of class and the collapse of socialism – to lead a united party hungry for power to three successive electoral victories with large working majorities. Those who do not welcome New Labour as well as those who do will find that this history of the rise and fall and transformation of Labour both enlarges their knowledge and enriches their understanding."

EDWARD ROYLE
Emeritus Professor in the Department of History
University of York

The Labour Party
and British Society
1880–2005
David Rubinstein

sussex
ACADEMIC
PRESS

Brighton • *Portland*

2 4 6 8 10 9 7 5 3 1

First published 2006 in Great Britain by
SUSSEX ACADEMIC PRESS
PO Box 2950
Brighton BN2 5SP

and in the United States of America by
SUSSEX ACADEMIC PRESS
920 NE 58th Ave   Suite 300
Portland, Oregon 97213–3786

British Library Cataloguing in Publication Data
A CIP catalogue record for this book is available from the British Library.

Library of Congress Cataloging-in-Publication Data
Rubinstein, David.
  The labour party and British Society : 1880–2005 / by
  David Rubinstein.
    p. cm.
  Includes bibliographical references and index.
  ISBN 1-84519-055-6 (h/c : alk. paper) —
    ISBN 1-84519-056-4 (p/b : alk. paper)
  1. Labour Party (Great Britain)—History. 2. Great
Britain—Politics and government. 3. Great Britain—
Economic conditions. 4. Great Britain—Social conditions.
I. Title.

JN1129.L32R7 2006
324.24107—dc22

2005017693

Typeset and designed by G&G Editorial, Brighton & Eastbourne
Printed by TJ International, Padstow, Cornwall
This book is printed on acid-free paper.

CONTENTS

PREFACE

The Labour Party has always been controversial. Historians have often been protagonists of particular points of view. They have adopted a variety of different approaches: celebration of the "forward march of Labour", anger or condemnation at its alleged lack of zeal for sweeping reforms, support for particular factions or groups, justification or castigation of the political trajectories of particular personalities. Taking sides has been inevitable since historians and autobiographers have themselves often been participants in Labour politics.

More recently historians have tended to see the party as an agent of conservatism or social stability. Whatever line they have pursued their work has often revealed as much about their own outlook as about the Labour Party. But there has also been a trend for historical writing about the party to try to explain rather than advocate particular policies. This book is intended as a contribution to historical understanding rather than an essay in awarding or subtracting points for the party's success or failure in conforming to any particular ideology or point of view.

I have written a narrative history which discusses the Labour Party against the background of the economic and social context in which it has moved throughout its existence. It is convenient to divide Labour history before 1997 into two periods. Prior to the 1950s one can discern four phases, the first being that of infancy and growth which ended with the general election of 1918. Second came the years of steady progress which ended abruptly with electoral catastrophe in 1931. There followed a short but turbulent phase when the Labour vote, though substantial, seemed destined to remain insufficient to form a majority government. This in turn ended with the formation of a wartime coalition in 1940 in which Labour members were prominently placed, and the triumphant election victory which allowed the first Labour majority government to assume office in 1945 and to remain there until 1951.

Between 1951 and 1997 Conservative governments dominated the political structure of the country. Only in 1966 did Labour win a convincing election victory and the party had by this time no larger ally as the Liberals had been in 1906. Much of the period was characterized by internal Labour dissension. The thirteen Conservative years between 1951 and 1964 were disastrous for Labour and the eighteen between 1979 and 1997 appeared to threaten its very existence, especially in 1981–2 when it lost a number of prominent members to the new Social Democratic Party.

The death of John Smith in 1994 was followed by the election of Tony Blair as party leader and with him the advent of a "New" Labour Party which won historic victories in 1997 and 2001 and a third, less convincingly, in 2005. The role of Blair and his entourage in transforming the party's aims and actions has not yet been definitively analyzed, inevitably in the case of a process which is still unfolding. There is evidence to suggest that the Labour Party after 1994 accepted the explicit reality of the position which it had occupied intermittently since its birth as a party of the centre. The Blair "revolution" on this reading was a public recognition of what already existed. There is stronger evidence, however, to support the contention that the party followed a new path under Blair and was primarily concerned to promote business and enterprise rather than trade unions and the working class. New Labour in this interpretation really was new and the old, ambiguous Labour Party was buried. It was changing economic and social circumstances which were primarily responsible for the changes in the party, but they should not be allowed to obscure the elements of continuity before and after 1994.

From its inception in 1900 until the 1980s the party contained a relatively large though not united body of socialists which sought to push it leftwards, but whose influence was never as strong as they hoped and the sensation-seeking media claimed to fear. Party leaders seldom promoted sweeping socialist measures as a means of attracting more votes at elections, since, as Roy Jenkins pointed out in 1964, at these times "the moderate section ... almost always triumphs".[i] Periods in opposition, though deeply unwelcome, have given Labour Party leaders the opportunity to reheat lukewarm convictions and renew links with activists, even to advocate left-wing causes. In government, parties of the political left or centre-left quickly realize that there are firm and narrow limits on the possible, limits imposed by the existing holders of power, the media, foreign nations and the electorate's fitful and languid interest in the political process. Hence such parties tend in office to edge forward with reforms in a manner which is intended to placate or disarm their opponents without angering their supporters. Activists are inclined almost inevitably to treat this behaviour as timorous and even treacherous.

Political scientists in Britain have often treated political parties and their leaders as relatively free agents. This view can be helpful since it reminds us that individuals make a huge impact on the political process. Sidney Webb, an influential figure in the early Labour Party, wrote in 1889: "Though our decisions are moulded by the circumstances of the time and the environment at least roughhews our ends, shape them as we will, yet each generation decides for itself."[2] Acts of parliament were not passed without legislators, he observed, nor municipal libraries erected without town councillors. Students of the Labour Party's history, of the strong leadership of Ramsay MacDonald, Hugh Gaitskell and Tony Blair, the impact of the left-wing dissidents Aneurin Bevan and Tony Benn, can be in no doubt about the importance of individuals in history.

But Webb was also well aware, as he wrote in the same place, that "we move with less resistance with the stream than against it". Individuals like institutions live in the context of their times and contexts change. The Labour Party has tried to represent the aspirations of the bulk of an electorate whose composition has altered, especially since the 1960s. Moreover, the alienation of much of the Labour-voting electorate from the political process has deepened over the years and in such circumstances it has been relatively easy for the media and political opponents to make plausible accusations that the party has acted in ways contrary to the national interest. Labour Party leaders have preferred to disappoint their activists rather than jeopardize their chance of elected office and, for most of the party's history, the support of conservative trade union leaders with their treasure chests and bloc votes. Leading politicians in progressive parties have tended to regard political conviction as an unnecessary luxury, and as their left wings have no other credible political home it is the left which can most safely be ignored or combated.

Kingsley Martin pointed out nearly sixty years ago: "A political party must be based on a desire for power. Its tactics must flow from a realistic analysis of the way to achieve power."[3] Prominent left-wingers in the Labour Party when faced with the prospects and pressures of party or elected office have generally moved towards the political centre. Although Labour governments have enacted important reforms their room for manoeuvre has usually been far more limited than they fondly supposed in opposition. It is not a glorious story but it is apparently an inevitable one, whatever the ostensible policies of particular individuals.

Britain, like other countries with representative forms of government, has gradually become increasingly democratic. The word is not used here in the media sense of an overnight transformation from autocracy to elected "democracy", but in terms of advancing with public opinion, however it is measured, and no further. The right-wing views of tabloid newspapers may, as is sometimes alleged, be unrepresentative of the population at large, but such papers continue to be widely purchased and read. The burden of proof appears to rest with those who claim that the outlook of the mass circulation press is not shared by the bulk of its readers. Voters who seek sweeping political change have never been more than a minority, usually a small minority. That is why the Labour Party in its search for elected office has always been gradualist and cautious. That is why its leaders and their allies have almost always been moderates, no matter how extreme the views of some of them may have been in the passion and irresponsibility of youth. This is the way that political parties operate in representative electoral systems, not only in Britain but in continental countries whose history shows much more similarity to the British experience than is often supposed. The essential argument of this book is that centre-left and left-wing politicians reflect their society more than they shape it. Nations change, in peacetime at least, more because of economic and social developments than because of the conscious actions of politicians. The Labour Party, since 1918 one of Britain''s leading political institutions, has been both cherished and reviled, but its policies have altered primarily in response to the transformation of the country's economy and society. The pages which follow seek to substantiate these claims.

ACKNOWLEDGEMENTS

This book has been written in unusual circumstances following serious illness. I am particularly grateful to those people who have sustained me during this period. The most important is Ann Holt, to whom I am married and without whose support the book could not have been written. I have thanked her in written acknowledgements many times over many years but this time her help has been something special and far beyond anything I had any right to expect. I hope that she knows how grateful I am.

The Nuffield Foundation awarded me a small grant in the social sciences when I was well and stood by me in illness. They have done even more for my morale than my pocket and I gratefully acknowledge their assistance. David Martin of the University of Sheffield, former student, then colleague and for many years a friend, has helped me by suggesting sources, advising me in countless ways and reading an early draft. I of course accept full responsibility for all errors and omissions, but I hope that David will not be embarrassed by his association with the book. My publisher, Tony Grahame, has been extremely helpful above all in the interest and support which he has demonstrated from the start of our association. I also thank my friend Nick Tucker, with whom I have discussed the Labour Party for more than forty years and who, despite or because of our frequent disagreements, has taught me a great deal about this as about other subjects. Like all academics I learned a great deal from the generations of students whom I taught, in my case labour history. More impersonally I am grateful for the assistance which I have received from librarians and archivists in York, Leeds, Manchester and London.

The brevity of this note is in inverse proportion to my indebtedness to the persons concerned.

DAVID RUBINSTEIN
YORK, MAY 2005

The Labour Party
and British Society
1880–2005

I THE BACKGROUND

1880–1900

The formation of the Labour Party in 1900, originally as the Labour Representation Committee, was an event which had long been sought by many socialists and trade unionists. The founding of the party, however, was more significant in the eyes of posterity than of contemporaries.

Britain in the later nineteenth century was a grossly unequal society. Town houses of the aristocracy could cost hundreds of thousand of pounds and vast sums were spent on the London "season". Writing in 1909 Lady St Helier recalled the shock which was caused, probably in the 1860s, by the rumoured expenditure of £1,000 on floral decorations for a London ball. "That sum, and double, is often spent nowadays in a single night on one entertainment; and the luxury of dinners and extravagant menus make the expenditure of those days seem a mere bagatelle."[1]

By contrast Charles Booth in his study of East London published in 1889 concluded that the standard wages of regularly employed workmen other than skilled artisans ranged from 22s. to 30s. per week. Most families which enjoyed this level of income, he wrote, were not among the 35.2 per cent of the population who lived in poverty in that part of London. Seebohm Rowntree in another and more detailed survey of poverty calculated that in 1899 the average male worker in York earned 24 shillings a week, male heads of families about 27 shillings and sixpence. Women workers earned less than half as much as men. Housing conditions were poor even by the standards of the day and by later criteria were abysmal. Rowntree found that only 12 per cent of the working-class population of York lived in what he termed "comfortable and sanitary houses"[2] and that nearly two-thirds of all the homes in the town had no more than two bedrooms. Few working-class families possessed a fixed bath and not all the 12 per cent who lived in comfort had a water closet. Where it existed it was not in the house itself but situated separately in the yard. These conditions prevailed in what Rowntree thought was a typical provincial town in economically prosperous times. He concluded that 27.84 per cent of York's population, 43.4 per cent of the wage-earning class, lived in poverty.

What mattered more to most of the working class than absolute income levels, however, was the trend of wages. According to the economic historian Peter Mathias, "in the crucial period from 1860 to 1900 the gain in real wages of the average urban worker was probably of the order of 60 per cent or more – even allowing for unemployment". The rise in incomes may in some cases have been too slow to notice but changes in patterns of consumption were more easily discerned. Mathias points out that the consumption of tea and sugar per head doubled between 1860 and 1910. Hamish Fraser chronicles in his *Coming of the Mass Market* the spread in the later nineteenth century of firms which remain household names, department stores, multiple shops and co-operatives. Membership of co-operative societies rose from 554,000 in 1880 to 1,707,000 in 1900. "Rising living standards among the working class", Fraser writes, "produced a demand for relatively cheap goods . . . A more self-confident working class was demanding better quality food, free from adulteration, than had previously been served up to them and this the multiples and the co-operatives offered."[3]

Working-class institutions grew steadily in the last quarter of the nineteenth century. By 1901 building societies had enabled an estimated 250,000 persons, most of whom belonged to the working class, to buy their own houses. In 1905 friendly societies offered to their six million members sickness pay, old age pensions, funeral benefits and other facilities. Trade unions had about two million members in 1900. This was probably no more than one in four adult male workers but membership had risen steadily in the past decade.

We are rightly struck by the fact that small-scale enterprises continued into the twentieth century and by the diversity and divisions within the working class. Sidney Pollard, writing of Sheffield, the home of the "little mester", makes clear that in 1890 "[t]he typical Sheffield firm was still the family concern", but subsequently "expansion and amalgamation greatly increased the average size of existing firms".[4] As the size of firm increased so did the potential for trade union growth and united action of the workforce, though actual progress was slow and uneven in most trades.

Mass entertainment was an important consequence of, among other things, increasing working-class prosperity. Asa Briggs suggests the importance of the date 1896 in the expansion of the entertainment industry. It was the year of the founding of the *Daily Mail,* of Marconi's first British patent for wireless technology and of the showing of the first motion picture in London. "The economic conditions for the development of a mass entertainment industry were all there in 1896."[5] There were five such conditions, Briggs writes: the growth of the urban population, rise in real incomes, an increase of leisure, improvement in urban public transport and the initial application of technology.

These features even in their early stages had implications for working people. The most important development in working-class entertainment in the late nineteenth century was professional football. Although an important motive in the establishment of football clubs was the desire of employers or churches to provide healthy exercise for the working class, the sport soon outgrew its paternalistic origins. The two Sheffield clubs played each other in a match in 1891 before a crowd of 23,000. The local newspaper commented: "the day might almost be looked on as a general holiday, for although the shops kept open, a great many of the workshops were closed for the day, while others threw the band off at dinner time."[6] Fifty thousand people saw Scotland beat England in 1896 and in 1901 over 110,000, almost all working men, attended the cup final at Crystal Palace. Florence Bell in her study of the iron workers of Middlesbrough and their families carried out early in the twentieth century wrote that thousands of spectators watched football, including a man earning 36 shillings a week, 17 of which were used to visit "a town some distance off, in cold, unfavourable weather, to see a football match". Writing at almost the same time Arthur Shadwell commented: "In all the larger industrial towns in the Midlands and the North games are played every Saturday during the season, at which from 10,000 to 20,000 spectators are present, consisting almost entirely of men and lads out of the factories, works and mines."[7] The growth of real wages and the gradual introduction of a shorter working week played an obvious part in this development.

Football, it was hoped by optimistic writers, did something to bring social classes together. Political developments followed a more complicated pattern but they also helped to make the national life more representative of the male population as a whole. Reform acts in 1867 and 1884 enfranchised many adult working men, though registration requirements and other restrictions meant that fewer of them enjoyed the parliamentary vote than was formerly supposed. Voting was by secret ballot from 1872 and the Elementary Education Act of 1870, supplemented by further legislation in 1876 and 1880, established a framework for universal compulsory elementary education. (At the end of the nineteenth century and beyond, however, national compulsion stopped at age 12; local education authorities could extend the period of schooling in their areas by passing by-laws.) Trade unions were given, or so it was thought, legal freedom by acts in 1871 and 1875.

The growing prosperity of the working class and its tentative moves towards unification assisted the desire for independent working-class politics. At the same time the new importance of the working-class voter brought trade unionists and the Liberal Party into closer contact and created a class of Liberal–Labour, or Lib–Lab politicians. The Liberals enjoyed mass support from the working class and W. E. Gladstone, their leader, was a popular hero. The young Arthur Henderson, who within a dozen years was to be a Labour MP and an important figure in the new party, was described by his early biographer Mary Agnes Hamilton as listening in "rapt attention" to the Grand Old Man speaking in Newcastle in 1891. "For the young Radicals of Tyneside," she wrote, "Gladstone was not only a hero: he was the hero." Frederick Rogers, the bookbinder who was to be the first chair of the Labour Representation Committee, had heard Gladstone speak in 1871 in the open air in south London. "I was only conscious", he wrote over forty years later, "of the presence of a great human personality under whose spell I was, and from whom I could in no way escape. The magic of sound was in the wonderful voice, and if the things he said were unintelligible to me, the voice brought with it something of inspiration and of uplifting power."[8]

Gladstone's personality and the Liberal Party's claim to stand for freedom and equality of opportunity secured the loyalty of large numbers of working men. But for some of their leaders there were more self-interested reasons to support the Liberals. Links between working men and the Liberal Party could lead to election to school boards, boards of poor law guardians and the new local government councils formed in the 1880s and '90s. A few working men, especially coal miners, could also hope to be elected to parliament. Two miners were returned as early as 1874, three working men in 1880 and as many as eleven in 1885. Harry Snell, a secularist and socialist who lived through the period, remembered not only Gladstone's unprecedented influence on trade unionists but the material benefits which seemed attainable through loyalty to Gladstone and the Liberal Party.

> [T]he effect of the appointment of [the trade unionist] Henry Broadhurst in 1886, of [the trade unionist] Thomas Burt in 1892, to [minor] ministerial positions, was to harness to the Liberal machine the whole of the trade union movement. A certain number of working-class leaders were to be assisted to enter Parliament as supporters of the Liberal Party, and nearly every trade union leader of the time promptly held out his hand and said: 'Here am I; send me.'[9]

Crumbs from the Liberal table did a good deal to inhibit the formation of an independent working-class party. Concessions of this kind were one factor which helped to ensure that when a Labour Party was finally formed it would retain close ideological and personal links with the Liberals. It is a curious fact that at a time when the gap between social classes was enormous, key figures across the class divide could work together politically, even in some places as Conservatives.

It was in this period of transition that British socialism made its appearance or, if earlier advocacy of pre-Marxist socialism is included, reappearance. The number of socialists was small but their importance was greater, since a political philosophy which could not be accommodated within Liberalism was an obvious source of a new party. The lineal descendant of the socialist movement was the Labour Party, a fact which does much to justify the attention paid to the tiny contemporary movement. There were other factors which gave socialists considerable contemporary attention. Much more powerful socialist parties existed on the continent of Europe, notably in France and Germany, during the same period and it was possible that their example could spread to Britain. John Rae, a well-informed contemporary observer, described the growth of socialism in other countries and, writing of England, warned: "[e]very requisite of revolution is there." The English working class, however, he reflected thankfully, had been persistently pacific: "the people will not rise". The same anomaly has been emphasized by historians. A century later, for example, Gordon Phillips pointed out that Britain had developed a larger urban and industrial population than any other European nation without "any comparable political transformation".[10]

The contemporary middle and upper class was concerned about the potential threat posed by working men who might possibly seek to overthrow the capitalist system. It was sensible for members of the higher social classes to treat their inferiors gently. By the end of the nineteenth century fear of a violent revolution had largely disappeared, but voices were still heard expressing the fear that adverse social conditions could lead to a popular rising. The fact that millions of working men enjoyed the parliamentary vote after the Reform Acts of 1867 and 1884 aroused apprehension about working-class domination of the political process. The Liberal Party, conscious both of social conditions and the need for electoral support, moved in the direction of social reform particularly after the retirement of Gladstone in 1894. Legislation which abandoned traditional adherence to *laissez faire* and implied higher taxation, however, angered the Liberal middle class who in some cases were large employers of labour and important contributors to party funds.

The years after 1880 were a period when social conditions received a great deal of attention from journalists and social researchers, though their researches produced more fruitful results in terms of shocking publications than effective movements for reform or ameliorative acts of parliament. Andrew Mearns's pamphlet *The Bitter Cry of Outcast London* (1883) is often given pride of place in terms of influence, but it followed George R. Sims's *How the Poor Live* of the same year and, as Mearns acknowledged, drew on Sims's work. There followed a number of local newspaper investigations of poor housing conditions, published under titles like *Squalid Liverpool* and *The Homes of the Bristol Poor*. In the dozen years which followed Mearns's pamphlet there were reports from royal commissions on housing (1884–5), elementary education (1886–8), labour (1892–4) and the aged poor (1893–5), to mention only the most prominent examples of their type.

The settlement movement whose best-known institution, Toynbee Hall, opened early in 1885, was another feature of the ferment of the time. The rise of socialism or at least advocacy of thoroughgoing social reform was one aspect of the ferment, both cause and effect of the attention to poverty and inequality which characterized the 1880s. The desire to improve social conditions was a sentiment which may have had a greater influence on some members of the middle classes than on the poor themselves. Beatrice Potter, soon to become Webb, did not announce her conversion to socialism to herself until February 1890, but she later reflected in a famous passage that others had strongly sympathized with socialist ideas some years earlier:

> The consciousness of sin was a collective or class consciousness; a growing uneasiness, amounting to conviction, that the industrial organization, which had yielded rent, interest and profits on a stupendous scale, had failed to provide a decent livelihood and tolerable conditions for a majority of the inhabitants of Great Britain.[11]

Beatrice Webb attributed the phrase "the sense of sin" to Samuel Barnett, the clergyman who was the first warden of Toynbee Hall, and there is no doubt that the Christian conscience was responsible not only for founding settlements but also semi-socialist organizations like the Guild of St Matthew and the more moderate Christian Social Union. These bodies were criticized and mocked in some quarters for doing too little about the injustices which they deplored. G. K. Chesterton, who was a prominent member of the CSU and a noted wit, wrote with gentle derision soon after the end of the period:

> The Christian Social Union here
> Was very much annoyed;
> It seems there is some duty
> Which we never should avoid,
> And so they sing a lot of hymns
> To help the Unemployed.[12]

Despite the gibes such bodies continued their ameliorative work. According to Stephen Mayor, the CSU had 27 branches with 2,600 members in 1897 and produced a good deal of literature. Its *Economic Review* was begun in 1891. Christian social reformers, most of whom were high Anglicans, wanted to stem the working-class drift away from organized religion and also to move the churches and chapels towards acceptance of the social gospel. They did not succeed in the first aim, but the work of such reformers helped to ensure that the Bible and elementary Christian beliefs retained an important place in working-class life and to make advocacy of the social gospel acceptable within the various denominations. Labour leaders, more frequently nonconformists than Anglicans, were often severely critical of organized Christianity and its official representatives, but not of essential Christian beliefs. Majority opinion in labour organizations as in the working class as a whole was not secularist.

The first recognizable British socialist party was formed in June 1881. This was the Democratic Federation, at first a radical organization which adopted a socialist programme in 1883 and the following year changed its name to the Social-Democratic Federation. It was generally known as the SDF and was not only socialist but Marxist. In 1884 it also adopted a programme advocating that the "MEANS OF PRODUCTION, DISTRIB-UTION AND EXCHANGE [should] be declared and treated as COLLECTIVE or COMMON PROPERTY". It had already declared in favour of a series of "stepping stones to a happier period",[13] including reforms in housing, education, working conditions and taxation. It also started a weekly paper called *Justice* in 1884, which was to survive many vicissitudes and last for over forty years.

Its leader, however, may have done as much harm through his over-bearing personality as good by his prolonged work for the cause. This was H. M. Hyndman, a Cambridge graduate and county cricketer who is sometimes described as a stockbroker but who would better be termed investor or capitalist. Hyndman antagonized almost everyone who did not unquestioningly accept his leadership, notably Karl Marx himself and the socialist movement's most celebrated recruit, the poet, designer and manufacturer William Morris. Bernard Shaw, who knew them both, reflected much later that they had in common only a privileged upbringing which encouraged a strong sense of their own rectitude. "Had Morris", Shaw wrote,

> been accompanied by Plato, Aristotle, Gregory the Great, Dante, Thomas Aquinas, Milton and Newton, Hyndman would have taken the chair as their natural leader without the slightest misgiving, and before the end of the month quarrelled with them all and left himself with no followers but the devoted handful who could not compete with him, and to whom he was a sort of god.[14]

What this entertaining characterization omits is that Hyndman was an energetic and determined figure who had a better idea of how to form and lead a Marxist party than most of his colleagues. It should also be borne in mind that he sustained a considerable financial burden, at least in the early years of the movement.

The adoption of a socialist programme and a name which at that period was associated with Marxism did not give the SDF a mass appeal, but even as a small pressure group it was unable to operate harmoniously. It is probably true that the passion of socialists for their cause made them particularly likely to disagree, as Morris was to observe ruefully a few years later in the opening page of *News from Nowhere:* "Up at the League . . . there had been one night a brisk conversational discussion . . . Considering the subject, the discussion was good-tempered . . . there were six persons present, and consequently six sections of the party were represented, four of which had strong but divergent Anarchist opinions."[15]

Quarrels over Hyndman's autocratic rule came to a head over the Christmas period 1884, when a narrow majority of the SDF executive passed a vote of no confidence in him. Instead of taking over the organization, however, the dissident majority founded a new body called the Socialist League and established a paper of their own, edited by Morris and called *Commonweal.* The rival papers carried articles by the leading socialists of the day but to posterity *Commonweal,* which continued on a regular basis only until 1892, is most significant as the source of Morris's most important socialist writings, *Justice* for the progress of the Marxist left in Britain.

That progress was at best disappointing. Hyndman was a partisan of electoral politics while Morris was then frankly hostile and, though somewhat softening his hostility in later years, remained sceptical until the end of his life. A decision had been taken earlier in 1884 not to put up candidates in elections, but the departure of the anti-parliamentary faction of the federation enabled the decision to be reversed the following year. The four members who stood in the London School Board election in 1885 were beaten but not disgraced. Soon afterwards three SDF members stood in the general election, in which justified charges were made that they had been assisted by "Tory Gold". The three failed miserably; only John Burns in Nottingham securing more than a derisory vote. Whatever the morality involved in taking money from one established party to defeat another, the catastrophic election result was, as G. D. H. Cole wrote years later, "a quite appalling tactical error". Internal dissension followed inevitably. The federation was severely embarrassed and membership declined. Although it did not abandon electoral politics it did not field candidates in the next general election, which took place in 1886. Hyndman later wrote a full and chatty autobiography but made no reference to the election of 1885. The SDF survived, however, while the Socialist League discovered that it could quarrel as well without Hyndman as with him and disintegrated at the end of the 1880s. It is not surprising that, writing in 1891, John Rae could proclaim that revolutionary socialism in Britain was no longer a threat to established institutions if it ever had been: "the height of the tide has been reached already, and the movement is now apparently on the ebb".[16]

The SDF had more success in its interventions outside parliamentary politics, as the Communist Party was also to do in later years. Both organizations were able to capitalize on deeply felt grievances and make alliances which could not be paralleled in the purely political sphere. Between 1885 and 1887 large-scale demonstrations which secured widespread publicity were held in London in defence of free speech and to protest against unemployment. Mass rallies caused more apprehension among the possessing classes than revolutionary utterances by a handful of Marxist socialists could do, and the reaction of the authorities was in turn conciliatory and harsh. A few of the most prominent events may be mentioned here. A crowd estimated by socialists at between 30,000 and 100,000 gathered at Dod Street in the East End in September 1885 to protest against a police attempt to close an established speaking site. They were left alone by the police and claimed triumph. Morris had earlier been arrested for strongly objecting to the behaviour of the police and a magistrate; his arrest and appearance in a police court were widely reported.

The following February a large meeting was held in Trafalgar Square by the SDF to protest against unemployment. The meeting, held to counter one called by the anti-socialist Fair Trade League, ended in riot and, two months later, in the trial for sedition of John Burns, Hyndman and two others. All four were acquitted and the SDF took the opportunity to reprint the speech which Burns made in his defence under the title *The Man with the Red Flag*. It included this passage:

> We are not responsible for the riots; it is society that is responsible, and instead of the Attorney-General drawing up indictments against us, he should be drawing up indictments against society, which is responsible for neglecting the means at its command . . . Well-fed men never revolt. Poverty-stricken men have all to gain, and nothing to lose, by riot and revolution.[17]

After the demonstration the Lord Mayor of London's fund for the relief of distress, which had been started immediately before, reached £62,000 by 24 February. The Lord Mayor commented bemusedly that he had never heard of so much money being raised so quickly.

Following more demonstrations the use of Trafalgar Square for protest meetings was banned. A huge rally was organized by radicals and Irish nationalists in defiance of the ban in November 1887, to defend free speech and protest against the government's Irish policy. Socialists joined in enthusiastically. The rally, long remembered as "Bloody Sunday", was dispersed by force by mounted police and soldiers but secured much more publicity than the SDF or Socialist League could have hoped to achieve from a unilateral effort. Some socialists drew the conclusion that the force used by the authorities on "Bloody Sunday" proved the impracticality of a policy of insurrection. A few years later, for example, Bernard Shaw wrote that "Insurrectionism, after a two years' innings, vanished from the field and has not since been much heard of."[18]

Whether "insurrectionism . . . vanished" because violence had failed or because trade had improved (Shaw believed that a new trade depression would lead to further militancy), there was now an opportunity for a new kind of socialism to make itself felt. This was propagated by the Fabian Society, formed in January 1884 and now Britain's oldest socialist body. Its political outlook was at first unclear and Edward Pease, the society's paid secretary and biographer, pointed out that the word socialism was slow in appearing. By 1887, however, its essential character had been formed and in its "basis" in 1887 it declared roundly: "The Fabian Society consists of Socialists." Writing in 1891 John Rae called it "a debating club of mixed socialism".[19]

Although some members belonged to the established middle class others, such as Sidney Webb and Bernard Shaw, its best-known and most influential recruits in its early years, belonged to the lower middle class of clerks, journalists and others whose numbers were rising noticeably during this period. Patricia Pugh, their centenary historian, comments shrewdly that the early Fabians illustrated their arguments "with what they knew of the social scene from precarious positions in the lower middle classes".[20] They sought to persuade by factual analysis, and the hundred or so "tracts" which they published by the end of the nineteenth century provided useful material for socialists of all views. They also published in 1889 the ambitious *Fabian Essays in Socialism* edited by Shaw, which was an immediate success. A thousand copies were sold in a month, by May 1897 the book was in its 35th thousand and, according to Pease, 46,000 copies were sold in English editions alone by 1916. The initial impact was particularly striking as the book was not only relatively expensive but demanded serious study, and the Fabians could justifiably be pleased with the notice taken of the *Essays*. Other editions followed in later years and the title was adapted for reuse in new collections of essays in later years.

It is difficult to assess how influential "the Fabian" was in its early years, partly because some of its best-known members lived into extreme and well-publicized old age, thus inhibiting for a lengthy period critical analysis of their achievements. Beatrice and Sidney Webb and Bernard Shaw did not die until 1943, 1947 and 1950, and Edward Pease lingered until early 1955, when he was in his ninety-eighth year. The importance of the early Fabians may have been exaggerated not only by themselves but also by temperamentally sympathetic politicians and historians. There is no doubt that their tracts provided useful information for socialist propagandists of all shades of opinion. But their ambivalence over labour independence meant they cannot be regarded without qualification as part of the movement to form the Labour Party.

An article in a periodical by Shaw and Webb in 1893 on behalf of the society committed it to advocating a labour parliamentary fund of

£30,000 or more and putting up 50 independent candidates at the next general election. It was soon printed in revised form as a Fabian tract, but the original article occasioned publicity, Liberal anger and the resignation of some members with Liberal sympathies. The formation of a Labour Party, moreover, was by no means settled Fabian policy. Breaking Liberal ties and forming a separate Labour Party was still adventurous in 1893, and if Beatrice Potter brought intellectual power and dedication to hard work to the society with her marriage to Sidney Webb in 1892, she also brought her social contacts with the older parties and an intention to use them. The Fabian commitment to the labour movement was much too insecure to be relied on by advocates of independent political action and many Fabians preferred the policy of "permeating" the older political parties with socialistic ideas. Beatrice Webb recorded in late 1894: "The truth is that *we want the things done* and we don't much care what persons or which party gets the credit."[21] Many socialists would have disagreed both about "the things" which needed to be done and, more particularly, the personnel required to do them, but to a predominantly middle-class group of people, access to the politically powerful seemed more effective and desirable than wholehearted co-operation with either working-class advocates of independent political action or sectarian champions of revolutionary ideology.

The Fabians were nonetheless socialists who were well aware of the anomalies and injustices of the society in which they lived. Sidney Webb wrote, for example in his *Fabian Essay* in 1889: "If private property in land and capital necessarily keeps the many workers permanently poor (through no fault of their own) in order to make the few idlers rich (from no merit of their own), private property in land and capital will inevitably go the way of the feudalism which it superseded." Most of the Fabians most of the time, however, wanted to work within the existing system of government and society. Above all things they were by the later 1880s gradualists who believed that socialism could come by instalments through municipal and other forms of public enterprise. Webb poked fun in a book published in 1889 at the "practical man" who complacently witnessed the gradual growth of publicly owned bodies while condemning socialist beliefs as "fantastic absurdities", and Shaw told an audience in 1888 that "the necessity for cautious and gradual change must be obvious to everyone here".[22] The Fabian Society was influential in making collectivist ideas acceptable in the late nineteenth century despite its lack of involvement in the process leading to the formation of the Labour Party.

The Social-Democratic Federation, the Socialist League and the Fabian Society all date from the initial phase of British socialism in the 1880s. The pioneering period continued into the next decade, but it was realized by that time that the road to socialism would be longer and more difficult than the pioneers had optimistically hoped. There was, however, a tantalizing glimpse of untapped possibilities when Robert Blatchford established his weekly *Clarion* at the end of 1891.

Blatchford was a former soldier and popular journalist on the Manchester-based *Sunday Chronicle*. He was an advanced radical who converted to socialism at the end of the 1880s, a move which led to a break with the proprietor of the *Chronicle,* Edward Hulton, and the establishment of his own weekly. The *Clarion* began life with a circulation of over 30,000. The paper moved to London in 1895 and its circulation rose to a claimed 83,000 copies by 1910, a figure which far exceeded that of any socialist contemporary. This was important, but it was less so than the ancillary activities which the *Clarion* spawned, the Cinderella clubs (which predated the paper itself), scouts, cyclists, glee clubs, holiday camps and other activities which spread over a wide area, particularly in the north of England Members were often young and always eager to spread the socialist message in any way they could, including, it was claimed, pasting advertising labels on the backs of unsuspecting cows. In 1895 there were 38 groups or "corps" of scouts. Their activities were described in song:

> Down to the haunts of the parson and squire
> Putting opponents to rout;
> Bestriding his steed with a pneumatic tyre.
> Through village and hamlet thro' mud and thro' mire
> Rideth the Clarion Scout
> Nailing down lies and disposing of fables
> Improving the landscape by sticking up labels . . .
> What is the message they bring? . . .
> A gospel of Brotherhood – that's what they preach.[23]

In 1897 there were 76 Clarion cycling clubs with 2,000 or more members, and in the same year a clubhouse was opened near Knutsford with celebrations which included dinner for 250 people.

Blatchford's most enduring achievement lay in articles from the *Clarion* reprinted periodically as short books. The first and most celebrated was *Merrie England,* which was published late in 1893 and addressed to "John Smith", supposed to be a typical Oldham working man. (Blatchford had written for or about John Smith as far back as his *Sunday Chronicle* days.) Blatchford himself was inspired by William Morris and drew much supporting detail from Fabian tracts. *Merrie England* cites the works of many other writers. But his writing style was his own and, with the enthusiastic assistance of Clarion scouts, enormous numbers of copies of *Merrie England* were sold. A penny edition was soon produced which sold over 700,000 copies in a few months. Writing in 1910 Blatchford's younger colleague Neil Lyons claimed that over two million copies had been sold in Britain and the United States and there were many translations.

The book still impresses by its simple and vivid style, notably in this passage relevant to the founding of the Labour Party:

> During an election there are Tory and Liberal Capitalists, and all of them are friends of the workers. During a strike there are no Tories and no Liberals amongst the employers. They are all Capitalists and enemies of the workers. Is there any logic in you, John Smith? Is there any perception in you? Is there any *sense* in you?[24]

Blatchford was a phenomenon and the sales of *Merrie England* unique. He undoubtedly did more to spread socialist ideas than any other individual in the period and showed that socialism had a ready audience if it was presented in an attractive and easily understood manner. But socialist transformation in a parliamentary system also required organization, continuous grinding work through forming political parties and campaigning for candidates in individual constituencies. This was work to which Blatchford was temperamentally unsuited and in which he had no interest.

The Independent Labour Party was founded in Bradford in January 1893. Here we meet James Keir Hardie, already a member of parliament. It is a curious fact that Hardie lived a much shorter life than Blatchford, a life which, though by no means devoid of success, was marked by severe disappointments and frustration. He could not present socialism in written form in as simple and compelling a form as Blatchford but he became a legend whose name is still invoked in the Labour Party while Blatchford was a meteor whose reputation burnt out and virtually disappeared during his own long lifetime.

Hardie, born in 1856, was a miner in Lanarkshire from the age of ten. Like most working men interested in politics he was originally a Liberal. As a young man he was both a trade unionist and a journalist, writing for the Ayrshire press from the beginning of the 1880s. It is worthy of note that he was from an early age a Christian without specific denomination and an advocate of temperance, two features which helped to shape his life and which he shared with other early members of the Labour Party. In 1888 he stood for parliament at a by-election in Mid-Lanark. He had hoped to be the Liberal nominee, but a Welsh barrister, J. W. Philipps, was chosen by the party. Hardie stood as an independent, with a confusing but not unusual mixture of labour, socialist and Liberal ideas. He was careful, Fred Reid points out, not to antagonize Liberals unnecessarily: "Hardie sincerely believed that the pristine goals of Liberalism, freedom and equality for every man under the constitution, were identical with the goals of socialism." He was thus able to tell the electorate: "On questions of general politics I would vote with the Liberal Party to which I have all my life belonged."[25] That he was able to hold these apparently incompatible beliefs simultaneously says much about both contemporary socialism and the mountain which advocates of independent labour politics had to climb. Hardie's vote in Mid-Lanark was small but he was to have much greater influence as the apostle of independent labour than he could have had as one more quiescent Lib–Lab MP.

Soon after the by-election Hardie took the lead in forming the Scottish Labour Party. As a political party it was of little importance. Its socialism was muted and it made "scant impact on Scottish, let alone British, politics", Kenneth Morgan points out. By the end of 1890 it "presented a sorry spectacle of self-indulgent sectarianism".[26] As the harbinger of a labour party independent of Liberalism, however, it was a significant straw in the wind. It was also important in Hardie's political progress. He moved carefully towards electoral success. At a meeting in West Ham in 1890 he secured support for a resolution favouring the election of "'a *bona fide* representative of working class interests, who in addition to being a Home Rule Liberal, will also strive to secure for labour a better share of the comforts and enjoyments of life'".[27] In the parliamentary election campaign of 1892 he stood for West Ham South as a "Labour, Radical and Home Rule" candidate, emphasizing both his support for temperance reform and his nonconformist credentials. He thus appealed across the entire progressive spectrum and was elected with a comfortable majority after a Liberal–Labour hopeful withdrew. His success against a Conservative demonstrated both that labour candidates were potentially popular and that it was electorally advisable to stress affinity with advanced Liberalism rather than hostility to it.

Hardie was not the only independent labour candidate in 1892. John Burns, the SDF firebrand of the mid-eighties, and Havelock Wilson, leader of the seamen's union, were also elected, both moving subsequently towards Liberal–Labourism and in Burns's case to a seat in a Liberal cabinet. Hardie's friend Frank Smith and the trade unionist Ben Tillett both polled creditably as independent candidates. But Hardie's victory was the most important success which independent labour had enjoyed until that time and it was followed six months later by the formation of the Independent Labour Party in Bradford. Socialist writers have stressed the growth of socialist ideas in Scotland and the north of England. E. P. Thompson, for example, wrote: "the two-party system cracked in Yorkshire because a very large number of Yorkshire working men and women took a conscious decision to form a socialist party".[28] Thompson acknowledged the importance of the defeated strike at Manningham Mills, Bradford, in 1890–1 but in contrast to other historians insisted that the growth of socialism was more significant.

This argument should certainly not be dismissed. Both socialist ideas and the belief that working people needed their own political party now had many adherents. Philip Snowden, who was soon to be a leading figure in the ILP, recalled: "Socialism to these men and women was a new vision, a new hope of relief from the grinding toil and hard struggle with poverty which had been their lot." David Howell points out that local labour unions and organized socialist groups already existed in many places and were well represented at Bradford. He also stresses the nonconformist roots of many ILP members which made natural a transition from religion to politics, the party's socialist convictions blending "simple warm enthusiasms with prudent pragmatism – the characteristic blend of the nonconformist chapel in which intention and good works counted for more than doctrinal exactitude".[29] But it was also significant that the word "socialist" did not appear in the title of the new party and that its programme was radical as well as socialist. Thus it anticipated by a quarter of a century the Labour Party constitution of 1918, adopted in very different circumstances.

The undogmatic nature of the new party helps to explain Hardie's willingness to be involved, indeed as the dominant figure at both the conference and in the ILP itself in subsequent years. Kenneth Morgan, acknowledging the socialist content of the programme adopted at Bradford, points out that "bridges were left open to radical Liberals and to trade unionists. The overwhelming majority of the items on the new party programme were part and parcel of the standard advanced radicalism of the day."[30] Hardie's early experience of parliament and his celebrity status at the founding conference may also have encouraged him to throw in his lot definitively with independent labour, but Fred Reid expresses the view that Hardie still hoped at Bradford to create the kind of alliance of trade unions, radicals and socialists which he had long desired. Events rather than Hardie's own intention were to move the ILP along a different path.

Flexible Marxists approved the formation of the party. The elderly Friedrich Engels, though increasingly suspicious of Hardie, wrote to his friend F. A. Sorge in the month that the ILP was formed, expressing his pleasure and support, and the "revisionist" German Marxist Eduard Bernstein, though initially provoked, was another supporter. The national SDF took a negative view of the formation of the ILP, but six of its Lancashire branches attended the founding conference and subsequent relations were often cordial between the two groups at local level.

The ILP, however, was necessarily a party whose eyes were firmly fixed on parliamentary elections, the only possible route to power in the British context. The party soon found that while it polled far better than the SDF had ever done, even undogmatic socialism did not attract the British electorate sufficiently to ensure parliamentary success. Two and a half years after its founding the party put forward 28 candidates in constituencies returning 35 members (7 stood in two-member seats) in the general election of 1895, a year of Conservative victory. All were beaten, including Keir Hardie, who was defeated by a Conservative in West Ham. Two of the ILPers secured over 4,000 votes, enough to have won in many places, and Hardie fell just short of that number, but half of the candidates polled below a thousand votes. The SDF put up four of its members and polled even less well than the ILP. The Liberals fought the ILP in all but four constituencies Twenty of the winners were Conservatives, fifteen Liberal. The moral seemed obvious. Socialists could not normally be elected to parliament without direct or indirect Liberal support. Where Liberal and Labour fought each other the Conservatives gained. If the ILP or any other socialist or labour party were to form a permanent presence in parliament it would have to strike a deal with the Liberals. John Burns and Havelock Wilson had done so and both were re-elected in 1895. The outlook for the ILP was gloomy.

By-elections increased the gloom. Four were fought by the ILP in the 1895 parliament and the result from its point of view was increasingly adverse. The last of the four was in October 1897 when the party took on the Yorkshire miners in Barnsley. The ILP candidate was Pete Curran, himself a trade unionist as well as a socialist. The successful Liberal was Joseph Walton, a colliery owner and coal dealer in Durham who had allegedly shipped Yorkshire coal to strike-bound Durham in 1892 and repeated this action in the opposite direction in 1893. Walton's associations did not prevent him from winning the support of the miners, in particular Benjamin Pickard, himself a Lib–Lab MP, president of the Miners' Federation of Great Britain and secretary of the Yorkshire Miners' Association. Pickard, whose influence with the miners was unassailable, acted as though the future of the union was at stake and appealed to his members to oppose the ILP as "men who have deliberately come into your midst to try and kill your power and influence both in politics and in combination".[31] Curran was apparently not stoned by the miners as later claimed by Hardie, but he finished a bad third in the election. The ILP had begun to learn that it could only operate successfully if it did not antagonize the unions.

Socialists in Britain in the 1890s were not only out of harmony with the unions but also with each other. Although ILP and SDF local branches often worked in amity as previously noted, the national leadership of the two bodies remained suspicious and hostile. First the SDF, then the ILP, blocked attempts to promote fusion. Graham Johnson, writing recently, describes a process in the second half of the 1890s whereby the SDF moved from opposition to frustrated attempts at co-operation while the ILP moved in the opposite direction. A ballot for fusion in 1898 had overwhelming support in both organizations, but the ILP leadership found grounds for ignoring it. Tom Mann, the left-wing trade unionist who was secretary of the ILP between 1894 and 1898, was a partisan of joint action between it and the SDF and wrote that both bodies wanted the same object. His later recollection was that "although there was no vital difference of principle, there was a considerable difference in temperament". Hardie and the rest of the ILP leadership, however, felt that important matters of principle were at stake. Kenneth Morgan points out: "Hardie's determined hostility towards any kind of union or even joint meetings with the SDF is apparent throughout." As Graham Johnson comments, "political pragmatism" and a "new realism"[32] within the ILP made the party search for more acceptable allies. Progress seemed impossible to the ILP leadership if they collaborated with the SDF which was regarded by Hardie and other leaders as sectarian, doctrinaire and not in tune with working-class ambitions.

The Fabian Society's differences with the ILP over strategy were undoubtedly exacerbated by personality clashes. The credentials of the two Fabian delegates who attended the founding conference of the ILP were almost rejected because of their scepticism about forming an independent labour body, though Bernard Shaw, who was one of them, made a significant contribution to the ILP programme as adopted. Many of the provincial Fabian societies turned themselves into ILP branches but the two organizations did not work closely in the later 1890s. Hardie, though himself a Fabian, strongly opposed the policy of "permeating" the Liberal Party and disliked Fabian intellectual snobbery. Beatrice Webb thought the ILP leaders, Keir Hardie in particular, emotional and intellectually confused. She told her diary early in 1895 that Hardie impressed her "very unfavourably . . . he knows little and cares less for any constructive thought or action". She admitted without dismay an element of truth in his remark that "we were the worst enemies of the social revolution". After the general election of 1895 she commented: "[T]he I.L.P. has completed its suicide. Its policy of abstention and deliberate wrecking is proved to be futile and absurd." Shaw, though later on friendly terms with Hardie, wrote to Sidney Webb in 1892: "My estimate of K.H. is that he is a Scotchman with alternate intervals of second sight (during which he does not see anything, but is suffused with afflatus) and common incapacity."[33] Fabians and ILP remained in contact with each other in the later 1890s, as Patricia Pugh comments, but the relationship was not close.

It became increasingly clear during the second half of the 1890s that despite the enthusiasm which socialists were able to arouse they could not without outside assistance form a significant political party. They could hope to succeed only in combination with the money and mass membership of trade unions. Thus the idea of a "labour alliance" was born.

To form an independent party based on the unions was a difficult task, though not quite so difficult as Curran's experience in Barnsley seemed to suggest. It is sometimes forgotten that the essential function of unions, then and later, was defensive. Their purpose was to improve their members' wages and working conditions, not to engage in socialist politics. They had then a greater role in mitigating the effects of unemployment and providing benefits in sickness and old age than in a later period. Union leaders were not socialist tribunes but functionaries who inevitably sought compromise, an unheroic position which infuriated both their own militants and outside agitators. Those who began their careers as firebrands often moderated their views and action as the realities of industrial life and the need for union survival and growth pressed upon them. Beatrice and Sidney Webb were given in 1893 and subsequently reproduced in their *History of Trade Unionism* a detailed description of the process whereby the activist became a bureaucrat, assimilated to the lower-middle class and gradually alienated from many ordinary members. This was a process which long remained recognizable.

Unions generally failed until at least the 1880s to recruit unskilled workers and casual labour. A London School Board attendance officer who was also a trade union official told the royal commission on elementary education in 1887 that his school board district was very poor, "not at all a district known to us by trade unionism".[34] Belief in conventional methods of self-help and respectability was widespread, and an enhanced role for the state was unpopular not only with union members but also with many of the lower paid, for whom it represented the poor law and other unacceptable forms of social coercion. In addition, the loaves and fishes of elected office, as we have seen, encouraged union leaders to form or maintain ties with the Liberal Party.

Given all these circumstances it is not surprising that unions seemed unfruitful ground to many socialists. Although the SDF, to take the most obvious example, was less hostile to unions than historians have often supposed, its leaders believed that socialism could not be obtained through strikes alone and said so publicly. In 1889, for example, *Justice* commented that "a strike is only guerrilla warfare for very small results . . . Social Democracy means that strikes shall become unnecessary and misery unknown".[35] This attitude was modified by time and recognition that unions were important working-class organizations, but the SDF necessarily believed that industrial action as such could not achieve socialist ends Both the ILP and Robert Blatchford, though generally expressing themselves more moderately, were also sceptical about trade union action, partly because they had little faith in "sectionalism" and agitation for improved conditions in individual industries.

On the other hand, unions did believe that they represented the whole working class and sometimes made pronouncements to this effect. Even leaders who rejected socialism were not impervious to the argument that it was the working class who created wealth and were denied its benefits. It was, moreover, obvious that many of the socialists were themselves of working-class origin. How could socialists persuade union leaders and members that their true interest lay in forming an independent political party pledged to socialist policies?

The first attempts to organize the unskilled pre-dated the 1880s, but it was in the later eighties that unions for such workers became prominent. The most important industrial action which took place in this period symbolized the awakening of unskilled labour. The strike of the Bryant and May matchgirls in East London in 1888 and the London dockers the following year achieved unprecedented publicity. Both strikes were led by socialists including Annie Besant, John Burns, Tom Mann and Ben Tillett, both roused sympathy among the socially conscious middle class, both showed unskilled labour the virtues of trade unionism and the fact that it was not beyond the reach of the poorly paid. "New" unions, as they were called, soon grew to resemble the old, with (for example) relatively high subscriptions, benefit funds and heavy expenditure on salaries and administration. New unionism was a bubble which soon burst in a number of industries, leaving romantic memories rather than permanent organization. George Howell, the "old" trade unionist who was a Lib–Lab MP from 1885 to 1895, wrote irritatedly in 1891: "There is scarcely a feature in which any of them differ from types of Unions long in existence." Yet something was left in terms of general unions of the unskilled, greater militancy and a growing sympathy among trade unionists towards socialism. The Trades Union Congress, founded in 1868, reflected the changing attitude and the resultant conflict of personalities.

Howell expressed his opinion of new unionist leaders at the TUC held in Liverpool in 1890 and also of a scathing commentary by John Burns, in a manner which hints persuasively that the older leaders had become absorbed into the political and industrial power structure:

> Perhaps the culmination of vulgar abuse, and of overbearing behaviour, was reached at the Liverpool Trades Union Congress; and of shameless misrepresentation subsequently, in the reports and speeches made thereupon. According to one "leader", tall hats and black coats, and also the size and stature of the delegates from the old Unions, were indications of a frightful state of decay, in the policy and management of the Old Trade Unionism. . . . A loud voice, impatient gestures, and persistent interruptions were in strong force at the Trades Union Congress of 1890. The exhibition was sad and pitiful to behold.

For the new unionists Will Thorne of the gasworkers later admitted that "perhaps one or two . . . were a little blatant", but he thought that they were a model of decorum compared to "the boorishness of the old school".[36] Socialist influence was felt in a number of older unions in the 1880s and at end of the decade the influence of the "new" unions in the TUC was temporarily strong. It was certainly the case that the frailer new unions realized that they needed the state whereas majority opinion in the better established unions felt able to cope without outside assistance, but this was itself a sign of the times. In 1890 at the congress just mentioned the TUC passed a motion in favour of the eight-hour day in all trades, a socialist demand for some years past. In 1892 congress voted in favour of independent parliamentary representation. In 1893 a motion was passed which committed the TUC to support public ownership of the means of production and distribution and in 1894 exchange was added. These resolutions did not commit individual unions or lead to decisive action, but they were at least an indication that belief in a political party separate from the Liberals and in collectivist ideas had become acceptable to much union opinion. The TUC by 1895 was no longer a reliable bulwark of Liberal–Labourism.

However, socialists could not expect a decisive shift in union attitudes without the impact of outside events. Strikes and lock-outs were important. A miners' lock-out in the second half of 1893 led to violence and the death of two miners in Yorkshire at the hands of the army. It also led to government intervention, an unprecedented step in industrial relations. The engineers' lock-out of 1897–8, which lasted for over thirty weeks, centred round the union demand for the eight hour day and resistance to technological change. If the powerful Amalgamated Society of Engineers could be defeated, as it was in this case, no union seemed to be safe from attack. In early 1898 the young L. T. Hobhouse, a labour sympathizer and later a prominent social philosopher, wrote in the *Manchester Guardian*: "The engineers have borne the brunt of an attack which in reality threatened the whole trade union world."[37] (He added optimistically that the resolute resistance of the engineers meant that other unions were unlikely to be attacked in the near future.) Other unions which had given financial assistance to the engineers shared the defeat.

The lock-out showed the effectiveness of employer organizations in combating the unions and the limited success that a union of skilled men could have without support from fellow workers who were excluded from membership. The Engineering Employers' Federation was founded in 1896 as the Employers' Federation of Engineering Associations; its membership rose from 180 at the start of the stoppage to 702 at its end. The offensive led to other union defeats which included the use of strike-breaking "free labour". A Free Labour Protection Association was formed in 1897. John Saville points out that free labour was of only marginal use in industrial disputes involving skilled labour but that its significance lay in the political context in which it operated. Unions were also attacked in the press, notably *The Times* which carried many anti-union articles in the 1890s, though the most influential series did not begin to appear until late in 1901.

Adverse legal cases were another feature of the 1890s. It had been thought that the legislation of 1871 and 1875 had safeguarded unions and protected them against legal prosecutions. After 1890 in a new climate of hostility to unions this supposition was proved to be false. New unionism in particular roused judicial hostility, though the first significant case did not take place until 1893. This was *Temperton v. Russell,* in which the Court of Appeal ruled against three trade unions in Hull which sought to interfere with existing contracts. *Trollope v. London Building Trades Federation* in 1895 held that unions could not publish a blacklist of building firms and damages were awarded against the union side. *Lyons v. Wilkins* in 1898–9 placed restrictions on picketing, and when the *Taff Vale* case was decided in 1901 against the Amalgamated Society of Railway Servants who faced an ultimate bill of £42,000, the judicial offensive against the unions reached an unmistakable climax.

This bleak reality was thus not fully revealed until after the birth of the Labour Party. The adverse trend of court cases, however, was clear to informed observers well before Taff Vale. Beatrice and Sidney Webb wrote in 1897:

> Unless these decisions are overruled, Trade Unionists will have to fight over again the battle for the right of combination which was believed to have been won in 1875. Collective Bargaining will become impossible if, whenever Trade Unionists are warned not to accept employment from a particular firm for any reason whatsoever, the Trade Union officials can be harassed by writs, cast in damages, and driven into bankruptcy. Unfortunately, the present generation of Trade Unionists, not excluding the responsible officials, are not alive to the gravity of the legal situation.[38]

The gravity of the situation was still not fully revealed in 1899, but that middle-class opinion was no longer as sympathetic as it had been in the 1880s was all too obvious. Frank Bealey and Henry Pelling in their detailed study of the formation and history of the Labour Representation Committee, ascribe to failed industrial action, press attacks, use of "free labour" and adverse legal judgments the explanation for "the marked growth of militancy in political questions" among union leaders at the end of the nineteenth century. A comment by W. C. Steadman of the bargebuilders, who chaired the founding conference of the Labour Representation Committee and was himself a Lib–Lab MP, was revealing. Steadman told the conference that the struggle for reduced working hours in his own industry had converted him to belief in working-class political action:

> [T]he leaders of the advanced movement who believed in political action were right and he was wrong. [Cheers]. Therefore he was now as ready as any man to take political action to redress the grievances under which the workers suffered. He gave way to no man in his desire to see Labour better represented in the House of Commons than it was to-day.[39]

This declaration did not prevent Steadman from standing again unsuccessfully as a Lib–Lab in 1900 and successfully in 1906, while claiming on at least one occasion to be an enthusiastic supporter of the Labour Party. Emotional and sentimental ties to Liberal principles endured and financial support for parliamentary elections was much more easily obtained from Liberal sources than from cash-strapped small unions.

Given the number of factors which tended to make trade unions growingly sceptical about their traditional allegiance in the 1890s, the Liberal Party would have done well to cultivate the unions and try to ensure that their loyalty was rewarded, above all by finding parliamentary seats for more trade union leaders. The Liberals in this period, however, had much to think about, including the continuing Irish home rule controversy, finding a successor to the aged Gladstone and the worsening situation in South Africa which led to war before the end of the decade. Leading Liberals were more concerned with these problems than with the electoral aspirations of their working-class supporters. H. H. Asquith, a relatively youthful home secretary in the Gladstone ministry of 1892–5 with a reputation as a radical, was urged at a Huddersfield meeting in 1894 to "Try a Labour Man" when he deplored the return of a Conservative in a by-election the previous year. He replied that he objected to "government by groups". In 1895 Asquith told working-class listeners in Hull that the Liberal Party was "in sympathy with your aims . . . breathes your spirit, and . . . has no selfish or class interest to serve". He contrasted it with "what must necessarily be for a long time to come a small, a comparatively weak, and an isolated organization", by implication the ILP.[40]

At local level social snobbery and the need for candidates who could contribute heavily to their election expenses were important. (A system of proportional representation in which individual working-class hopefuls would not have had to face the local Liberal middle class and its social prejudices might have led to a larger number of Lib–Lab MPs.) In addition, the political measures advocated by many labour men, as previously mentioned, were anathema to important Liberals. These factors helped to alienate some able working-class radicals from their Liberal roots, though often reluctantly and incompletely. George Lansbury was pushed from the platform when he tried to move a resolution for the eight-hour day for government employees at the National Liberal Federation in 1889. "[T]hus ended my connection with Liberalism", he wrote.[41] Ramsay MacDonald was incensed by the Liberals putting up two candidates in the two-member Southampton seat for which he stood in 1895, however illogically in view of the fact that he was the ILP candidate. Gladstone's retirement in 1894 and his death four years later encouraged Arthur Henderson to break his Liberal links; so too did Liberal failure to nominate him for the Newcastle constituency in 1895. The general election of that year was disastrous for Liberals and socialists as previously noted, with the result that a number of Lib–Labs were defeated at the polls.

Lib–Lab MPs, nine in 1886, were no more numerous in 1895 while the problems facing trade unionists were increasingly severe. Three by-election victories in 1897–8 made little difference to the underlying situation, although the Lib–Lab route must have seemed more fruitful than the ILP's failed attempts in 1896–7. Liberal–Labourism, it seemed clear, would never be more than an insignificant tail to the great Liberal dog.

The hostility of employers, the press and the courts of law, and the apparent indifference or wariness of the Liberal Party about giving the aspiring working class increased parliamentary representation added up to a formidable case for a trade union-based independent political party. But it would be easy to exaggerate the number of working men who were convinced of this point of view in the later 1890s when defeating the triumphant Conservatives seemed to many trade unionists to be a more important aim, and dividing labour from Liberal a policy of despair. It would also be easy to exaggerate the importance of the special conference in February 1900 when the Labour Representation Committee was established.

The crucial decision to hold the founding conference was taken in September 1899 at the annual meeting of the Trades Union Congress at Plymouth. The Amalgamated Society of Railway Servants, the union which would bear the brunt of the Taff Vale decision in the near future, put forward a motion calling for "the co-operation of all the co-operative, socialistic, trade unions, and other working organizations" to convene "a special congress" to devise methods of "securing the return of an increased number of labour members of the next Parliament".[42] The motion had originated in its Doncaster branch, where the moving spirit, Thomas Steels, was a member of the ILP. At the TUC itself the case was put by James Holmes, another ILP-er and a notable speaker. The most important opponents of the proposal were the miners, whose representatives formed the largest bloc of Lib–Lab MPs, and the cotton unions among whom Conservative sympathies were strong.

The young Margaret Bondfield, representing the shop assistants, was later the first woman member of the TUC general council and the first woman cabinet minister, but was then the only woman among nearly 400 delegates. She won applause for an effective contribution on behalf of those unions which lacked the power and influence of the miners and cotton workers. "She appealed for support on behalf of the resolution, believing there were many grievances which could only be remedied by legislative enactment, and because they were not likely to get redress in the House of Commons until the labour members formed an appreciable party in that assembly."[43] This was the majority sentiment of those who contributed to the debate and of the unions represented at the congress. Philip Bagwell, historian of the railwaymen, writes:

When the President began to announce the result of the voting there was a breathless silence. He slowly read: "Five hundred and forty-six thousand for the resolution, against four –" but he got no further. The next moment men were on their chairs raising their hats and cheering with indescribable enthusiasm. It was only considerably later that most delegates learned that the vote against the resolution was 434,000.[44]

The passage of the resolution shows how far advocates of independent labour organization had progressed in the trade unions, but also how little had been achieved after twenty years of agitation. Although the resolution referred to the co-operation of "socialistic . . . organizations" there was no reference to forming a socialist party, and the terms of the motion could in theory have been fulfilled by electing an increased number of Lib–Labs. The big battalions at the TUC were sceptical about the resolution but did not organize to defeat it, in part no doubt due to the apparently vague and innocuous terms in which it was worded, in part because increased labour representation as such was a generally agreed aim of working-class bodies. Robert Taylor points out that four of the five trade unionists appointed to the preparatory committee to organize the conference were Lib–Labs; as we have seen one was W. C. Steadman, who was an MP. On the other hand, the unions which supported the resolution were the ones in which socialist influence was most marked and the passage of the resolution was regarded correctly as a victory for socialists.

The founding conference in February 1900, though in retrospect momentous, hardly seemed so to contemporaries, as noted at the beginning of this chapter. Only 129 delegates representing fewer than 570,000 members were in attendance, a number little greater than the TUC majority which had supported the crucial resolution in 1899. The conference was held in dripping rain at the Memorial Hall in London, and the official report of the debate on establishing a new organization barely covered two pages. The decision to form such a body had in effect already been taken at the TUC and the problem which faced the delegates was how to form an effective organization without alienating potential support. James Macdonald of the London Trades Council and the SDF moved that a party be formed "upon a recognition of the class war" to which an amendment was moved, which would have left a free hand to Lib–Lab policies. Keir Hardie moved a second amendment which replaced the first and called for the establishment of

a distinct Labour Group in Parliament, who shall have their own Whips, and agree upon their policy, which must embrace a readiness to co-operate with any party which for the time being may be engaged in promoting legislation in the direct interest of labour, and be equally ready to associate themselves with any party in opposing measures having an opposite tendency.[45]

The amended motion was carried unanimously.

Like the successful motion at the 1899 TUC, the amendment as passed showed the limits of the agitation of twenty years. The class war was not to be recognized and, more important, there was no reference to socialism, though the executive committee was to include representatives of the SDF, ILP and the Fabians. Nor was there necessarily to be a Labour Party as such. David Marquand points out: "The Memorial Hall conference had not created a Labour Party: at most it had opened the door to one."[46] The first challenge to the new Labour Representation Committee was to be a general election, held less than a year after its formation.

2 LABOUR IN PEACE AND WAR

1900–1918

Although the years between 1880 and 1900 may be regarded as the heroic phase of British socialism, they were largely unsuccessful in electoral terms. The period from 1900 until the end of the Great War was one of modest but real progress for the Labour Party. At the start of the period "Labour" was a committee which did not yet dare to call itself a political party; by the end of 1918 it had become, however uncertainly, the second party of state. It can be argued that both in 1900 and 1918 a misleading picture was presented. Even at the earlier date Labour was potentially a strong force, and in 1918 its prominence was more fortuitous than the result of extensively increased public support.

The secretary of the new Labour Representation Committee was James Ramsay MacDonald, then aged 33, the dominant figure in the Labour Party in the first third of the twentieth century and a man whom the party had trouble in ignoring even after his death in 1937. The legend circulated that MacDonald had become secretary because he had been mistaken for James Macdonald of the SDF. This appears less likely than the more prosaic version that MacDonald, who had married into the established middle class, was the only candidate who could work without a salary. He was a man of obvious ability and lived in London, an essential qualification for the secretary of a political party, though some of the northern delegates appear initially to have thought otherwise.

MacDonald's character and political views have received attention from many writers, but his prominence within the party for so many years and his role in expounding its beliefs mean that these features cannot be ignored here. He was a man of personal magnetism, his Scottish accent ensuring that it was more difficult for the party to be despised and ignored than would have been the case if a cockney or English provincial working man had been leader. He was a self-made intellectual, willing to expound his cloudy beliefs in writing and able to do so at greater length than party leaders in a later, less leisurely age. He was a socialist and a member of the ILP, but he believed that socialism should be introduced by consensus, a belief which was likely to cause less alarm among the possessing classes than if a more militant leader had been in place. His first book, *Socialism and Society* (1905), expounded his views. These did not change and MacDonald was able to provide the Labour Party with an intellectual foundation for a gradualist policy to which it too remained loyal.

To MacDonald socialism was a philosophy which should appeal to all people of good will regardless of social class, provided that they believed in democracy and social evolution. His advocacy of democracy was not always consistent when parliamentary votes for women were at stake, but in 1905 his reservations about the women's demands were not yet apparent. "The Socialist appeal", he wrote,

> may find some people in poverty, and they may follow because it offers them economic security; but it will find others in wealth, and they will follow because it brings order where there is now chaos . . . Socialism marks the growth of society, not the uprising of a class. The consciousness which it seeks to quicken is not one of economic class solidarity, but one of social unity.[1]

Here was socialism without tears, an ideology which could potentially attract the electorate and unite a party many of whose potential supporters were at best lukewarm about any form of socialism or other ideology.

It might have been expected that the general election of 1900 would see a reaction against the ruling Conservative (or Unionist, because it represented those who opposed Irish Home Rule) Party. This in fact did not happen, mainly because Britain was engaged in her first major war since the Crimean conflict nearly fifty years previously. The South African war led to a sweeping Unionist victory in a so-called "Khaki" election and was an unfortunate time for a new party to appear on the scene. Eight Lib–Labs were elected, among them five miners and John Burns, who had effectively cut his ties with independent Labour. As for the LRC, it put up fourteen candidates to fight fifteen seats, as Keir Hardie stood in two constituencies. Five (including the socialist Will Thorne) were supported by trade unions or trade councils while in eight of the remaining seats the Independent Labour Party sponsored the candidate. The other two were in one case supported by the SDF and ILP jointly, in the other by the SDF alone. Richard Bell of the Railway Servants, one of the two victorious LRC candidates, faced only one Liberal opponent in Derby, a two-member seat, but Keir Hardie won a seat against two Liberals in another two-member constituency in Merthyr Tydfil. Some of the other LRC candidates, though not MacDonald, were given a clear run by the Liberals, but a party which claimed to speak for millions of working men had suffered a marked defeat, even given its extreme youth, even given the impact of foreign war.

One hopeful sign was that some of the LRC candidates polled strongly. Philip Snowden recalled in old age the enthusiasm of his meetings in Blackburn, his many voluntary helpers and the fact that he won more votes than any other socialist had done up to that time. There was no Liberal candidate, however, and some local Liberals gave him their support. Other Labour candidates made clear their Liberal sympathies and also their hostility to the war, which was opposed by many radical Liberals.

The fact had to be faced after the election that a committee had been established to forward Labour's political fortunes, that it had returned only two candidates at its first attempt, and that one of those two was in reality a Lib–Lab. Richard Bell is portrayed in his union history as a hard-working parliamentarian, determined to do his best for his constituents and his union colleagues, and convinced that this should be carried out by supporting the Liberals. He made clear to the House of Commons that he represented "a very large body of organized workmen". He demonstrated that a working-class MP sympathetic to Liberalism could give effective publicity to the shackles placed on trade unions in the existing state of the law, insisting that unions were permitted to be no more than friendly societies. But his Liberal links remained unshaken. "What possible influence on legislation", he asked, in the paraphrase of the union historian, "could be exerted by two members who insisted on cutting themselves adrift from the progressive wing of the Liberal Party?"[2]

The answers to this question were various, but the young Labour Representation Committee survived. The SDF withdrew from membership in August 1901 and though Edward Pease continued to represent the Fabian Society on the LRC executive he recalled that most of his Fabian colleagues "showed little interest in the new body".[3] Many trade unions, however, felt otherwise. The *Taff Vale* case established in July 1901 that trade unions could be sued as corporate entities and the case was finally settled in March 1903 with a total cost to Richard Bell's Railway Servants, including damages, of £42,000. This case, reinforced almost immediately by *Quinn v. Leathem*, demonstrated that all unions and their funds were at risk. The leading Liberal barristers and politiciams H. H. Asquith and R. B. Haldane observed separately that it was impossible to advise unions how to conduct strikes legally. The French historian Elie Halévy, who observed closely the contemporary British scene, later declared: "[A] public opinion favourable to the claims of the unions . . . did not exist" in 1901. "The middle class had declared war upon the unions."[4] Valuing their Liberal links unions did not turn immediately and unanimously to the Labour Party, but some did and others were increasingly inclined to do so. Trade union affiliation to the LRC rose from 41 unions and

353,070 members in 1900–1 to 165 unions and 956,025 members in 1903–4, a small percentage of the total number of unions but nearly half their membership.

Increased numbers were mirrored by increased parliamentary representation. The LRC contested seven by-elections during the life of the parliament elected in 1900, only two against Liberal opposition, and won three of them, in one case in a three-cornered contest. All of the victors were Labour men who won Labour victories, but all had Liberal ties which had not been broken. One was David Shackleton, returned in August 1902, who was Liberal in his outlook and attitudes; another, Will Crooks (March 1903), was heavily involved with the Liberals in London, and the third, Arthur Henderson (July 1903), had his feet firmly in both camps as a Liberal Party agent and an LRC adherent. On the other hand, where was the LRC to find its candidates if not from the ranks of Liberal working men? These Liberal ties added to a certain gloom about the short-term progress of the Labour cause, and persuaded Keir Hardie, supposedly the firm advocate of Labour independence, to appeal at different times between 1900 and 1906 to the Liberals John Morley and Lloyd George, and the former socialist John Burns, to lead a progressive coalition. Independent Labour policy was both complicated and flexible in these years and links of various kinds with the Liberals were not only inevitable but in many cases cherished.

If Taff Vale and other events concentrated the minds of union leaders, Liberals looked back at the beginning of the new century on a sad record. Since the party split on the Home Rule rock in 1886 it had formed only one short-lived and unsuccessful government, in 1892–5. Although it still had its Gladstone, he was no hugely popular leader but a chief whip and negotiator. It was this (Herbert) Gladstone, son of the Grand Old Man, who in negotiating with MacDonald assisted by Keir Hardie sought to help the LRC while also benefiting his own Liberal Party. It was a difficult and complicated task in which Jesse Herbert, Gladstone's secretary, played an important part.

The Liberal leaders concluded that if their party stood down in favour of Labour in certain vulnerable Conservative seats, they could hope for an overall Liberal–Labour parliamentary majority in which the victorious Labour candidates would owe their seats to Liberal forbearance. Thus any tendency to independence displayed by Labour MPs could be countered by a reminder of how and why their party had succeeded, reinforced by the Liberal sympathies of so many members of the Labour Representation Committee. The case for collaboration was strengthened by the fact that many Liberals supported a greater role for Labour in parliament than seemed possible via the Lib–Lab route. On the other hand, an enlarged Labour faction in parliament would carry with it the potential for greater independence and hence represent a significant threat to the Liberals. This was an obvious problem for the Liberals from a later perspective, but that the Liberals were likely to be superseded or even seriously challenged within the foreseeable future by a group of miners, cotton workers and miscellaneous working men was not regarded as a realistic threat by contemporaries.

MacDonald and Gladstone reached agreement in the summer of 1903. Labour was to be given a free hand in thirty seats but not to put up candidates in other constituencies where to do so might stand in the way of Liberal success. The pact had the added advantage for MacDonald that it made possible a Liberal–Labour rapprochement, an attractive prospect to him since he was attracted both by Labour independence and by the prospect of friendliness to the Liberals, a policy which he had long advocated and was not to abandon definitively until after 1918.

In the meantime the LRC met annually in conference and passed resolutions which most historians regard as being of little importance. Resolutions opposing the South African war and imperialism indicated which way the new party was moving, though the apparent absence of discussion of many of them makes it difficult to estimate the impact of the measures passed. In 1903 a resolution demanding "the overthrow of the present competitive system of Capitalism" was narrowly defeated with no reported debate and the same decision was reached the following year, this time by a larger margin. In 1905, however, the anti-capitalist resolution was adopted without discussion and without a recorded vote. This does not appear to be the action of a political party which regarded policy matters seriously. More convincing were lengthy discussions dealing with the administration of the LRC itself and its operations. Perhaps most significant were the defeats of resolutions in 1903 and 1904 calling for the adoption of a party programme. Keir Hardie and the ILP trade unionist Ben Turner spoke against the resolution in 1903 and D. C. Cummings of the boilermakers' union and also an ILP-er called for its defeat in 1904 because the aim of the LRC was, he said, to return Labour members to the House of Commons and "not to formulate programmes. They had also to face the fact that many of the Trade Union workers had only just realized the need for direct Labour representation, and were not yet sufficiently educated to swallow a full Labour programme wholesale."[5]

The first years of the twentieth century were an exciting period in British politics. The Conservative government of A. J. Balfour, beset by internal disputes over free trade and under attack over many issues including the labour of indentured Chinese workers in South Africa, resigned late in 1905. The new Liberal government promptly called an election in January 1906 and won a striking victory, though as in our own day the disparity of votes was by no means as great as suggested by the distribution of seats. The issues of the election were mainly the Liberal ones of free trade, Chinese labour, education, licensing reform and Irish home rule, though the repeal of the Taff Vale decision was also prominent. The LRC election manifesto was reformist in tone and varied little from progressive Liberal themes. Ironically there would seem to have been no need for the victorious Liberals to exercise generosity to the LRC, which changed its name to the Labour Party after the election, for even if all the Labour seats had gone to the Conservatives the Liberals would still have won a great victory. However, would-be Labour voters voted Liberal in many cases in which the MacDonald–Gladstone agreement had resulted in a Labour candidate not standing. With no pact the Liberal–Labour vote would probably have been split and more Conservatives returned, as happened in a number of seats in which Labour or independent labour/socialists as well as Liberals stood. As it was there were 399 successful Liberals, 156 Conservatives, 82 Irish Nationalists and 30 Labour MPs, one of whom did not stand as an LRC candidate and joined the party only after the election, in a house of 670 members.

The thirty Labour victories attracted much attention. *The Times* referred editorially to "the new cleavage introduced by Labour, cutting across the lines of traditional parties, and yet for present purposes throwing its weight into the Liberal scale". It published an article by an anonymous Liberal who mused that Labour would want to turn its victory to its own account. He added the striking prophecy: "I will hazard the prediction that the Labour party has introduced into the organism of middle-class Liberalism, now perhaps for the last time triumphant, the seed of inevitable disintegration."[6] The prediction was uncannily accurate, though in large part for reasons which the writer could not have foreseen.

Only six of the successful Labour candidates faced Liberal opposition in a single-member constituency or two Liberals in a two-member seat. Several of the first generation of Labour Party leaders now joined Hardie and Henderson in the House of Commons, including MacDonald, Snowden, J. R. Clynes and Fred Jowett. In all, fifty LRC men stood and 32 did not fight a Liberal or, in two-member constituencies, two Liberals. At the same time the Lib–Labs returned a record 24 of their candidates, thirteen of whom were miners. Among their other MPs were John Burns, now a cabinet minister, Havelock Wilson and Richard Bell. Perhaps most significantly, where labour and socialist candidates stood independently of the LRC, all failed; they included the eight candidates of the Social-Democratic Federation and ten others. These candidates faced Liberal opposition, which supported the contention that socialists could not be elected without Liberal co-operation.

The election was a thunderbolt, however viewed. Even the Conservative leader, A. J. Balfour, was defeated and his party temporarily rendered politically impotent. Balfour himself mistakenly blamed the election result on the repercussions in Britain of revolutionary and socialist manifestations on the continent of Europe. Some socialists at least experienced a temporary sense of euphoria as the account of H. M. Hyndman, who attended "the great [Labour] meeting of congratulation and jubilation" held after the election, makes clear. "I looked round the crowded hall, surveyed the blaze of scarlet decorations, and read the telling mottoes inscribed all over the walls in praise of Socialism as 'The Only Hope of the Workers,' 'Workers of the World Unite' for the Social Revolution, and so on. A wave of enthusiasm temporarily swamped my critical faculty."[7] A less exultant note was struck by Bernard Shaw, who pointed out that Labour was more dependent than ever on Liberal votes, doubted that the party would be more than "nominally independent", and though he may have been the first, was certainly not the last socialist to "apologize to the Universe for my connection with such a party."[8]

The Liberal government elected in 1906 turned out to be a great reforming administration which took the first steps to establish a welfare state, although this development had not been expected either by many of its supporters or by most contemporary commentators. Its success was probably one of the reasons why the new Labour members exhibited little independence. The longstanding friction between the Liberals and the House of Lords, however, which developed into open conflict shortly after the election and was particularly severe from 1909, and the loss of the Liberal majority in 1910, were also important factors. By this time a pattern of Labour quiescence and subordination had already been established, for taken as a whole the calibre of the Labour members was not high and many were not strikingly active. Their election to the House of Commons was in some cases, as it long remained, an end in itself. Parliamentary debates often "transcended [the] professional competence" of Labour members; they were not class warriors but "devout Christians and moderate patriots".[9] They were in origin all working men, and although most had left the shop floor or the pit face before their election, few had risen into the middle class by occupation or marriage. The relatively low calibre of the Labour men, their general subservience to the Liberal government and their lack of concern with ideological purity renders almost irrelevant the efforts of historians to discover how many of the thirty MPs should be classified as socialists. What mattered was not their politics but their social class. They were not, it should be emphasized, the left wing of the parliamentary Liberal Party but the larger part of its working-class wing.

The relationship between Liberals and Labour was complicated and in turn complicated relations within the Labour Party. Labour MPs were necessarily conscious of the fact that without enlightened Liberal self-interest many, perhaps most of them would not have been elected, and they were in consequence eager not to incur Liberal hostility. Moreover, as has been emphasized previously, many members of the Labour Party were sympathetic to historic Liberal beliefs as understood or imagined, above all free trade and the opportunity for talented men of working-class origin to climb the social ladder. For its part the Liberal Party was less sentimental about its ties to Labour but conscious of the fact that its ally could not be ignored. The new Labour MPs represented a social class which was unprecedentedly prominent in the years before war broke out in 1914. Liberals were aware that Labour represented the bulk of the nation, even the voting nation, as the older parties could not hope to do. Liberal recalcitrance in the face of Labour demands might lead to a haemorrhage of voters to Labour, in the middle if not the short term. As Lloyd George, the most important Liberal social reformer of the period, observed in a speech delivered in Cardiff in October 1906 while he was President of the Board of Trade:

> If at the end of an average term of office it were found that a Liberal Parliament had done nothing to cope seriously with the social condition of the people, to remove the national degradation of slums and widespread poverty and destitution in a land glittering with wealth . . . then would a real cry arise in this land for a new party, and many of us here in this room would join in that cry.[10]

Lloyd George was anything but disinterested, but he was a strong supporter of social reform and his words were to be more prophetic than he intended.

At first the new Labour Party seemed to be a considerable success. The *Taff Vale* decision was speedily reversed in the form of the Trade Disputes Act of 1906. A complex Liberal bill giving conditional protection to trade unions was replaced by a simple Labour proposal which prevented a union from being sued for the illegal acts of its members. This was certainly a Labour victory in which the influential role played by David Shackleton was acknowledged publicly by Liberal and Conservative parliamentary leaders, but it should be noted that it was a trade union measure which united and enthused the party. Moreover, a series of Liberal backbenchers, particularly Sir Charles Dilke, gave the Labour bill their support, without which its passage would have been in doubt. (It should be added that these backbenchers were mindful of promises made to their constituents and the likely adverse consequences had a bill satisfactory to Labour not been passed.) Indeed, Dilke thought the Labour men "[t]oo easily satisfied",[11] while, according to the account of a contemporary activist, they thought him an extremist. The essential point was that the measure was supported not only by the Labour Party but also by many Liberals and that among them was the prime minister, Sir Henry Campbell-Bannerman. The Conservatives too were unwilling to oppose the bill wholeheartedly. No other measure of vital importance to Labour in this parliament had such impressive force behind it.

There was, however, further legislation of interest to Labour in this first year after the election. ILP members worked hard for a bill passed in 1906 which permitted the feeding of necessitous schoolchildren, and also for one which introduced medical inspection of schoolchildren in 1907. Labour was also active in strengthening the Workmen's Compensation Act of 1906, itself a measure which consolidated and extended an earlier act of 1897. But once these measures were passed there was little else to suggest that parliament was influenced by the election of thirty Labour members, the majority of whom claimed to be socialists.

The most obvious characteristics of the parliamentary Labour Party during the parliament of 1906 were weakness and division. Many complaints were made by Labour leaders about each other; Snowden, Hardie, Henderson and MacDonald were all among the backbiters and the bitten. By 1908 Ben Tillett, the mercurial trade union leader, was asking pointedly whether the parliamentary party was a failure and claiming that it was a lion with "no teeth or claws . . . and losing its growl too".[12] Hardie was a deeply disappointed man, criticizing the party for its subservience to the Liberals and early in 1910 insisting privately that his preference was to resign from it because of its lack of fighting spirit. There was a complicated relationship between ideological consistency and political reality. Even Hardie seems to have been prepared during the budget crisis of 1909 to agree to give open support to Liberal candidates in constituencies in which no Labour man was standing in order to defeat the Conservatives and the Lords.

Left-wing, socialist or even reformist parties are often suspicious of the autonomy of their leaders and the result has sometimes been, as in this case, to weaken their effectiveness. The parliamentary Labour Party was presided over by a chairman who was not described as leader. Hardie was narrowly elected to this post over David Shackleton in 1906. He was replaced by Henderson in 1908 and George Barnes of the engineering union followed in 1910. It was not until MacDonald succeeded Barnes in 1911, Henderson replacing MacDonald in turn as secretary, that the party had firm or apparently long-term leadership. Hardie's period as Labour hero had ended with the election of 1906. As Henry Pelling comments, he was "an indifferent parliamentarian, rather inclined to play the lone wolf, and by no means ready to adapt himself to collective decisions". He was prone to associate himself with prominent though unsuccessful causes, including Indian nationalism and women's parliamentary suffrage, and thus became an easy target for ridicule. *Punch*'s parliamentary correspondent, an unsympathetic observer, described Hardie as a "self-appointed champion [in this case a lone supporter of imprisoned suffragettes] particularly alive to opportunity of asserting himself when gratuitous advertisement is forward".[13] The "slippery skills of the parliamentarian"[14] were not his. His dislike of parliamentary manoeuvres and negotiations was probably both the cause and the result of his disaffection from the party in these years.

Inadequately led, the Labour Party did not escape incident, reverse and temporary eclipse in these years. Parliamentary by-elections were a fertile source of friction. In August 1906 Robert Smillie of the Scottish miners contested Cockermouth for Labour in a by-election. Labour had not contested it in the general election of 1906 but Smillie's intervention cost the Liberals the seat. Christabel Pankhurst's indifference or hostility to the Labour cause in this election and Hardie's known sympathy with women's suffrage led to anguish and bitterness within the party.

In 1907 Labour and socialist candidates won two seats. Jarrow had seen a straight fight in the general election of 1906 between Sir Charles Palmer, the Liberal member who owned the prominent shipyard in the town, and Pete Curran, an ILP member and a hardened veteran of Labour and ILP politics. Palmer had won an easy victory. Upon his death in 1907 four candidates stood for the vacant seat, and although Curran lost nearly 400 votes from his 1906 total he won convincingly against a Liberal, a Conservative and an Irish Nationalist. The Liberal press argued that his victory was not due to his socialism but rather to the death of the dominant MP and the multiplicity of candidates, and there was much to be said for this claim.

The second 1907 by-election, in Colne Valley, differed from previous elections in being won by a professed and independent socialist, Victor Grayson, who was not endorsed by the official Labour Party but who narrowly won a previously Liberal seat in a three-cornered fight. Grayson was born in 1882 in Liverpool and followed an engineering apprenticeship there, but by 1907 he had been a student both in Liverpool and Manchester and was scraping a living as a socialist lecturer and journalist. In one election leaflet he told the Colne Valley electorate: "I am appealing to you as one of your own class. I want emancipation from the wage-slavery of Capitalism . . . The time for our emancipation has come."[15] Although the Labour Party officially remained aloof, the local ILP branch supported Grayson, Snowden spoke for him, Bruce Glasier, another ILP leader, raised money for him and MacDonald was benevolently neutral. Hardie also supported Grayson with a personal message, but his subsequent absence on a world tour did nothing to endear him either to the pro or anti-Grayson factions.

In the event Curran made little impact on parliament while Grayson secured much publicity at the price of dissension within the Labour Party and in particular within the ILP. Both men lost their seats to Liberals in the general election held in January 1910, Curran narrowly and Grayson by a larger margin. Their by-election victories, one challenging the

Liberals in the name of Labour and a muted socialism, the other as an independent socialist, appeared to have achieved little in the aftermath. Curran died later in 1910 while Grayson faded away. His memory was long cherished, but neither he nor Curran had done much to suggest that Labour or socialism was a steady electoral force unless it could attract Liberal support. Labour did manage to win another by-election in Sheffield in 1909 despite the opposition of a Liberal and two Conservatives. This election was won by Joseph Pointer who, significantly, retained the seat in both general elections of 1910 in straight fights with a Conservative. Another dozen by-elections were lost in one of which, Bermondsey, the Labour vote in 1909 for the ILP-er Alfred Salter exceeded the margin of the victorious Conservative over a Liberal.

The general election of January 1910 was a sign to Labour that the progress it could hope to make without Liberal support was limited. On the surface the party made important gains, for its thirty MPs elected in 1906 became 40, an increase of a third. In fact the increase was wholly due to the fact that the Miners' Federation of Great Britain had formally affiliated to the Labour Party in 1909, bringing with it the bulk of the 13 miner members elected as Lib–Labs in 1906. Seven sitting Labour MPs were defeated including Curran and a former Lib–Lab. Most significantly, no successful Labour candidate faced a Liberal opponent or two official Liberals in a two-member constituency. All the Labour and socialist candidates who faced Liberal opposition, however, numbering over 40, were defeated.

Political problems of the time, which included a parliament with virtually equal numbers of Liberals and Conservatives, led to a second general election in December 1910; not until 1974 were there to be two elections again in a single calendar year. This time the results of the Labour campaign were no more gratifying than in January, and the overall parliamentary situation was almost unchanged. Labour gained a net two seats (five new members and three losses) but only one of its successful candidates was opposed by the Liberals. Only 14 others stood, a decline in the total number of Labour candidates of over a quarter since January, and almost all of the 14 faced Liberal opponents.

As 1910 ended, therefore, the number of Labour MPs seemed to have reached a ceiling of well under 10 per cent of the House of Commons, even if the Irish members are disregarded. The outlook was bleak. The political situation was dominated by Liberal causes, above all the prolonged struggle over the Lloyd George budget of 1909 and the subsequent campaign to restrict the legislative powers of the House of Lords. This was the great political battle of the day and Labour members were forced to play the role of junior ally. Even here they were heavily outnumbered by Irish Home Rulers, though Labour support was not conditional on Liberal advocacy of a single cause and hence was more reliable than that of the Irish. The fight with the Lords, the passage of national insurance legislation in 1911 which sharply divided Labour opinion, and Lloyd George's land campaign in the last prewar years ensured that causes identified with the Labour Party like its Right to Work bills received little attention outside its own ranks. The social reforming radicalism of the Liberals, acceptably "socialistic" rather than socialist in MacDonald's view, may have been as influential for inter-party relations as the Liberal instincts of many Labour men and their knowledge that they owed their seats to Liberal benevolence. In any case, Labour was closely bound to the Liberals in these years. Hardie, as seen above, was dissatisfied with the Liberal alliance, but the more important MacDonald was on friendly terms with several Liberal ministers, an advocate of Liberal measures and at least willing to consider a formal Lib–Lab coalition. Such a coalition might not have restored the deferential relationship which existed between Labour men and the later Gladstonian Liberal Party, but it would have imposed a strong barrier to real Labour independence then and later.

The parliamentary Labour Party was largely quiescent in 1910–14. It was to a considerable extent made up of formerly Liberal trade unionists, amongst whom miners were especially numerous. If MacDonald the theorist thought the true Labour role lay in providing strong support for the Liberals, why should practical trade unionists dissent? They knew far more about their working-class voters than MPs of other parties could hope to do, but, as David Martin who has closely analysed the first Labour MPs points out, "the strongest impression created by the early Labour Party is one of vague good intentions in so far as its wider philosophy was concerned".[16]

The political situation did not favour Labour independence, and one important feature was Labour's lack of money. This was partly the result of the Osborne judgment of 1909. W. V. Osborne was a Liberal member of the Amalgamated Society of Railway Servants who took court action to oppose being compelled to support the Labour Party through his union subscription. Whoever gave financial support to his action it was nevertheless successful, and unions were unable to contribute funds for political purposes until the law was changed. Henceforth the Labour Party would have to rely upon voluntary contributions and depend financially as well as politically on the Liberals. The Osborne judgment was highly unwelcome, deplored publicly and privately by Labour and union leaders and potentially extremely menacing, but it may have had less immediate impact on Labour fortunes than was once thought. The opinion of Neal Blewett, the author of a study of the two general elections of 1910, is that the judgment did not inhibit the Labour Party from putting up as many parliamentary candidates as it wished in the two elections of 1910, even in December when there were only 56 Labour candidates. "[T]wo elections in the one year imposed a heavy strain on Labour's resources.

Neither the [party leadership] nor the prudent union executives were likely to throw money away on contests in which, judging from January, the chances of success were non-existent."[17] In Liverpool unions were accused of hiding behind the Osborne judgment in cases in which "through indifference or hostility, [they] preferred to save their coppers".[18]

One crucial difficulty was solved when in 1911 the Liberals introduced a yearly salary of £400 for members of parliament, a surprisingly high figure for the day. But the Liberals were slower about taking legislative steps to reverse the Osborne judgment itself and thus assist Labour Party funds, and the Conservatives were no more eager to do so. It was not until 1913 that the Trade Union Act was finally passed, allowing unions to create a fund to be spent on political objectives if members voted in favour, but with safeguards for dissenters. Andrew Bonar Law, the Conservative leader in the Commons, expressed the view that it was "not in their interest" for unions "to identify themselves with any political party". A similar sentiment had been expressed by Winston Churchill, then Liberal home secretary, speaking to an earlier version of the bill in 1911. "[T]he advantages of trade unions", he declared, should not be "reserved for persons of one political creed."[19] Nor did the large minority of union members who opposed the establishment of a political fund in ballots held in the next few years suggest that the organized working class was overwhelmingly supportive of the Labour Party.

Labour was not helped, though it might be thought that it would have been, by the fact that the years 1910–14 were a period of unprecedented industrial unrest. The young George Dangerfield made an apparently imperishable reputation amongst historians by insisting in *The Strange Death of Liberal England* (1935) that Liberalism was fatally damaged by the economic and political unrest of these years, but in fact most progressive political parties have suffered, in the short term at least, during periods of industrial turmoil. The Labour Party leadership were embarrassed witnesses and opponents of the strikes and violence of the period. MacDonald and Snowden, while emphasizing forcefully adverse living and working conditions and the political conservatism which had given rise to the unrest, made abundantly clear their opposition both to violence and the "syndicalism" which put industrial emancipation before the party political struggle. MacDonald denounced "the flashy propaganda of impatience, of heroic action, of anti-social methods" as well as "narrow class prejudice" and "the feeble force of Syndicalism". Snowden made clear his view that syndicalism was "fundamentally different from Socialism" and that it was as a form of industrial organization "utterly impractical and undesirable".[20] Both authors denied absolutely that industrial workers without broader political support could create a just society by a policy which set out to divide one social class from another.

There is no doubt that they spoke for their parliamentary colleagues. They were decisive figures in the party leadership and they probably spoke for most Labour voters as well. Even the maverick Hardie, though sympathizing with the strikers, urged the case for political action rather than relying on industrial militancy.

Recent decades have seen a lively debate among historians about the position of the Labour Party at the outbreak of war in 1914. Was Labour a growing political force or the tail of the Liberal dog?

The books and articles that have discussed the subject are well researched and persuasive on both sides. The case for the Labour Party is well summarized by Henry Pelling, in whose view non-political workers, a majority in their class, were coming to accept "a sort of undogmatic Labourism . . . which consisted in little more than the opinion that the Labour Party, and not the Liberal, was the party for working men to belong to . . . By 1914 the Labour Party was the party with the centralization to take advantage of twentieth-century political conditions."[21] This is a view which has found support among a significant number of other historians.

By this time other European countries had strong working class-based political parties eager for power, and the British working classes had gained in self-confidence and political understanding. How long could middle-class Liberals, most of whom had little sympathy with socialism or involvement in working-class politics, continue to be an adequate expression of working-class aspirations? Pelling also cites "long-term social and economic changes" which divided Britain on class lines and benefited the Labour Party. Gordon Phillips, writing more recently, admits that before 1914 the party had difficulty in attracting votes but draws attention to Labour's stronger organization and the possibility that it would have put up many more candidates in an election in 1915 had one taken place than it had done in 1910. "Though still very much a third party, it was now a far more formidable one."[22] Local election results too suggest that the party was making steady if not spectacular progress. It should also be noted that there was a radical fringe of the Liberal Party inside and outside parliament sympathetic to Labour policies such as a minimum wage. Some of these Liberals might have joined Labour even if war had not broken out in 1914.

The pro-Liberal point of view is put by, among others, MacDonald's most important biographer David Marquand, who maintains:

> The notion that the Liberal Party was doomed and that the Labour Party was bound by some inexorable sociological law to replace it as the main anti-Conservative party in Britain would have seemed absurd [in 1912–14], not only to most Liberals but to most Labour men as well. The Labour Party seemed to be stuck in the doldrums, its energies consumed by petty personal bickering and ideological feuds.[23]

This argument appears to be more plausible than the opposing view, though personal bickering and ideological feuds were apparent not only in 1914 but also at other periods of Labour history.

The pro-Liberal case is strengthened by an analysis of by-elections in the years 1911–14. The Labour Party had from spring 1912 the support of the non-militant National Union of Women's Suffrage Societies, which claimed somewhat optimistically that Labour, "alone among the parties in Parliament, is UNITEDLY determined to fight the women's battle through".[24] Despite the support of the NUWSS at by-elections, however, the Labour Party finished bottom of the poll in every one of the sixteen seats which it fought or which had previously been Labour-held between March 1911 and May 1914. Four of the sixteen had been Labour but two were now won by the older parties, a third candidate, though a trade unionist, stood as a Lib–Lab and the fourth was George Lansbury, who had resigned his seat over women's suffrage and lost as an independent Labour candidate to a Conservative in the by-election fought on the issue. The co-operation between Labour and suffragists was a tactical one, based on Labour's consistent though not always enthusiastic support for women's suffrage. A few Labour MPs, notably Keir Hardie and Lansbury, were impassioned supporters of women's suffrage but the majority of their colleagues were less convinced. Some historians have suggested that the Women's Liberal Federation was increasingly mutinous before the outbreak of war and that many of its members were no longer willing to support the party, but there is little evidence to suggest that their defection would have helped the Labour Party. Nor was support for women's suffrage an issue which would ensure Labour popularity with a male electorate.

The historian Ross McKibbin claims that in some of the by-elections "Labour made some significant gains", but the party's position at the bottom of the poll suggests that there was still a steep hill to climb before significant gains would be transformed into election victories. Nor were unions under heavy pressure from their members to develop closer links with Labour at the expense of the Liberals. Some members and some unions were firmly attached to the Labour Party but Beatrice Webb was probably correct in concluding that "the closer the Labour member sticks to the Liberal Party the better . . . [t]he British workman . . . is pleased".[25] Labour had not won a special place for itself with the working-class electorate by 1914.

Two more Labour members, miners who had always been Lib–Labs at heart, drifted away from their Labour allegiance, and although there were gains for the party in trades council and local Labour Party affiliations as well as more elected members of local government bodies in these years, it lost about 15 per cent of its parliamentary party. It was a body devoted above all things to parliamentary representation, and "the doldrums" or at the very least a temporary halt to progress fairly describes its position during the summer of 1914. Even G. D. H. Cole, a socialist historian and strong Labour partisan who lived through the period, acknowledged later in his *British Working Class Politics 1832–1914* the political moderation and acceptance of capitalism of the ordinary worker and the dominance of Liberalism on the political left in 1914. The Liberal Party, after all, had formed the country's government since 1906, and had enacted a number of important if somewhat tentative social and political reforms, including old age pensions and legislation to limit working hours, which much of the working class valued highly.

On this reading it was the Great War, in which Britain joined early in August 1914, which made an unsuccessful pressure group into an important party of state. It would have been hardly possible for political observers in 1914 to have thought of Ramsay MacDonald as prime minister of a Labour government within ten years, but in the early summer of 1914 few people imagined that the dynamic chancellor of the exchequer, David Lloyd George, would break with Asquith, his prime minister, and form a coalition with the Conservatives – and Labour – less than three years later. In 1914 the Labour Party was not, Duncan Tanner writes, "on the verge of replacing the Liberals . . . As things stood, Labour's progress would be slow . . . Despite potential fissures in the Liberal and Labour coalitions, it appeared that an immediate and fundamental realignment of forces was unlikely."[26] This is also Andrew Thorpe's conclusion; the Labour Party was well established in 1914, unlikely to decline and able to take advantage of the unexpected opportunities offered by the war, but in no position to overtake the Liberals either. It is hard to dissent from this view. Although labour and socialist parties were strong political forces in other European countries, it needed the cataclysm of war for Britain to follow the same pattern.

Labour would have had to achieve a complete reconstruction of the election system in order to supersede the Liberals. A parliamentary system dominated by two political parties had gradually developed in the course of the nineteenth century, most constituencies from 1885 returning a single member of parliament. Twenty-four two-member constituencies remained, enabling both Liberals and Labour to gain parliamentary representation without fighting each other. Labour profited considerably from the existence of two-member constituencies, ten or more of its members of parliament, including Hardie, MacDonald and Snowden being elected in these seats at each of the elections from 1906. Hardie, as seen above, had also been elected in such a seat in 1900, though he had faced two Liberal opponents as he did again in 1906 and January 1910, one of them an independent Liberal. In most constituencies, however, a single member was returned, an almost insuperable obstacle for a ambitious young political party.

The Labour Party could not hope to transform its fortunes by judicious exploitation of the electoral system alone. Such manoeuvres could not lift its status above that of a pressure group, as it still was in essence in 1914. A significantly stronger Labour Party might benefit the Conservatives, and British political history for many years after Labour overtook the Liberals as a political force did little to suggest that division in progressive ranks was a sensible strategy to follow. Thus in addition to the personal and ideological ties which bound many working men to the Liberals a practical consideration arose; a Liberal government was much to be preferred to the Unionist alternative.

The existing political structure could not have survived socio-economic reality if there had been a strong demand for more working-class representation in parliament. Contemporaries and historians have calculated that in the early years of the twentieth century as many as three-quarters of the population belonged to the working class and were socially distinct from the established middle class. They did not, however, form a homogeneous political group, as Jose Harris among others points out. Social class was only one factor influencing political behaviour, the appeal of patriotism, religious affiliation, local issues and personal considerations remaining important influences. "Class division was not an inexorable process . . . [W]hat needs to be explained is not the speed but the slowness with which assertion of specifically working-class interests caught up with the formal reality of working-class power."[27] Although the working class was numerically dominant it was too divided, socially as well as politically, to make use of its power. Many of its members were fatalistic and uninterested in the political process. As the American historian Standish Meacham comments: "Political commitment demands a consciousness that change is both desirable and possible – a consciousness foreign to most men and women trapped at the level of 25 shillings a week."[28] It is unlikely that in such circumstances the British political system would soon be overturned by a triumphant Labour Party.

The astonishment of the British people at finding themselves at war with Germany in 1914 has been stressed in many accounts of the period. Labour shared the general surprise but most of its parliamentary representatives were strong supporters of the war effort, despite the fact that this meant loyalty to a society in which much of the working class was poor and exploited. The party appears to have followed the wishes of its working-class voters, whose enthusiasm for war was generally acknowledged at the time as it has been by historians subsequently. Indeed, trade union leaders and many of their members, on whose votes the Labour Party was dependent, appear to have been among the greatest supporters of war. David Marquand points out that older Labour belief in internationalism and the newer hope that the working class would stand together against war were now swept aside. "[T]hese attitudes ran alongside a deeper vein of old-fashioned patriotism; they were easily overwhelmed by the wave of abhorrence and indignation which was let loose in Britain when the Germans invaded Belgium." "The invasion of Belgium", Philip Snowden recalled, "came as a veritable God-send to the embarrassed British Government, who were conscious that it would have been difficult to get popular support for a war on behalf of France and Russia". Beatrice Webb, who was not an opponent of the war, wrote in similar terms in her diary two days after Britain entered the war: "If this little race [Belgium] had not been attacked the war would have been positively unpopular – it could hardly have taken place."[29]

Snowden was one of several Labour leaders who, though they did not go out of their way to appear unpatriotic, deplored the war. These men had long been members of the Independent Labour Party which, at least at national level, was not carried away by war fever as was the Labour Party itself. Keir Hardie had a long record of opposition to war, but during the period of ill health and distress which preceded his premature death in September 1915 he was more prominent in attempts to mitigate its effects than in outright opposition. Despite his general anti-war sentiments, several statements during the last year of his life suggested a resigned support for this war and in particular for forcing the Germans to retire behind their pre-invasion borders. As for MacDonald, he was more concerned to secure a just peace than to campaign against the war, but his position was subtle and easily misunderstood. He resigned from the chair of the parliamentary Labour Party soon after the outbreak of war and was subjected to the worst kind of obloquy, including the charge in the jingoist journal *John Bull* in 1915 that he was a "Traitor, Coward, Cur", who, it demanded, should be courtmartialled, "'taken to the Tower and shot at dawn".[30] That his ambivalent anti-war stand would stand him in good stead after 1918 could hardly have been guessed at the time. His successor was Arthur Henderson, who was not an ILP-er. Henderson supported the war but equally wanted to keep the Labour Party united, an aim in which he was largely successful.

Without expressing opposition to the initial British war aims there was plenty of work for ILP MPs to do in opposing government abuse of wartime powers and in supporting conscientious objectors and a negotiated peace. Snowden, though like his colleagues not demanding peace negotiations in the early stages of the war, was particularly active in the struggle against conscription, in seeking exemptions and helping objectors. In January 1916 he told the House of Commons that conscription would be "a strong weapon for enforcing the chains of slavery on the democracy". It was "an attempt to get cheap soldiers". Three months later he protested "in the strongest way possible" against the claim that the few men who had given up their attempts to become recognized as conscientious objectors and joined the army had done so from a change of conviction. "Nothing could be further from the truth."[31]

Snowden's efforts were supplemented by those of MacDonald, Fred Jowett, W. C. Anderson and Thomas Richardson, who after Hardie's death comprised most of the small ILP parliamentary contingent. The Labour Party as a whole threatened to withdraw its members from the first coalition government in opposition to conscription but was persuaded not to do so by a personal appeal from Asquith and its general support for the war effort. J. R. Clynes, an ILP member, and some other Labour MPs voted for a parliamentary amendment which would have strengthened the position of men who faced examination of their refusal to fight before tribunals, but there was no vote by the parliamentary Labour Party against conscription as such. Most "political", as opposed to religious, conscientious objectors were influenced by the ILP which is not surprising since it was the only political organization which unambiguously opposed conscription. The ILP MPs worked closely with the somewhat larger group of anti-conscription Liberal MPs, most of whom favoured a negotiated peace and some of whom were to join the Labour Party after the war. The two groups collaborated in forming the Union of Democratic Control, whose views influenced Labour Party foreign policy in post-war years.

Some historians have suggested that the intervention of the government in the economy in wartime conditions was influential in moving the mind of the British electorate in the direction of the Labour Party, which believed in such intervention in principle. Such a shift in public opinion was probably less important than the fact that wartime developments brought greater opportunities for working-class civilians and greater understanding of the indispensability of their class to national life in both war and peace. The governments of Asquith and especially of Lloyd George were convinced of the need to meet the demands of trade unions and their members and to ensure their continued support for the war. The result could be seen in higher wages, at least for those engaged in war production, greatly increased trade union membership and an unprecedented number of trade unionists in government office or related positions. Alan Bullock, biographer of Ernest Bevin, points out: "For the first time, the unions were taken into partnership by the State; their leaders (a short time before denounced as agitators) were invited to join the Cabinet and brought on to one committee after another."[32] Bevin himself was from March 1914 one of three national organizers of the Dockers' Union, an important though not pre-eminent position in a union of 43,000 members. By the end of 1918 he was a prominent figure and a coming man, partly because of his own talents, partly because of the new opportunities offered by the war.

The years 1915–18 were full of important political developments. In

May 1915 Asquith formed the first wartime coalition government, with Arthur Henderson, at the time a much more important figure than Bevin, as president of the board of education. There were also two Labour junior ministers. Henderson's office had in fact little to do with education and much with labour relations; he was subsequently translated to the post of paymaster-general, a ministry without portfolio which left him free to concentrate on labour questions. The ministerial appointment caused dissension within the Labour Party, but he won the majority support of its national executive and of the parliamentary party. The historian Kenneth Morgan asserts that Henderson's assumption of office while actively carrying on his party work was "a classic instance of the insider-outsider role that Labour acquired during the first world war, to its great good fortune".[33] As a member of the cabinet he accepted the need for conscription as a military necessity, although the party opposed it in principle at its conference in 1916. (The threat of industrial conscription was, however, its major concern.) This was the first example of what would become a not unfamiliar process, the conference making a decision which pledged the party to a line which was ignored or evaded by its members in government. Policies which appeared urgently straightforward to activists were inevitably seen in a different light by leaders, especially those who were in a position to become government ministers.

In December 1916 Lloyd George replaced Asquith as prime minister, an event over which an enormous amount of ink has been spilt. In fact Asquith, widely charged with being an inadequate war leader, had been prime minister since April 1908, longer than any predecessor since the 1820s, and had presided over greater loss of life than would have been thought possible before August 1914. The surprising point is not that he was superseded but that it should have taken well over two wartime years to force him out of office. The change of leader, which put Lloyd George in charge of events for six years, shattered the Liberal Party and heralded its death as an important party of state. As such this event was one of the most fortunate for the Labour Party in its entire history, though it took time before this new political development could be fully appreciated.

Labour entered the new, smaller Lloyd George coalition, its participation approved by the party conference in January 1917 by nearly two million voting members to just over 300,000. (This was an early example of the value to the leadership of the union bloc vote.) Henderson became a member of the five-man inner war cabinet and was joined by five Labour men in more junior roles. The party thus achieved unprecedented prominence, but in August 1917 Henderson resigned when the war cabinet refused to accept his recommendations on preventing Russian conquest by Germany and Bolshevik assumption of power in Russia itself. The Czarist regime had been overthrown in March and Henderson strongly but vainly advocated supporting participation in a conference at

Stockholm of international socialist parties at which peace terms would be discussed. He was replaced in government by George Barnes of the engineering union, but a gift of enormous significance to the party had inadvertently been made. The Liberals had split irrevocably, Henderson had been raised to the position of a national figure, and was then effectively dismissed, leaving him free to spend his considerable energies and ability on reshaping the Labour Party. Seen in a longer perspective than was available to contemporaries the party had been presented with a golden opportunity by its opponents which it did not waste.

The aftermath of Henderson's return to domestic politics was to be the creation of a new constitution for the Labour Party which after initial rejection was accepted at the end of February 1918. This was the constitution that introduced individual membership of the Labour Party and was a harsh blow to the ILP which, like the Fabians, lost its own representatives on the national executive. There was to be, at least potentially, a local Labour Party in each constituency as well as the continuing and assured primacy in the party at national level of the trade unions. The constitution also contained the famous Clause Four, the socialist objective which committed the party to "secure for the producers by hand or by brain the full fruits of their industry . . . upon the basis of the common ownership of the means of production". Distribution and exchange were to be added to this formulation by an amendment in 1929. Five positions on the executive were reserved for the new local parties and four for women, but their election by the whole conference did nothing to loosen union control. The new constitution was devised largely by Henderson with the assistance of Sidney Webb. As F. M. Leventhal, one of Henderson's biographers points out, it was he who most clearly "saw the need not merely to devise a bargain with the trade unions, but to appeal to a wider constituency, including women as well as men, intellectuals no less than manual labourers".[34]

Ross McKibbin, who has made a detailed study of the adoption of the new constitution, concludes that the unions did not object to a socialist objective since they retained control of the party organization. Samuel Beer, the American scholar, sees Clause Four as a bid for independence from the Liberals by adopting "a set of beliefs and values distinguishing [Labour] from other parties".[35] These views seem to be accurate, as does the assertion made by some writers that the progressive section of the middle class and the trade unions had moved to the political left during the war and, it was hoped, would be attracted by a bold programme. What cannot be accepted is that the leopard had changed its spots and that the Labour Party had suddenly been convinced of the need to find a coherent fixed doctrine or that the men who had worked happily with the Liberals for so long had discovered that only independent Labour socialism would respond to the needs of the nation. Clause Four, far from committing the party to an early drive towards socialism, was an ultimate aim. Labour was to remain a party seeking consensus and popular reforms, responding to the desires of a non-ideological electorate. Nevertheless, Tudor Jones's reminder that common ownership of the means of production had been "a central strand of British socialist thought" since before the beginning of the twentieth century should be borne in mind. So should his further comment that the adoption of Clause Four "did at least imply some kind of official socialist commitment". As Jim Tomlinson points out, nationalization would remain "at the core of Labour's economic programme . . . until the 1940s, and crucial to its rhetoric until the 1990s".[36]

Post-war Britain was clearly going to be a different society in important respects from the years before 1914. The older landed class had lost much of its domination. Working-class organizations and their members had gained greater confidence and unity. Working-class aspirations had risen and the life styles of the different social classes began to bear greater resemblance to each other, if not by 1918 then in the years which followed. The wages of unskilled workers had risen in both absolute and relative terms. As Duncan Tanner points out: "Earnings were more regular, overtime more common, and supplementary work for family members was more freely available."[37] Above all, the nation had undergone a collective trauma after which huge swathes of the population could claim and receive greater recognition and respect from the holders of power than in the past. The symbol of this recognition was the massive widening of the franchise in 1918.

The changes should not be exaggerated. Craft privileges had been "diluted" by wartime conditions to a certain extent, but innovation was less sweeping than sometimes believed and the unions of skilled workers were by no means reconciled to the loss of their privileges. The war, traumatic as it was, did not transform the British class system nor, at a stroke, unify the different strands of the working class. Four years brought no revolution but it did bring changes which benefited the Labour Party.

The party had a new, centralizing constitution, an agreed objective which was clear in principle though vague in practice, and an expanding number of local parties. It also published a party programme called *Labour and the New Social Order*, drafted by Sidney Webb. This programme, which included full employment, measures of public ownership, progressive taxation and social reforms, was designed both to identify Labour with progressive policies and to appeal to the mass electorate of both sexes which had been created earlier in 1918. The Representation of the People Act of that year enfranchised those men over 21 who had previously remained voteless and the bulk of women over 30. The electorate was thus nearly trebled by a single act of parliament giving Labour, at least potentially, "a substantial new basis of support"[38] and an advantage over the Liberals. Some historians are sceptical of the claim that

Labour gained markedly from expansion of the franchise. The Edwardian Labour Party assumed that its support came particularly from already enfranchised skilled workers and trade unionists and did not regard extension of the parliamentary vote before 1914 as an urgent priority. It can be accepted, however, that the revision of constituency boundaries in 1918 was unequivocally beneficial to Labour.

The new electorate had been subjected to severe deprivations in wartime and promised a better future. Its employment prospects were uncertain, its housing conditions poor. It was asked to vote for a national Labour Party, no longer a federation, which intended to bid for independent political power. The party's trade union affiliated membership nearly doubled during the war years and by 1918 stood at nearly three million. Henderson had persuaded the party to adopt a new constitution far enough to the left to ensure that when the Communist Party was formed in 1920 it would be small, and reassuring enough to most union leaders to prevent them from succumbing to the potential appeal of a purely trade union party. He had appealed for the support of the middle class. What he needed now was a general election and Lloyd George was soon to oblige.

The election of December 1918 had two principal results. First, despite the overwhelming victory of Lloyd George, "the man who won the war", it paved the way for a Conservative-dominated period between the two wars. Conservatives, known for the last time as Unionists, formed nearly two-thirds of the victorious parliamentary coalition. It took them four years to get rid of Lloyd George, but they could have done so at a much earlier date had they wished. Second, it marked the advent on the national scene of the Labour Party as one of the main parties of state. Its election manifesto demanded "a peace of reconciliation", withdrawal of foreign forces from the new Russian republic, "[f]reedom for Ireland and India" which did not imply imminent independence, "[a]t least a million new houses" paid for by the state, abolition of conscription, improved education and health, a capital levy and "nationalization and democratic control of vital public services, such as mines, railways, shipping, armaments, and electric power" and also land. A special appeal was made to women voters. The manifesto concluded: "Labour's programme is comprehensive and constructive. It is designed to build a better world, and to build it by constitutional means . . . . Labour confidently appeals to the country to support its programme of social justice and economic freedom."[39]

The result contained elements of both disaster and triumph. The parliamentary party was shorn of most of its ILP or supposedly left-wing leaders, for MacDonald, Snowden, Fred Jowett and W. C. Anderson were all defeated at the polls. Even more serious, Arthur Henderson was also beaten. Sidney Webb, George Lansbury and Ernest Bevin, none of them parliamentarians during the war years, failed to win seats, and J. R. Clynes, who had been a minister in the Lloyd George coalition, was the best-known survivor. What was left was a trade-union dominated party without much imagination or a strong ideological purpose. The short-lived National Democratic Party, composed mainly of pro-war trade unionists, formed part of the coalition and defeated both MacDonald and Henderson at the polls. Thirteen candidates, four of them government ministers, were elected by "coalition Labour" or the National Democratic Party.

On one level this was clear defeat, and regarded as such. Beatrice Webb told her diary that the 25 miners' representatives were "dead stuff", and that William Adamson, the miner who led the parliamentary party, was "respectable but dull-witted". Other Labour MPs were in her view "fat-heads" or "buffoons, simpletons and corrupt persons", the parliamentary party itself "a very tame lion". MacDonald, no doubt influenced by his own heavy defeat, noted in less flamboyant terms: "[T]hough there are one or two good men in it, the Labour team is altogether inadequately equipped for the part it ought to play".[40] But on another level there were gains, as Beatrice Webb also recognized. Labour was able and willing to put up candidates in places where it must have known it could not win, for their number rose more than six-fold though Labour MPs increased by less than half. Thanks to the greater number of candidates, the new voters and Liberal divisions Labour polled over 20 per cent of the vote, a respectable percentage for what was in important respects a new party claiming to be the official opposition in conditions of post-war turmoil. It returned 57 of its candidates, a number which rose to 61 with a Co-operative Party ally and the subsequent adherence of three unofficial Labour MPs. Labour polled less than half the vote of the coalition candidates but over half again as much as the independent Liberals, still led by Asquith, and elected many more MPs. It had emerged from its chrysalis stage. Moreover, at a volatile time it had more control over its parliamentary party than Asquith had over his.

The election was bound to be a walkover for the successful coalition. Social issues, however, played an important part, with Lloyd George and Bonar Law, the Conservative leader, jointly promising land reform, better housing and education and improved standards of employment, and Winston Churchill, another leading coalition figure, offering railway nationalization, state control of monopolies and "a decent minimum standard of life and labour".[41] The electorate was now markedly more democratic and politics would for the next two generations at least be dominated by social issues as it had not been during the period of Liberal power. It is obvious in retrospect that Labour, a party which claimed to have a socialist aim, was going to have great opportunities in post-1918 Britain. In the event the next dozen years would be marked by a single-minded drive by Labour for political office which would end its age of innocence and relegate socialism to the political margin. When socialism came to the fore as a specific aim rather than a pious aspiration the party would have suffered its worst electoral catastrophe.

3 LABOUR BETWEEN TWO WARS

1918–1939

The interwar years, with their important changes, set the pattern for the Labour Party for a prolonged period. In 1918 the party was led by men, originally Liberals, who had lived through the period when it was a small pressure group at least semi-subordinate to the Liberal Party. By 1939 Labour was a party with its own structure and a detailed programme, while the Liberals were no longer a great party of state. Women had a small but important role among the rank and file and in a few cases were backbench members of parliament, though they were uninfluential in the leadership. The first generation of party leaders – Hardie, Henderson, MacDonald, Snowden – were all dead, and in the latter two cases had broken with the Labour Party before their deaths. Their former colleagues, men like J. R. Clynes, Fred Jowett, George Lansbury, J. H. Thomas (who like MacDonald and Snowden had left the party in 1931) and Sidney Webb were elderly and no longer important politicians. The party was led by a new generation, hardly known before 1918 and not elected to parliament until 1922 or later. There had been remarkable changes of personnel in a short period.

The Labour Party changed significantly between the wars. The party of the 1920s was destroyed by the catastrophe of 1931, when the number of Labour and allied MPs suddenly fell to little more than a sixth of its previous total. The party was painfully reconstructed in the 1930s. The earlier period was marked above all by the efforts of the party leadership to show that Labour could be trusted by other politicians, the press and holders of economic and political power to run the country's affairs without either ruin or revolution. Its electoral base lay in the working class, but not enough working people, in particular not enough women or workers in the new industries of the period, voted Labour to make its electoral position other than precarious. Leaders like MacDonald, Snowden and others made frequent derogatory comments about the political awareness of the working class and their love of drink and gambling.

Christopher Howard has shown that progress was also unsatisfactory at local level, since constituency parties were chronically short of workers, supporters and money.

A majority Labour government between 1918 and 1931 had it existed would probably have enacted significant social reforms, but it is unlikely that it would have passed such sweeping and novel measures as the Liberals had done in the period 1906–14. The keyword was respectability. MacDonald, who was still writing influential books, declared in 1921 that socialism did not lead to antagonism between classes but harmony, and that property would not be abolished under socialism but based on "social utility . . . The Socialist State is already appearing within the capitalist state . . . The construction of Socialism is a development of tendencies already in operation."[1]

Such sentiments did not differ significantly from what MacDonald had written well before the Great War, but he had then been writing in the circumstances of a seemingly perpetual peace and a tiny Labour Party which had no prospect of forming a government. His first publications were written in a period of relative social peace. Now he was writing after mass slaughter in the trenches, the transformation of the Labour Party into an important political force and in conditions of international social turmoil. Though MacDonald was not to resume leadership of the party until after the 1922 election, his words illustrated the general desire within the labour movement to cool the passions of class war. As the historian Philip Williamson emphasizes, his socialism was "always . . . more concerned with 'community' than with 'class'".[2] These attitudes should be seen as typical of the views of Labour leaders, not merely as a bid for support from unlikely sources.

Arthur Henderson, the central figure in the party bureaucracy, was another leader who sought class co-operation. He attempted to attract middle-class recruits to Labour, both to strengthen the young party and to encourage harmony between social classes. Class collaboration was congenial to him, and in the conditions of postwar Britain it was also tactically sensible to make an appeal for middle-class support. As his early biographer Mary Agnes Hamilton pointed out, Henderson tried to make Labour a national party by "seeking the support of all who work, regardless of their class or kind of work". In 1935, at the end of his life, Henderson himself insisted that the Labour Party was faithful to "the traditional democratic and constitutional doctrines of the English-speaking peoples".[3] Class war was thus to be avoided both on principle and for tactical reasons.

The "forward march of Labour" no doubt seemed irresistible from the vantage point of 1945 or even when the first Labour government was formed by MacDonald in 1924, but it was not obvious in 1918. A parliamentary party of about sixty which had lost its leading figures, facing a government with over 500 supporters or sympathizers, was not in a strong position. This situation differed from pre-war days, when Labour had for nearly ten years supported the main legislative proposals of the dominant party. Moreover, if it was true that progressive parties did not profit during periods of civil unrest, Labour had little to expect. The years after 1918 were marked by boom and bust and major labour unrest at home, turmoil abroad, war in Ireland and an unstable government coalition until the Conservatives decided that they no longer needed Lloyd George and voted to abandon his coalition in October 1922. Wage demands struggled to keep up with rising prices; employment rates were high until 1920–1, when the postwar slump succeeded previously high levels of economic activity.

The government, though Conservative-dominated, passed a number of measures of social reform, particularly affecting housing (1919) and unemployment insurance (1920). All this made the Labour Party seem insignificant in some eyes. Beatrice Webb, an intermittently harsh critic of the party, wrote in her diary in December 1919 that William Adamson, who chaired the parliamentary party, was "ugly, ineffective, almost mentally deficient relative to his position as leader of His Majesty's Opposition". Later in the same month she wrote of herself and Sidney: "We are not convinced that there is in the newcomers sufficient character and intelligence to lead the people in the direction of social democracy."[4]

Voters were probably less influenced by considerations of character and intelligence than by social class. In addition, economic adversity may have turned some of them from industrial towards political solutions. In any event Labour won fourteen by-elections in the parliament of 1918–22 for the loss of one, while the coalition parties were heavy losers. Labour's organization in the country, with the formation of local parties, the appointment of paid agents and of parliamentary candidates also proceeded steadily though by no means adequately, facilitating progress at the polls. Thanks to its by-election gains Labour's strength during the first post-war parliament rose by over 20 per cent. The party also gained the adhesion during this parliament of Josiah Wedgwood MP, formerly a Liberal, and such prominent extra-parliamentary Liberals as Arthur Ponsonby and Charles Trevelyan. All three were to serve in the first MacDonald government in 1924.

In August 1921 the coalition government headed by Lloyd George appointed Sir Eric Geddes, a businessman and member of the coalition, to head an economy campaign which, when its details were made public in February 1922, became known as the "Geddes axe". The unsophisticated decision to reduce government expenditure at a time of economic adversity was not unusual then or later, but it was a useful propaganda tool to the Labour Party in the election of November 1922 when its manifesto attacked "the notion of economies at the expense of the poor for the benefit of the rich". It was a reasonable delineating line between a business government and a Labour Party which had the luxury of being able to criticize cuts in the social services and public sector salaries without needing to devise a detailed alternative to government policies.

By this time J. R. Clynes, a trade union leader and wartime minister, had replaced William Adamson as chair of the parliamentary party and it was Clynes who held this position at the time of the election of 1922, though MacDonald had returned to a position of prominence and authority within the party. The result of the election, in which the manifesto insisted that the party was "the best bulwark against violent upheaval and class wars", gladdened Labour hearts. All of the previous leaders who had been defeated in 1918 were returned except Arthur Henderson, who soon won a seat in a by-election. The Labour tally rose to nearly 30 per cent of the voting electorate, and its number of MPs increased to 142. For the first time the parliamentary Labour Party had a small middle-class element including Clement Attlee, who was much later to be the first prime minister of a majority Labour government. The party had more votes and more seats than the Lloyd George and independent Asquith Liberals put together. The Conservatives held a majority in the House of Commons, though they had less than 40 per cent of the vote, and formed a government under Andrew Bonar Law. It should have been obvious that a Labour government was no longer unimaginable and indeed that it might be in office before very long, though it apparently took some time for many in the Labour Party to grasp that a new political landscape had been created.

The party's first task was to choose the official whom it now termed "chairman and leader of the parliamentary party". Clynes stood again and most of the trade union MPs gave him their support. His opponent was MacDonald, who was in the advantageous position of seeming to be left wing because of his wartime record, thus gathering the support of ILP MPs, while in reality remaining the moderate that he had always been. He was also seen by his supporters, probably accurately, as a better organizer and more vigorous leader than Clynes. Emanuel Shinwell, the ILP-er who nominated him at the parliamentary Labour Party meeting and became a junior minister little over a year later, preferred the charismatic political figure to the quiet, self-effacing trade unionist: "[T]here was no one else either worthy or capable", he recalled. "Socialism in the Palace of Westminster . . . needed an experienced guiding hand." Beatrice Webb gave him her grudging approval: "If he is not the best man for the post, he is at any rate, the worst and most dangerous man out of it!"[5] MacDonald's supporters in this leadership election, who included Attlee, regretted their vote in 1931 but MacDonald was undoubtedly a more appealing figure to the electorate than Clynes would have been and it is doubtful that the policies of the two men would have differed significantly in time of crisis.

The problem for a party which thought of itself as socialist was not so much a question of individuals as of how to transform one kind of society to another, a problem which caused MacDonald and later leaders little concern once they had reached positions of eminence. And in fairness, leaders until the 1990s, by which time Labour had effectively dropped its socialist commitment, were too concerned with urgent economic problems to consider longer-term ideological questions.

The party to whose leadership MacDonald was elected by a majority of five parliamentary votes would have been difficult for the ablest leader to have controlled. The passions of wartime had cooled and the Labour Party was no longer challenged by a purely trade union party of the kind which might have become a serious rival at the end of the war. It contained men and women, however, of widely varying social class origins and political views. Four prominent Labour MPs and future ministers, to take one example, differed considerably in a 1924 symposium in their definition of what the party was thought to have agreed was a common goal. To Frederick Pethick-Lawrence socialism was "[t]he organization of society on the basis of mutual service", to Herbert Morrison "[o]wnership by public authorities of land and the essential means of production and distribution", to George Lansbury "a society within which there will be neither rich nor poor", to Ben Turner "the abolition of class warfare and class hatred and the uniting of all the peoples".[6] Catherine Ann Cline, who has studied converts to Labour from other parties between 1914 and 1931, quotes definitions of socialism as enunciated by some of her recruits. Their definitions, like those already cited, were varied and vague: "a determination to put the interests of the people before the interests of property", "freedom of development" and, in the case of Josiah Wedgwood, "a land (or a time), when we shall not need policemen".[7]

It was not the case that the party's left wing was to be found exclusively among its middle-class converts from other parties or that the whole of the Labour middle class had left-wing sympathies. The former Liberals in the party's councils, some of them landowning members of the traditional governing class, were often supporters of left-wing causes, but their contribution to the party was more significant in enabling Labour to claim to be a truly national party than in terms of new policy. Disagreements and indeed consciousness of class distinctions within the party seem to have been more common in the 1930s than in the twenties.

Women in the 1920s began to play an important though always subordinate part in the labour movement, with women's sections in local Labour parties, women members of some trade unions and other bodies, women in local government, a National Conference of Labour Women raising without great success in the wider party "women's issues", and the publication of the *Labour Woman*. Susan Lawrence, one of the best-known Labour women of the 1920s and in youth a Conservative member of both the London School Board and the London County Council, belonged to the upper-middle class but worked unremittingly for the Labour cause. She was one of the most intellectually competent members of the inter-war party, a junior minister in 1929–31 and, if she had been younger would have been a strong candidate for a cabinet position in a later Labour government. Her niece Lesley Lewis wrote sceptically of a weakness of which many socialists have subsequently been accused: "Aunt Susan combined intense goodwill towards the human race in general . . . with a total inability to get on comfortable terms with more than a very few intimates." Lewis remembered that Lawrence had a long-serving "general maid" named Wordley. "Aunt Susan thought it insulting to call a person by her christian name just because of her occupation but I used to reflect that although we never called our maids 'Miss' we would never have thought of working them quite as hard as Aunt Susan did Miss Wordley."[8] Lawrence was not an adherent of left-wing policies, which was fortunate for a woman seeking office within the MacDonald Labour Party and a Labour government.

Virginia Woolf, another upper-middle class intellectual, was not herself politically active but assimilated to the Labour Party thanks to her marriage to Leonard Woolf and friendship with Margaret Llewelyn Davies of the Women's Co-operative Guild. She observed in a lecture delivered in May 1924:

> The Victorian cook lived like a leviathan in the lower depths . . . [T]he Georgian cook is a creature of sunshine and fresh air; in and out of the drawing-room, now to borrow the *Daily Herald* [the newspaper which was by this time closely associated with the Trades Union Congress and the Labour Party], now to ask for advice about a hat.[9]

This passage does not suggest that even within Labour ranks a classless society was at hand.

In contrast the party contained members like Jack Jones, MP for Silvertown and a former builder's labourer who in youth had been a strong adherent of socialist policies. Later he was an unqualified supporter of British participation in the Great War, a "pro-war Socialist", as he said. Jones had stood for parliament in 1918 without official Labour endorsement but joined the parliamentary party after the election. He told the party conference in 1919 that he and his friends were "tired of these continual sneers at those who represented so-called industrial unskilled labour – they did not claim of course to have the intelligence of the long haired men and the short haired women . . . the friends whose heads were evidently bursting with the brains they could not use."[10] Jones was something of a licensed jester, but he spoke the words that other trade unionists and some of their leaders thought. Patriotism extending in some cases to xenophobia, sentimentality and the "aristocratic embrace" in parliament were a powerful combination and helped to ensure that many working-class Labour representatives would be sympathetic to a conventional cast of mind. Jones, though by origin an Irish Catholic, said in 1918: "The country they lived in, bad as it was, was the best he knew of."[11]

Social antagonism between Conservatives and Labour at local level was a feature of the time, but many Labour MPs succumbed to the blandishments of parliamentary life and the social invitations of Lady Astor and others. Clydesiders, who saw themselves as the socialist spearhead of the early 1920s, were often also sentimentalists. James Maxton, with his tendency to weep or joke, was a House of Commons favourite who could fill the debating chamber without antagonizing or frightening the opposing parties. All were willing to acknowledge his burning sincerity, since all knew that his views would find no place in the actions of the Labour Party. David Kirkwood, another Clydesider, was dazzled by the cordiality of Tories and Liberals, beginning with Winston Churchill who as a wartime minister "had been big enough", Shinwell wrote, "to recognize the honest purpose of Davie".[12] Kirkwood asked Churchill to write a foreword to his autobiography in 1935, a book which contained lavish praise for such leading Conservatives as Bonar Law, Stanley Baldwin, Churchill and Neville Chamberlain. He concluded with the contented observation "that the major injustices are fading and that reason is winning".[13]

This type of progression was common. Tom Forester points out astutely that parliamentary comfort, ambition and "the cumulative weight of the British political–cultural tradition" worked a powerful spell: "The history of the Labour Party is littered with examples of radicals who have gone into parliament with a view to changing the world overnight and have later modified their approach, or who, elected as socialists, end up looking, speaking and acting like Conservatives."[14] It is easy but often mistaken to blame such a progression on simple careerism. Desire for sweeping social change is often weakened when the life of an agitator is first modified by working-class apathy and later exposed to power and influence. Passion for replacing existing society is superseded by concern for what are seen as the common interests of a whole nation. It should be noted that many socialists in other countries have followed the same path towards the political centre.

A significant factor of this period was Beatrice Webb's attempt to acclimatize the many Labour wives whose husbands were new MPs in the early twenties to London life and to break down the isolation and loneliness which many would otherwise have felt. Her vehicle for carrying out these aims, founded late in 1920, was termed the Half-Circle Club. It has been derided as a means of encouraging social climbing or at least accepting the norms of upper-class behaviour, but Beatrice Webb's own austere outlook and her diary entries suggest otherwise. She expressed in her diary her concern that "some of the frailer vessels"[15] should not succumb to the blandishments of duchesses and millionaires, and was pleased to be told by the assistant (later general) secretary of the TUC that some of the wives felt they were part of the labour movement for the first time.

A party as variegated as Labour in the early 1920s was difficult to lead as a united team but easy to dissuade from open rebellion since so many members disliked the personalities or politics of others. MacDonald could therefore safely ignore most manifestations of inconvenient opinions. He had other things to think about. In the autumn of 1923 Stanley Baldwin, who had replaced Bonar Law as Conservative leader, called a general election on the issue of protective tariffs as opposed to free trade, a tactic generally seen as a bid to appeal to the various groups within his party. Though taken by surprise Labour fought a strong campaign, winning 200,000 more votes, an additional one per cent of the vote and nearly fifty more parliamentary seats. The first three Labour women MPs, Margaret Bondfield, Dorothy Jewson of the ILP and Susan Lawrence, were returned at this election. The nominally united Liberals were again eclipsed by Labour and though the Conservatives remained the largest party their loss of over 80 MPs prevented them from continuing in government. The new prime minister was Ramsay MacDonald.

His Cabinet was constructed with some care, so that Labour stalwarts like Snowden, Henderson, Clynes and William Adamson were included together with the former Liberals Trevelyan, Wedgwood, Noel Buxton and Richard Haldane, now a peer, and former Tories like Lords Chelmsford and Parmoor. John Wheatley represented the contemporary ILP and Fred Jowett its older element. George Lansbury, another left winger, incurred the hostility of King George V and was omitted from the cabinet.

Historians have quoted some of the naïve or deferential comments of former working men who now found themselves cabinet ministers. They have also spoken of the fondness of some ministers for royal occasions and court dress. It would have needed men (Margaret Bondfield, a junior minister, was the only woman member of the government) of exceptional independence of mind not to be swallowed up by flummery and formality, and by and large the new Labour ministers, led by their chief, did not resist their social opportunities.

The Labour government of 1924 has not had a good press. But given the problems – under two hundred MPs and consequent dependence on Liberal support; inexperienced, deferential leaders with no clear policies in several fields; an unruly parliamentary party; a widespread feeling within the electorate that the Labour Party represented class interests while the Conservatives stood for "the public";[16] and a tenure of less than a year – the performance of the Labour Government of 1924 was surprisingly competent. Its best-known measure was Wheatley's Housing Act, which sought to make council housing a permanent feature of public policy and in good measure succeeded. In the eyes of a knowledgeable historian this was "by far the most successful"[17] of the nine housing acts passed between the wars. Unemployment insurance was increased, and advances were made in education under C. P. Trevelyan. MacDonald, who was his own foreign secretary, had a number of successes on the international scene and even the Agricultural Wages Act, though emasculated in passage by Liberal amendment, was important in some areas in organizing rural workers and raising wages. It should, however, be borne in mind that Labour under MacDonald was a moderate party of social reform and that, like later Labour governments, this one seemed less of a threat to capital and the established order when it surrendered office than when it assumed it.

The modest but real achievements of the 1924 government have been overshadowed by the manner of its fall. The arrest and subsequent release of J. R. Campbell, editor of the communist *Workers' Weekly*, the consequent loss of Liberal parliamentary support, a bungled election campaign, the effective use by the Conservative press of the influential "Red Letter", signed by Zinoviev, the leading figure in the Communist International (a "letter" now generally thought to have been a forgery), to make it seem that the Labour government was allied to revolutionaries, were the most striking events. In fact the principal reason for the Labour defeat in the general election of 1924 was that there were over one hundred fewer Liberal candidates than in 1923. This was a move which was of major benefit to the Conservatives, though Labour gained over a million votes and could now boast the support of a full third of the participating electorate. The reduction of the Liberals to forty MPs and little more than a sixth of the vote effectively ended their threat to Labour, and should have made the Labour Party regard the election result not as a qualified disaster but as a qualified triumph, despite the loss of office and forty MPs.

The most important event in the life not only of the labour movement but of the British nation between 1924 and 1929 was the general strike of 1926. It was called off after nine days because, historians maintain, trade union leaders believed government and other claims that they were revolutionaries and consequently sought any pretext to end the strike. In fact the strike was solid, the leaders had never wanted it and sought to end it. But the charge made by militants of treason is misleading. Trade union officials were accustomed to negotiate on behalf of their members, not to challenge governments or the British constitution, whatever was meant by that term. They had been drawn into a strike to defend the living conditions of the miners who refused to compromise or to put their case into the hands of the TUC and continued their action long after the general strike had ended. Union leaders feared for their membership numbers and their funds. There was a great deal of confusion during the strike, some genuine, some the result of wishful thinking. Page 3 of the *British Worker*, the official TUC strike bulletin for 15 May 1926, contained the sentence: "Accordingly, on the strength of the assurances which it had obtained, the General Council felt justified in calling off the General Strike and thus permitting the reopening of negotiations." The next page admitted: "There are no official undertakings and no official assurances. But the position is one where the basis of agreement obviously satisfies men of honour concerned to make peace." With this degree of self-deception at the centre, it is not surprising that the rank and file had little idea of what was happening and that cries of treason were heard.

The course of the strike showed not only that a sudden event could not make class-conscious warriors out of pacific trade union officials. It was also clear that with much hostile public opinion, with motor vehicles available to opponents and middle-class youths eager to drive buses and trams, and with the government wholly supportive of the employers, the strikers could not win. They could not do so, at least, without great diffi-culty, singlemindedness and a prolonged strike. (In the same way Labour Party leaders were parliamentarians; their militant past, if it existed, lay far behind them. To deplore their moderate attitudes is to misunderstand the political and social environment.) The general strike was doomed before it began, though its termination on terms which ensured the virtual unconditional surrender of the unions was certainly encouraged by trade union leaders sympathetic to class collaboration like J. H. Thomas of the railwaymen, also an important Labour Party leader and former minister.

The Labour Party was embarrassed by the general strike, about which its leaders said little and from which they sought to distance the party. Snowden remained silent during the strike while MacDonald attempted to support the miners and industrial peace simultaneously, while claiming with some justification to be an outsider. One important problem for the party resulted, however, from the passage of the Trade Disputes and Trade Union Act of 1927, which banned general strikes and forced trade union members to "contract in" rather than "contract out" of their unions' political funds. Almost at a stroke the party lost over a third of its affiliated trade union membership, a suitable illustration of the lack of political commitment of many workers.

The second half of the 1920s was an eventful period in terms of Labour and socialist politics in Britain. The most important development was the crisis that developed between the party and the Independent Labour Party, which had in earlier years produced several figures who had become leaders of the main party. Such important personalities as MacDonald and Snowden were unwilling to follow the ILP prescriptions for "Socialism in our Time". These were a series of policy proposals put forward in stages and finally enunciated in full in 1926. The centrepiece was a plan for a minimum "living wage" guaranteed to every citizen, accompanied by measures of nationalization and family allowances. The programme was in a sense Keynesianism before Keynes, since the plan for higher wages especially associated with the economist J. A. Hobson, a former Liberal, would have increased consumption by means of stimulating demand. It also had similarities to the "right to work" policies put forward by the infant Labour Party of Edwardian days. However, in the context of the 1920s the ILP proposals were seen as extreme socialism, anathema to MacDonald for political reasons, to Snowden for economic ones and also to many trade unionists, who felt themselves potentially excluded from policy making. In the upshot the ILP proposals were watered down or defeated, Snowden resigned from the ILP and MacDonald was deeply alienated, although he did not yet resign. The ILP was to continue down the road which led to its disaffiliation from the Labour Party in 1932. It was not the last organization to discover that a close link with the Labour Party led to frustration and that ending the link consigned it to insignificance.

The general election of 1929 was preceded by a new Labour Party programme entitled *Labour and the Nation* (1928), based on a draft by the economic historian and educationist R. H. Tawney. On one level it was a socialist document, asserting without qualification that Labour was a socialist party, committed to the replacement of capitalism by a more equitable system, as MacDonald made clear in the preface. Land, coal, transport, power and life insurance were all to be taken into public ownership, though there was no commitment to do so within a specific timespan. The Bank of England was also to be nationalized, though Snowden insisted that it should not be controlled by politicians. The joint stock banks, however, were to remain in private hands: "if you give me the citadel, you may keep the outposts for a time", Hugh Dalton declared to the party conference. (It should be remembered that in 1929, with a Labour government in office, the words "distribution and exchange" were added to the commitment to the public ownership of the means of production agreed by the party in 1918.)

On the other hand, the programme was vague and gradualist and gave the next Labour government a free hand. James Maxton's warning that "the approach to Socialism" could not realistically be "a long, slow process of gradualistic, peaceful Parliamentary change" was ignored and an ILP amendment was overwhelmingly defeated. Herbert Morrison, like Dalton a rising star of the new generation of moderate Labour leaders, aimed at an easy target in insisting that "some of our Members of Parliament are inclined to put themselves and their own views and their own individuality before marching in step with the general policy of the

Party". J. R. Clynes, an older party leader, pointed to a problem which the Labour Party was never to solve: "[M]y belief is we shall get Socialism in Britain just as soon as the majority of the people of Britain want it, and that our job still for the present is to go on making Socialists."[18] How that was to be done, especially by a party many of whose leaders had made their peace with economic orthodoxy and high society, was unclear.

The general election of 1929 marked a new level of success for the Labour Party, a high-water mark which was not to be exceeded until 1945 after another gruelling war had been fought and the existing party leadership replaced. The party won for the first time more seats than any other in the House of Commons, reaching 287 out of the total of 615. The Conservatives secured nearly three hundred thousand more votes than Labour with 21 more candidates but returned only 260 of them. Labour had over 37 per cent of the vote, continuing the progress made since 1918, when it won under 22 per cent with its Co-operative Party ally. As James Cronin points out, the election showed both how strong the Labour appeal had become to the working class, or at least sections of it, and how far the party remained from a parliamentary majority. Perhaps most gratifying was the fact that the Liberals, now led by Lloyd George (Asquith had died the previous year), had won only 59 seats and while a minority Labour government would be dependent on Liberal support, it was hard to see any circumstances in which the Liberal Party could resume its former political predominance. (Although the party split in 1916 had given Lloyd George the premiership it also ensured that he would be the last Liberal to be prime minister in the twentieth century.) Yet in little more than two years the Labour government would collapse and the party be decimated at the polls.

The second MacDonald Labour government was not a success and its fall in 1931 was a catastrophe for the party. Soon after its assumption of office in 1929 the Wall Street crash took place, helping to ensure that economic slump and unemployment became the greatest issues facing the British government. After more than a year of sharply rising unemployment the government appointed in March 1931 an economy committee under Sir George May of the Prudential. This was done at a time when government borrowing to finance unemployment benefit helped to unbalance the national budget, a phenomenon unacceptable to orthodox economic and political opinion. The May committee consisted of seven men, most of them members of the business community, who were certain to produce a majority report favourable to business and financial opinion. This they did at the end of July. (The two-member minority report, blaming deflationary policies, accepting the case for some reductions in public salaries and proposing to tax investment income, was generally ignored.) Its solution to the problem of the budget, which it estimated to be heading for a deficit of £120 million (Snowden, as in 1924 chancellor of the exchequer, informed his cabinet colleagues that the true figure was £170 million), lay largely in measures to make access to unemployment benefit more difficult and to reduce its level. Its other preferred policies consisted largely of lower salaries for teachers and other public servants.

By the end of August MacDonald had formed a National government dominated by Conservatives with Liberal support. His reasons for doing so have been endlessly debated by historians and others. It would perhaps be more profitable to ask why the May committee with its bias in favour of orthodox economic opinion was appointed, since once it reported the break-up of the government was in the light of hindsight highly likely. The reasons are fairly clear. First, the Liberals had been frightened away from their previous slump-fighting policies and were putting pressure on the government to effect economies. A minority government was in a weak position to deny them even if it had wished to do so.

Second, this government like others was heavily dependent on its prime minister and chancellor of the exchequer. Writing in early 1929 Egon Wertheimer, London correspondent of the German socialist paper *Vorwärts*, referred to MacDonald's "schoolmasterish condescension, his hypersensitiveness and vanity". MacDonald's "general attitude towards life", he added, seemed to be that of a Conservative. Yet he was the dominant figure within his party, and as Wertheimer said in an often quoted phrase, "the focus of the mute hopes of a whole class".[19] When one adds to this mix MacDonald's belief in class collaboration rather than antagonism, his ignorance of economic thought, his indifference to sentiment within the Labour Party, his contempt for the ILP and his love of high society, his subsequent defection seems hardly surprising. Snowden was a different type, "small, thin, bitter",[20] hostile to many of his colleagues in the Labour Party, including MacDonald. David Howell says in a telling phrase that "[h]is style blended evangelical socialism and financial rectitude",[21] but by 1929 there was little apparent trace of socialism remaining in his outlook. He was unsympathetic to trades unions, opposed to the ILP and temperamentally inclined to economic orthodoxy including free trade and balanced budgets. He hoped that the May committee's report would encourage his own party to accept heavy cuts in public expenditure.

Snowden and MacDonald were supported by J. H. Thomas, the railwaymen's best-known leader, whose conventionality, vulgarity, snobbery and patriotism appealed to many voters who did not otherwise support the Labour Party. These characteristics meant that Thomas could boast a common touch and an easy popularity which neither MacDonald nor Snowden possessed but found useful. David Low the cartoonist habitually portrayed Thomas wearing evening dress to typify, he wrote, "the new respectability of the Labour Party" Yet he was much more than a comic buffoon, a stage working men transfixed by wealth and rank. As

LABOUR BETWEEN TWO WARS

G. D. H. Cole imagined Thomas saying in a skit written in 1926 but published much later: "And though it seems odd, I'm a little tin god to the boys of the N.U.R."[22] For many he remained so, even after the end of the Labour government in 1931.

The final reason for the appointment of the May committee and the events which followed was that in August 1931 there seemed to be no alternative. MacDonald's biographer David Marquand is persuasive on this point and so too is the historian Ross McKibbin. Keynes's counter-cyclical theories were not yet fully enunciated, Keynes himself was not certain about the wisdom of leaving the gold standard, Britain was behind other countries in adopting deflationary policies. Reflation would have meant state control of the economy, "the then British ruling classes"[23] would not have agreed to it and it was inconceivable that a minority government led by MacDonald and Snowden would either have wished or been able to challenge directly the ruling classes. Philip Williamson, writing more recently, concurs. Keynes equivocated at the crucial time and appeared to MacDonald to accept, however, unwillingly, orthodox views. Although leading trade unionists like Ernest Bevin and Walter Citrine had a better understanding of economic problems than either MacDonald or Snowden, the unions as a whole were regarded by the Labour leaders as demanding only that the brunt of the economic collapse should not be borne by their members. They were consequently condemned by unsympathetic contemporaries and historians as selfish and negative.

Defence of MacDonald, who was once comprehensively condemned by virtually all Labour sympathizers, has over the decades become accepted orthodoxy. Reginald Bassett, his first academic champion, asserted in 1958 that he was "moved primarily by his sense of duty". Harold Wilson defended him when he spoke as Labour prime minister at a MacDonald centenary celebration in 1966. "MacDonald made his decision – I believe . . . because he sincerely felt he was putting the survival of his country above the survival of his party". David Marquand put a similar view. MacDonald introduced anti-Labour policies in the national interest and attached importance to the wishes of the king, though Marquand admitted that MacDonald had "a large . . . bump of vanity". The historian Kenneth Morgan put a more sophisticated gloss on this view, saying that divisions within the party, patriotism, urgings from the king and political leaders played their part: "But the decisive factor lay in something deeper, in MacDonald's outlook and psychological make-up . . . On domestic issues he was fundamentally a consensus man". Philip Williamson also expresses a more nuanced view, but he concludes that MacDonald felt that the cabinet had "destroyed the Labour party's claims to be a party of government, by declining to do what seemed necessary in the 'national interest'".[24] It should be noted that when crisis arose MacDonald thought of Labour policies as incompatible with the national interest. Leaders of other parties were not under similar pressure to separate party from nation.

Labour politicians and others put a different view, often in simplistic terms. Recent historians have generally not criticized MacDonald, though Keith Laybourn asserts that he "remained too wedded to the values of Victorian Liberalism", perhaps unsurprisingly given that he was in his mid-thirties when Victoria died. David Howell notes his "conservative characterization of the national interest", though he also refers to MacDonald's "strong sense of duty".[25]

Some contemporaries who did not support MacDonald's action in ending his Labour government attempted subsequently to criticize him more analytically than abusively. The writer Gilbert Thomas, who knew MacDonald as MP for Leicester before 1918 and afterwards, summed up his character as a combination of "a love of power and a childlike vanity mingled with a sincere altruism [and] a genuine passion for social righteousness". Kingsley Martin, who was closely involved with the political scene from the editorial chair of the *New Statesman & Nation,* wrote immediately after MacDonald's death that he had long since used up his "large store" of intellectual and political capital. "He did not add to it, and when it was exhausted there was nothing left but emptiness and the hollow echo of great words which had once moved multitudes." Mary Agnes Hamilton, a writer and political figure who was a Labour MP in this period and knew MacDonald well, pointed to his "deep conventionality" which, she added, "made it impossible for him to render constructive service of a lasting kind, either to Socialism or to Internationalism. His international ideas resembled his Socialist ideas. In general, they were noble; when you came down to action, they dissolved." Hamilton is surely correct in saying, probably drawing on her own experience, that MacDonald "broke hearts, right and left" and that "[i]t took years for the Labour Party to get him out of its system." Jon Lawrence, writing recently, makes the related point that "the events of 1931 etched the idea of 'betrayal' into the party psyche"[26] where it remained for several decades.

More important than individuals, however, is the undoubted fact that the Labour Party led by any possible substitute for MacDonald would have been unwilling in 1931 to challenge the economic orthodoxy or the social and political establishment of the day. It was under MacDonald and his colleagues a party which sought a policy acceptable to most shades of opinion at a time when political opponents were in no mood to compromise. It is also important to realize that the Labour leaders were not economists of a new school of thought able to work out novel policies at a time of panic and that few of them sought an unconventional solution to urgent problems in the face of overwhelming conventional advice. When the policies they had advocated in opposition "crumbled or seemed inappropriate in office"[27] they had no alternative to offer.

A National government was formed at the end of August 1931 after MacDonald's Labour cabinet failed, largely because of trade union pressure to avoid cuts in unemployment benefit, to agree on economy measures and consequently fell. Nearly half the cabinet refused to support the proposed reductions. Arthur Henderson, though ambiguous in his earlier analysis of the economic crisis, led the opposition to the new government which contained four Labour men in its cabinet of ten; MacDonald as prime minister, Snowden initially as chancellor of the exchequer, J. H. Thomas as dominions secretary, and Lord Sankey as lord chancellor. Its dominant political tendency was Conservative and MacDonald and his three colleagues were almost without support from the Labour backbenches. The new government lost no time in introducing economies in both unemployment benefit and public salaries, though less extensive reductions than May had advocated. More controversially it both abandoned the gold standard ("No one ever told *us* we could do that!"[28] Sidney Webb, who had a reputation as an economic thinker, was reported as saying) and devalued the pound, measures which helped to forestall an even more disastrous slump. It then proceeded to call a general election. Labour Party speakers advocated socialism, but their speeches were notable more for rhetoric than for detailed policies. Labour's socialism had failed to solve the mounting economic crisis and seemed to have little to offer when the crisis reached its climax.

For the new government it was an ideal moment to win a sweeping public endorsement. The Labour Party had lost its three best-known figures to its political enemies, and the electorate was according to different interpretations either in the mood for sacrifice in what was thought to be the national interest or in a state of panic. The press was overwhelmingly anti-Labour and a great victory could be anticipated by the supporters of the National government.

The first signs of the more socialist Labour Party of the 1930s were apparent in an election manifesto which attacked the House of Lords, made menacing noises about seeking "such emergency powers as are necessary to the full attainment of its objectives", and promised to bring banking and credit "under national ownership and control". This statement reflected a widespread belief within the Labour Party that the government had been brought down by a "bankers' ramp". The party was attacked by Snowden in a broadcast for enunciating a programme which he termed "Bolshevism run mad". Andrew Thorpe, the historian of this election, comments: "perhaps no other political broadcast in British history has achieved such immediate and lasting fame or notoriety". Snowden's own later gloss was that he had attacked his former colleagues "in no vindictive spirit, but because I was firmly convinced that it would be a national disaster to give power to a Party which had shown itself unworthy to be trusted with the responsibility of office".[29]

MacDonald played his part by displaying at election meetings German marks of high denomination from the super-inflation of 1923, and Walter Runciman, a National government supporter who joined the cabinet after the election, warned with support from MacDonald and Snowden that a Labour victory might threaten the millions of accounts in the Post Office Savings Bank. The election entered Labour mythology as having been won by lies and manipulation of a panicked people, a claim strongly rebutted by Thorpe, who writes: "[I]t was ludicrous to claim that the electorate had been panicked by National scares. The charge was an insult to the intelligence of the voters; that it had to be resorted to was an indictment of the recent performance of the Labour Party and its leaders."[30]

Whatever interpretation is put on the election, and my own view is that Thorpe exaggerates the sophistication of the electorate, the result was arguably a victory for the British electoral system, for Labour's catastrophe in terms of seats did not reflect its vote. Its support remained reasonably solid in the circumstances at almost 80 per cent of its 1929 total with 53 fewer candidates. It retained its working-class following, writes James Cronin, despite or because of its lack of theory. The few Labour members who followed the new government were not to be the nucleus of a new mass party, for they mustered only twenty "National Labour" candidates. (Thirteen of them were returned, including MacDonald, his son Malcolm and J. H. Thomas. Snowden, who did not stand, was soon made a peer.) But the Labour Party itself suffered a catastrophe. Every ex-cabinet minister who remained loyal to the party was defeated except George Lansbury, already aged 72 and a minor figure despite his popularity. The party returned only 46 members (52 with the nearly disaffiliated ILP and one independent; three of the six later rejoined Labour). Its talented pre-election group of ten women MPs, two of whom had been returned at by-elections, was obliterated and none of its other women candidates was returned. (Four of the group elected in 1929–31 were later returned, three after a lapse of fourteen years.) The Conservatives alone had nearly twice Labour's vote, the National government had over 550 supporters in the House of Commons, the independent Liberals had virtually disappeared. There was no comfort unless it was to be found in the disappearance of MacDonald and Snowden from the Labour Party. Professor Harold Laski, who had drafted Labour's election manifesto, wrote to his aged American friend Oliver Wendell Holmes that Labour had been defeated by panic, that there was an "atmosphere in which reason had completely abdicated and no lie was too great to be believed. I don't take our defeat tragically," he added, putting the best possible face on the débâcle, "even though I think five years of Tory government a heavy price to pay for a moment's panic. But five years is a small period in the life of a people."[31] In the event the price in electoral terms was to be much heavier for the Labour Party.

Labour suddenly entered a new phase of its history in the early 1930s. Henry Pelling in his short history of the party calls his chapter on the 1930s "Convalescence: the general council [of the Trades Union Congress]'s party", and there is no doubt that a parliamentary party of less than 50 members, reeling from the shattering defeat which it had suffered, was in need of aid and support. Walter Citrine, the general secretary of the TUC, and Ernest Bevin, secretary of the Transport and General Workers' Union, were competent and dominant personalities, Citrine more discreetly than Bevin. The National Joint Council, renamed the National Council of Labour in 1934, included members of the General Council, the parliamentary party and the party's executive. But the parliamentary party, led by Lansbury with the former junior minister Clement Attlee as deputy (though Arthur Henderson, no longer an MP, retained for a time the position of titular party leader) did what they could to make up for their lack of numbers. They were reinforced by the return of Arthur Greenwood, formerly minister of health, at a by-election in April 1932. Attlee was prominent in the House of Commons while Stafford Cripps, who had been a party member only since 1929 and a member of parliament since early 1931, was also active in parliament and supplied money, assiduity and good will. Cripps, with Attlee, was the only former junior minister who had kept his seat, and his unofficial position within the party leadership gave him both the prestige and the opportunity to press his newly-found socialist views without inhibition. Such vocal figures provided a continuous if inevitably inadequate opposition.

The belief that the Labour Party was a socialist party until the 1990s owes a good deal to its behaviour in the early 1930s. The ILP finally disaffiliated in 1932 but its place was taken within the party by other left-wing groups of which the Socialist League, founded in the same year and led from 1933 by Cripps, was the most important. The numerous middle-class recruits to the Labour Party ran into suspicion and even hostility in the party, for which they were themselves at least partly responsible. Kingsley Martin, himself middle-class and left-wing, recalled Charles Trevelyan, no new recruit but a wealthy former Liberal and former Labour minister, urging a general strike on Ernest Bevin in protest against the foreign policy of Neville Chamberlain in the late 1930s. At the time Trevelyan was Lord Lieutenant of Northumberland. "'You want a strike?' said Bevin, 'O.K. I am to call out 600,000 [sic] dockers; will you call out the Lord Lieutenants?'"[32]

Walter Citrine's view was similar. He and Arthur Pugh the trade union leader met Cripps, G. D. H. Cole and other left-wing luminaries at an informal meeting at the London School of Economics in July 1933. At the meeting Citrine referred to a previous statement by Cole advocating the extension of death duties to all property worth over £1,000. His self-righteous recollection continued:

I did not think this was the way in which the middle class would be converted. I said that it seemed to me hypocritical, and I doubted whether any man in the room, other than Arthur Pugh and myself, was paying on a life insurance policy for less than £1,000 . . . [W]e were discussing ultimate Socialist objectives of a theoretical character. I did not propose to waste my time further in doing so.[33]

The middle-class recruits to the Labour Party were mainly sincere and hard-working, and many of the prominent ones were well to the left of the trade unionists and party loyalists. To some extent the reason for the apparent paradox of trade union conservatism was that union leaders often had little imagination and limited horizons, but more important was the fact that however far they had moved from their roots they understood the working class far better than party members who "dressed for dinner" and enjoyed each other's company at their weekend cottages while simultaneously finding Labour policies unadventurous and inadequate. Patrick Seyd, who has studied the Socialist League, points out that its leadership consisted predominantly of people who had enjoyed a privileged and expensive education. This was a factor which did not increase the popularity of the policies they advocated.

John Strachey, the socialist intellectual who was close to the Communist Party in the 1930s, invited to lunch a neighbour who discovered that one of the party was the family cook. "She sat silent throughout the meal, and, thought the guest, [was] rather more embarrassed than he was by the novel encounter." Margaret Cole later reminisced about living conditions in the house in Hampstead to which she and G.D.H. and their three children moved at the end of the 1920s: "[We were] a standard middle-class professional family, with a nurse for the children and an out-of-work miner from Barnsley and his wife to do the house-work." Naomi Mitchison was a prominent writer in the period and long afterwards. She and her husband Dick, an old Etonian future Labour MP, were described years later as "in the thick of the 1930s upper crust socialist intellectuals who embraced the cause of the workers". She wrote in an autobiography:

You may well ask how people like us – and there were a good many – came to call ourselves socialists and to join the Labour Party but without altering our way of life very much. We did alter it to some extent but we still took holidays, still had a big house with staff to run it as we expected them to do, still gave parties, were recognizably ourselves.[34]

The Labour Party could not hope to be an oasis in the still powerful British class system and different life styles inevitably created social barriers. It was also inevitable that at a time of strongly held views about national and international affairs, opponents of the left naturally used all the weapons available to them. "Sir Stafford Cripps is a rich man with rich pals around him", John McGurk of the Miners' Federation told the Labour Party conference in 1937, "and they are the biggest danger to the Labour Party in this country. You will find those chaps where [Oswald] Mosley [a former wealthy Labour left-winger, subsequently a fascist] is before much longer."[35]

The policies adopted by the party were more specific and, as previously stated, more socialist than in the days of MacDonald and Snowden. Geoffrey Foote, who has studied the Labour Party's political thought, gives the name "corporate socialism"[36] to the beliefs of most members of the party in the period. These were a mixture of convictions which in their original forms had often been regarded as incompatible. In practice they boiled down to an efficient planned economy, nationalization without socialist transformation of certain industries, trade union participation in national affairs and the amelioration of class conflict. The policies seemed radical in a period when the national and international political climate was more fevered than it had been in the 1920s.

The party conference in 1932 supported the nationalization of the joint stock banks against the wishes of Hugh Dalton and his executive colleagues, though with the support of Stafford Cripps. It also carried a resolution moved by Charles Trevelyan and supported by Attlee for legislation of a socialist character to be an immediate priority of the next Labour government. Arthur Henderson, who was still nominally party leader as well as secretary, opposed the resolution. He resigned subsequently as leader in favour of Lansbury, whether because of the resolution or not (his biographers differ) but remained active as an MP from September 1933, as party secretary until 1934, specially in working for world peace until his death in 1935. With the departure of Henderson came to an end the first generation of Labour Party leaders and Labour as a party led predominantly by men of working-class birth. He had been above all things loyal to the party and the trade unions and as Chris Wrigley points out, "epitomized many of the strengths and weaknesses of the British Labour movement in the first third of the twentieth century".[37]

In 1933 Stafford Cripps moved a resolution urging "[t]he immediate abolition of the House of Lords", a decision already unanimously agreed by the 1932 conference. The resolution also advocated the passage of an emergency powers act which would enable a Labour government to introduce socialist legislation to control "the financial machine" and socialize industry, convert rapidly capitalist society into a socialist one and adopt an economic plan "to abolish unemployment and poverty"[38] These intended commitments were harmlessly referred to the executive.

The party policy statement *For Socialism and Peace* (1934) was an unusually incisive document, advocating extensive measures of public ownership and the abolition of the House of Lords, but its left-wing character did not forestall large numbers of amendments from the Socialist League, which sought to commit a future Labour government to enact not social reforms but socialism within a short period. The amendments not accepted by the platform were voted down by heavy majorities. The League had raised widespread animosity within the party and, as seen above, it could be vilified as an attempt by the wealthy and privately educated to move the party in its preferred direction. This condemnation of the League's leaders posed an additional burden to the acceptance of its policy proposals.

Britain in the mid-1930s remained a country of enormous contrasts in wealth and poverty and unemployment remained high. There was, however, no doubt that conditions were improving. Real incomes, productivity and living standards were rising and unemployment of insured workers was falling, though it did not drop to the 1929 percentage until 1939. Salaried employment was rising and the number of wage-earning workers began to decline. Shopping became easier and less class-bound. A figure equal to nearly half the population of York, Seebohm Rowntree discovered in his second social survey of the town, entered Woolworth's, Marks and Spencer or British Home Stores on one day in 1936, the great majority of them working people. "Moreover", Sidney Pollard points out, with a degree of exaggeration,

> statistics fail to take full account of the difference made by electricity instead of candles, and gas cookers instead of coal or coke ranges, as standard equipment in working-class homes; of improved housing, including indoor water and sanitation; or of radio, the cinema and newspapers within almost everybody's reach.[39]

This type of development did not go unnoticed at Labour Party conferences, where few delegates opposed social amelioration because it discouraged socialist enthusiasm, though this was a problem for the Socialist League in the 1930s as it had been for the first Socialist League fifty years earlier. Herbert Morrison told the party conference in 1934 that working-class voters were in some cases more interested in their "little investments" in the Post Office Savings Bank than some capitalists were in their more extensive holdings. Another delegate pointed out that not every working-class family lived in poverty: "There are in my constituency railwaymen – good socialists – who have a share or two in the railways."[40] Over fifty years later the riposte to the left would be couched in terms of second homes near Marbella (see p. 159), but the dominant party view was the same; manual workers had a stake in capitalism. As the historian Richard Lyman has pointed out, to "achieve a mandate for revolutionary change in a profoundly unrevolutionary society"[41] was a conundrum which the left was unable to solve.

Lansbury had after illness resumed the leadership of the party, but his type of socialist pacifism seemed outmoded in the conditions of the mid-thirties. Moreover, at 76 it was time for him to go. After an attack on his pacifist beliefs at the party conference in October 1935 by Ernest Bevin, "the one man powerful enough and brutal enough to spoil the effect Mr Lansbury had produced"[42] as Kingsley Martin pointed out a few days later, he resigned to be replaced as temporary leader by Clement Attlee. Stanley Baldwin, who had replaced MacDonald as prime minister the previous June, took the opportunity to announce a general election. As in 1918 the election was a significant advance for the Labour Party while simultaneously being a disappointment. Labour, which had gained ten seats in by-elections since 1931, now returned 154 candidates. Its 38 per cent of the vote was the greatest share it had ever won, and party leaders old and new like J. R. Clynes, H. B. Lees-Smith, Fred Pethick-Lawrence, Hugh Dalton, Herbert Morrison and Emanuel Shinwell (who defeated Ramsay MacDonald) were returned, together with many non-trade union candidates. It was no longer a rump but a genuine national party.

On the other hand, the relatively happy days of the 1920s were gone. The government, overwhelmingly Conservative but still calling itself National, had over half the vote and 429 MPs. The middle-class Liberal vote had been won by the Conservatives, apparently irrevocably. The Tories had in Stanley Baldwin the most trusted leader in British politics. The elderly but still acute Beatrice Webb recorded: "Over the larger part of Great Britain there is not the remotest sign of any widespread discontent with the existing social order. The leadership of the Labour Party during the election was ineffectual and divided."[43] Labour's young candidates were mostly defeated. The most important reason for the party's defeat was probably the previously mentioned fact that the slump was now having a less severe impact than it had had a few years previously. G. D. H. and Margaret Cole reflected soon after the election:

> It is especially difficult to win men and women over by a Socialist appeal when the actual conditions under which they are living are by no means intolerable in their eyes . . . Regarded in [the] light [of past experience] the condition of the majority of the British electorate does not look so very bad . . . There is in consequence some disposition to say that the British people, having come through the economic crisis better on the whole than most other peoples, will be wisest to leave things as they are and to avoid all rash and untried experiments.

The view of Harold Laski, another of Labour's leading intellectuals, was similar: "the result of the election was essentially a refusal to take risks".[44]

Such explanations seem as plausible as the assertion that Labour had failed to attract the middle-class vote. One must remember that even in an intensely political decade like the 1930s the interest of the British people as a whole in the political process remained sporadic. Football and "motor-bandits" were of more interest to the average voter, in the view of G. D. H. Cole writing in 1937, than the activities of Hitler: "An electorate as unpolitical as the British in its ordinary habits of thought weights the political dice heavily in the side of the status quo." Moreover, unemployment continued in the staple industries while more workers entered new, often light industries, in which employees characteristically had weaker social class and trade union loyalties than those employed in older industries. There was also a question of loyalty to institutions created in the past. "The Trade Union means less to the typical modern factory worker than it meant to the generations which built it up", wrote the Coles.[45] The party, which was widely regarded as the political voice of trade unionism, was in danger of being regarded also as the voice of the past.

Attlee was confirmed as party leader after the election, though not without opposition. Another candidate for the post, Arthur Greenwood, was elected deputy leader. The third candidate, Herbert Morrison, hoped to replace Attlee during much of the latter's twenty-year tenure of office. But the new generation of leaders knew that without the party they were nothing. They could not and in most cases did not wish to ignore it or fight it as MacDonald and Snowden had done. Attlee wrote in a passage more characteristic of an opposition leader than a prime minister: "I am not prepared to arrogate to myself a superiority to the rest of the movement. I am prepared to submit to their will, even if I disagree."[46] No one would have regarded the unassuming Attlee or any of his more ebullient colleagues as "the focus of the mute hopes of a whole class" as Egon Wertheimer had described MacDonald at the end of the 1920s. Even the politically cautious, noticeably complacent Dalton declared in 1935, "The next Labour government must start off with a well-planned rush."[47] (He later pointed out that this was what in fact happened in 1945.) To that extent the party was stronger than it had been in the 1920s.

The second half of the 1930s was a tragic period in European history, and it was an unhappy period for Labour. The passion for socialism on the left evident in the first half of the decade turned into a passion for a united front of all anti-capitalist parties against fascism and Nazism, and, later, a popular front to include the Liberals and anti-fascist Conservatives. The official Labour Party would have none of this, partly because it was unwilling to admit that it needed to work with other parties, partly because of its strong anti-communism, which was understandable especially among trade unionists who faced internal communist challenge. Thus Ellen Wilkinson, again an MP and leading the Jarrow "crusade" in 1936, the inter-war hunger march which persisted most prominently in popular memory, found that both the central Labour Party and the TUC frowned on local assistance, with curious results. "So in places like Chesterfield, where the Trades and Labour Council obeyed the

[TUC] circular, the Conservative Party weighed in with hot meals and a place to sleep."[48]

The Spanish Civil War also caused division within the party, with the left committed unequivocally to the republican side and much of the right supporting "non-intervention" and concentrating its attention on the need for British rearmament. Hugh Dalton, who had become an expert on foreign affairs as well as finance, was the leading opponent of Labour involvement in the Spanish crusade. He was not interested in the threat from Franco, seeing in Hitler a much greater potential danger. He wrote later: "They [the Labour Party partisans of republican Spain] had no clue in their minds to the risks, and the realities, for Britain of a general war. Nor did they, even dimly, comprehend how unrepresentative they were, on this issue, of the great mass of their fellow countrymen."[49]

The Socialist League was disbanded in 1937 after it had signed a "unity manifesto" with the Communist Party and the ILP, and the Labour executive had consequently voted to expel it. This did not prevent individuals from advocating the united or the popular front. Early in 1939 Cripps, who had continued to urge the case for the popular front, was expelled from the party and was soon followed by Charles Trevelyan, Aneurin Bevan, George Strauss and two others. (All those named were later readmitted, and Cripps, Bevan and Strauss became post-war Labour ministers; Trevelyan, who was 70 in 1940, was no longer actively involved in politics.)

The Labour Party did not cover itself with glory in these years. It devoted to internal dissent energies which might have been expended on positive policies. It put forward an *Immediate Programme* in 1937 which contained specific pledges but marked a retreat from previous commitments in some respects. The party won another twelve seats from the Conservatives in by-elections before the war, but these results did not necessarily imply victory in the general election scheduled for 1940. G. D. H. Cole wrote in 1937 that the Labour Party was "not even in sight of an independent majority" and more recently Andrew Thorpe has written of the later 1930s: "Labour seemed to be condemned to Opposition for the foreseeable future."[50] As the inter-war years drew to a close, therefore, the Labour Party could not look to the immediate future with much confidence. It had lost its first generation of leaders and found more suitable ones, but it remained divided and impotent. Another great war would change its prospects as much or more than the first war had done, but that was not apparent in 1939.

LABOUR IN WAR AND PEACE

1939–1951

Britain's participation in the Second World War began on 3 September 1939, two days after the Germans invaded Poland. This time there was no astonishment on the part of the British people, nor general excitement at the prospect of war. The public mood was no longer typified by such phrases as "swimmers into cleanness leaping", with which the poet Rupert Brooke had greeted the European conflict in 1914. Interestingly the writer and journalist Harold Nicolson MP, an establishment figure and, with reservations, a government supporter, observed in his diary on 3 September: "The Labour Party will be hard put to it to prevent this war degenerating into class warfare." [1] As the comment implies, the Labour Party was no keener on class warfare than Nicolson.

Labour was handicapped at the outbreak of war by the fact that its leader had not recovered from a prolonged illness, but Attlee's place was taken by Arthur Greenwood. The party made clear from the outset its support for the war effort, even more strongly in consequence of the signing of the German–Russian Pact a few days before the invasion of Poland. Although the first months were known to the press as "the bore war" or "the phoney war" because of the lack of military action in western Europe, the corridors of Westminster were alive with gossip and manoeuvre. It was in a sense curious that Neville Chamberlain, the prime minister who had to make way for a more vigorous successor once the Nazis turned their attention to the West, should have been replaced by Winston Churchill, who was heavily implicated in the defeat in Norway in April 1940. The government, however, was led by Chamberlain and he had given, it was claimed, too little authority to Churchill to carry out the Norwegian job properly. Moreover, Churchill had been the most prominent advocate of rearmament in the later 1930s.

By early May a coalition government was increasingly being demanded. The Labour Party executive made clear its unwillingness to serve under Chamberlain. It was at this point on the day that the Germans attacked in the west, 10 May 1940, after the Conservative Party realized that Churchill was the only person both available and acceptable across the political spectrum, that he became prime minister and leader of a five-man war cabinet in which Attlee was Lord Privy Seal (and later deputy prime minister) and Greenwood minister without portfolio. The Labour Party, whose annual conference was meeting in Bournemouth at the time, gave overwhelming approval to working with the Conservatives; suddenly Labour provided 40 per cent of the inner core of government. If this development was as unexpected as it was unprecedented, so too was the fact that by the end of June of the same year the Germans were the masters of virtually the whole of the continent of Europe, either as conquerors or as dominant "allies". Within less than a year of the outbreak of war the German aims of 1914–18, never achieved in that war, had been more than fully realized.

Previously accepted opinion about the home front in the war years has been increasingly subject to attack by revisionist historians. This makes difficult a generally acceptable summary of Labour history during the war. Nonetheless, two points do stand out: first, that Labour leaders became ministers, familiar with the problems of government and known to the public, and second that public opinion was given a sharp push to the political left by events in and after 1940.

Ernest Bevin entered the cabinet and then the war cabinet as minister of labour in 1940, a parliamentary seat being quickly found for him. He was followed into the war cabinet in 1942 by Sir Stafford Cripps, who had not yet rejoined the Labour Party, and by Herbert Morrison as Home Secretary. Greenwood resigned and left the government in the same year. Hugh Dalton was also a minister, first of economic warfare and later at the Board of Trade and so too were A. V. Alexander and William Jowitt, who had served under MacDonald and were to serve again under Attlee from 1945. It was Labour ministers who were most prominent on the home front and they pushed within the government for distinctive Labour solutions to economic and social questions. Only Greenwood was judged a failure and even he appointed Sir William Beveridge to write the report on social insurance which proved to be an enormous success with public opinion. It is hard to see how Labour ministers, in office for five years and becoming household names, could have done other than help Labour to election victory. As R. B. McCallum and Alison Readman pointed out in the first scholarly study of the 1945 election, Labour had previously seemed to be a sect or faction, but could now rightly claim to represent the whole people.

Revisionist historians have plausibly claimed that the war did not lead to harmony amongst social classes and, more controversially, that the Labour Party followed by the time of the election in 1945 a conservative strategy. It is fair to assert that a social revolution led by the servant-keeping class, from whom much was heard of social harmony, was unlikely to be either sweeping or long-lasting. But the Labour share of the vote rose between 1935 and 1945 from 38 per cent, its previous best performance, to over 48 per cent, while the Conservatives fell from over 53 to under 40 per cent. Labour, which represented the mainstream political left, won a landslide victory in 1945, though the Conservatives were led by the victorious and hugely popular war leader. As we have seen, had there been a general election in 1940 it seems unlikely that a Labour government would have been elected. Something must account for such a change during the war years and it seems certain that the "something" resulted from developments during the war itself. If the Labour programme of 1939 was perceived as moderate by 1945, this too says much about the swing of opinion in wartime. Policies which could be dismissed as too left wing in 1939 became more generally acceptable in war-time conditions.

Politicians were forced to promise "a better future" to working-class voters, some of whom had recently been unemployed while many still lived in slums, as bombs rained out of the sky from the summer of 1940. Even Churchill, who deprecated domestic controversy during wartime, was willing to preside over planning for postwar prosperity. In the summer of 1940 socialistic propaganda of various types was already circulating in official and unofficial circles, and staff of the Ministry of Information were being told that the needs of war production demanded better working and living conditions. Paul Addison, one of the most careful students of the home front in war time, refers to Penguin Specials, "abrasive meritocrat[s] . . . progressive churchm[e]n, and J. B. Priestley" as helping to establish the national mood and concludes that the Conservatives could not have won a general election at any time after June 1940. Mass-Observation, the social research organisation, wrote in 1943 of "the leftward drift in political outlook which has continued at a steady rate throughout the war". Rationing, introduced at an early stage of the war "to make more certain that you get . . . fair shares with everybody else",[2] reinforced the egalitarian sentiment stimulated by shortages affecting almost everyone. It seems difficult to deny that there was a swing in wartime opinion, especially in 1940–2, towards collectivism and left-wing views.

The new interest in a collectivist approach to government policy reached an apex late in 1942 with the publication of *Social Insurance and Allied Services,* the Beveridge Report, essentially a lengthy official document dealing with the social services, closely printed and packed with tables and charts. Under the terms of its proposals social insurance was to cover the whole population through a flat-rate contribution and a uniform benefit. The report advocated an enlarged maternity benefit and a funeral grant, and the basic unemployment and retirement benefits were to be a far from lavish £2 per week for a married couple. (Average weekly men's earnings rose to over three times this level by July 1944.) It also advocated family allowances, a national health service and an approach to full employment, though its assumptions, notably that most married women would be content to remain housewives and mothers after the war, were in the main conventional in their time. This may have been an advantage in appealing to conservative views. The report sold hundreds of thousands of copies, an unprecedented number for a government "blue book" and however much publicity Beveridge himself and the Ministry of Information organized prior to publication, as it was claimed that they did, its reception suggested that the public were determined that Beveridge's "five giants"- want, disease, ignorance, squalor and idleness – should be slain. James Griffiths, Labour's postwar minister of national insurance, recalled that the report "fell like manna from heaven". Lady Beveridge later remembered "[t]he fantastic limelight in which we lived" and how even more than ten years later she was often asked whether she was "the wife of the famous Report".[3]

The main proposals of the Beveridge report were not adopted as government policy until the later stages of the war, and the failure of the wartime coalition to endorse the report immediately may well have contributed to a public mood of cynicism. "People had thought it too good to be true", wrote Chuter Ede, a Labour junior minister, recording the view of his constituency election agent in February 1943; "they now believed they were being deprived of it for selfish reasons."[4] Privately Conservative backbenchers were often hostile and some Labour ministers unenthusiastic at best about Beveridge's plan. But the most important aspect of the report was surely its initial reception rather than the machinations of politicians after its publication. It played an important part in the election of 1945. The Conservative manifesto promised "a nation-wide and compulsory scheme of National Insurance", while Labour attacked the prewar social security policies of the Conservatives and declared: "A Labour Government will press on rapidly with legislation extending social insurance over the necessary wide field to all." Labour had in fact adopted a comprehensive policy on social security, health and family allowances as early as May 1942, several months before the Beveridge Report appeared: "the Labour Party is deeply committed to social insurance",[5] Chuter Ede noted on the day following its publication.

The wartime economy also absorbed the unemployed. Further, many workers moved into occupations which brought them within the sphere of influence of trade unions and Ernest Bevin as a leading minister was an influential advocate of union membership. The numbers in unions rose, though not by as much as they had done in the first war, more than 1½ million between 1939 and 1945. The newly recruited members often saw Labour as the party most likely to prevent a return to mass unemployment and hence they were inclined to vote for it when they were given an opportunity to do so.

Attlee, Bevin and Dalton were willing for the wartime coalition to continue until the defeat of Japan, but there was little sentiment within the party to support them once Germany surrendered in May 1945. Herbert Morrison, a key figure, was among the advocates of an early election. Labour, again in conference soon after the war ended in Europe, agreed to continue the coalition until the autumn (the war's sudden end in August not being then foreseen), but the proposal was unacceptable to Churchill and the general election took place in early July. The principal author of the Labour statement, *Let us Face the Future*, was Morrison himself with the assistance of Michael Young, secretary of the party's research department. They did not, however, have an entirely free hand. The party members in government had been gradually converted to the view that public ownership was not necessarily the only or even the best form of state control of industry, but much of the rank and file did not share their outlook. A motion proposed by the future MP Ian Mikardo, representing Reading at the conference in December 1944, committed the party to sweeping measures of public ownership, while Mikardo himself declared that "our rank and file comrades . . . will be appalled and disappointed" by what he termed the "un-Socialist character" of the executive's own imprecise resolution. Not all the industries and services specified in the Reading resolution survived the drafting process, but Morrison's biographers admit that it "gave an extra impetus towards nationalization, if any were needed, and made it much more difficult to retreat from nationalization commitments".[6]

Let us Face the Future was published in April 1945, before the end of the wartime coalition and was adopted as the party's election manifesto. It promised to nationalize the Bank of England, fuel and power (coal, gas and electricity), inland transport (road freight, transport by rail, air and canal) and iron and steel, which Morrison did not want to include, and again opposed taking into public ownership in later years. Although the majority of these industries had been included in *Labour's Immediate Programme* in 1937, that document was not an election manifesto. *Let us Face the Future* declared: "The Labour Party is a Socialist Party, and proud of it. Its ultimate purpose at home is the establishment of the Socialist Commonwealth of Great Britain", though it was careful to add: "But Socialism cannot come overnight, as the product of a week-end revolution. The members of the Labour Party, like the British people, are practical-minded men and women." Speaking to the party conference in May 1945 Morrison urged delegates to argue the case for the nationalization of each industry. "That is how the British mind works. It does not work in a vacuum or in abstract theories. You must prove your case each time".[7]

Despite the qualifications and reservations Labour's programme in 1945 is striking, more particularly early in the twenty-first century when none of the industries named above is publicly owned except the Bank of England and none is likely to be nationalized by a Labour government. The emphasis on socialism is also striking to modern readers. In presenting itself to the public a political party shows itself the creature of its time. Its leaders are men and women who usually follow the line of least resistance rather than remaining loyal in changing circumstances to the principles of their youth. Winning elections and forming governments must, as previously pointed out, be a political party's first and guiding principle. It is therefore plausible that if a party puts forward a programme which does not appeal to the intermittently attentive electorate it is serving neither itself nor those whom it wishes especially to help.

At the end of the war the public was ready for change. Homes, jobs and social security were what mattered to the electorate in 1945, and were identified more with the Labour Party than with any other political organization. Nationalization was not a prominent issue in the campaign. When *Let us Face the Future* wrote of jobs, housing, personal freedom and modernization of social services, factories, machinery and schools, it proclaimed: "All parties say so – the Labour Party means it." This was a point to which the electorate could and did respond. The Labour Party's programme was not conservative in 1945, but the party had moved closer to the political centre ground, finding a moment when its proposals were hard to caricature as extreme. "[T]he party's main argument", Andrew Thorpe points out, "was the need to develop and extend the measures which had helped to win the war."[8] It seized the moment and fought a successful campaign.

The general election of 1945 produced a Labour landslide, a result which astonished many observers. "Nobody foresaw this at all", Harold Nicolson, who was among the defeated pro-Churchill candidates, told his diary.[9] Among those surprised were most of the Labour leadership, who had feared that Churchill's appeal would be irresistible. But the vote, the counting of which was delayed for three weeks to include the ballots of overseas service personnel, was decisive. Labour made gains all over the country, winning well over 200 new seats while the Conservatives and allies lost over 200. Some former MPs were startled to find themselves without parliamentary seats, while other candidates were equally startled to find themselves in the House of Commons after having allowed their names to go forward in bravado or without serious thought.

Historians have been more convincing in discounting previously accepted reasons for the Labour victory than in explaining why the party won. Labour did not, despite claims to the contrary, have large numbers of full-time agents during the war years while Conservatives went patriotically off to fight. The Army Bureau of Current Affairs, though regarded by some writers as a nest of left-wing ideas, has been viewed by others as a better recruiting agent for rest and recuperation than for socialism. The service vote, though strongly pro-Labour, was not large enough to explain a landslide. Political interest was not great and fewer than three-quarters of eligible voters actually voted, a low poll reinforced by the fact that the electoral register was seriously inadequate. The pendulum, that hoary explanation of political change, could not be relied upon to swing. The election was fought principally over practical issues, and the number of voters who sought socialism by voting Labour, though not insignificant, was relatively small.

Familiarity of office helped Labour, but the shift in wartime sentiment outlined above was probably the main reason for the Labour landslide. Public perception that Labour favoured social reform and that Conservatives were indifferent or hostile was of crucial importance. Thus Kevin Jefferys writes that "the social experience of a 'people's war'", and government prevarications over social reform from early 1943 increased Labour's popularity: "the swing to the left was clearly unstoppable by the time of the election". Labour's social agenda differed from the Conservatives' and "embraced a positive vision of the welfare state".[10]

But there was another reason for the Labour victory which should be cited here. This was the fact that the social class system had by 1945 created a working class in Britain united enough to vote together and sufficiently self-confident to vote Labour rather than abstain or support the Conservatives. "In class terms, therefore," writes Roger Eatwell, "Labour's victory was basically a working-class one, a culmination of the growth of class consciousness". Ross McKibbin's more recent formulation is that in wartime the middle class was "much weakened [politically] once progressive politics became inextricably associated with the organized working class; and for that the Second World War was responsible."[11] Working-class people voted for what they took to be "their own", even though a sizeable number of parliamentary seats and some of the leading positions in the party were held by public school-educated graduates of the old universities. The growth of class sentiment over a prolonged period had helped Labour, together with the development during the war years of an at least temporarily less deferential society. When one adds to this solid base the transient adhesion of a number of conscience-stricken middle-class voters, Labour's victory seems natural, even inevitable.

Hugh Dalton was told shortly after the election that the American president Harry Truman had said to King George VI that there had been a revolution in Britain. Truman was assured that Britain did not have revolutions, and the king's view was more perspicacious than the president's. There was no revolution by consent in any European country after the war, and if the British people had voted for one, as the Labour left asserted, they were to be sadly disappointed. A government led by Attlee, Bevin, Dalton and Morrison, all of whom were "gradualists – orthodox Fabians" who regarded the nationalization proposals as "a measure of social reform", or in Stephen Brooke's words "the highest form of physical planning",[12] believed in sweeping change but not in revolution. The newly readmitted Labour Party member Stafford Cripps had shifted to the right while his compatriots were moving left, and other members of the government, few of whom were political figures of stature, were too borne down by departmental work to consider root and branch reconstruction of British society. Stephen Brooke's detailed study of the Labour Party in the Second World War points out that six years of war produced a new form of socialism in which the public good was seen by the party leadership as national, not class-based, a vision which they adopted with some enthusiasm. Only Aneurin Bevan, at 47 the baby of the cabinet, was a "potential red revolutionary socialist",[13] and he was too isolated, distracted and ambivalent to lead a successful socialist campaign from within the government.

To the older generation in the party, who had worked within it since 1918 or earlier, a majority Labour government presiding over full employment throughout the country was itself a revolution. To this fact must be added their years in wartime government, which had increased Labour's appeal to the electorate at the price of cooling such socialist ardour as remained in 1940 after years of internal party struggles. Attlee was a product of Haileybury, the nineteenth-century public school. Seeking a parliamentary private secretary he deliberately chose an Old Haileyburian from the Labour benches. With his passion for cricket and his belief in tradition he was an unlikely British Lenin. Dalton and Cripps were also consciously if less explicitly loyal to their public schools, Eton and Winchester. Ernest Bevin, chosen to be foreign secretary, was as anti-communist as Attlee himself, inclined to behave, it was said, as if the Soviet Union had resulted from a breakaway from his own Transport and General Workers Union. Within a week or two of Bevin's appointment Harold Nicolson wrote of him: "He is a realist, in that he believes that facts are more important than theories . . . He would not be tempted to subordinate vital British interests to some ideological conception of party sympathies or dislikes."[14] Bevin kept in contact with Anthony Eden, his Conservative predecessor, and his foreign policy was often severely criticised by his own left wing. It was said, as seriously as jokingly, that he was a fatter version of Eden. Dalton as chancellor of the exchequer prided himself on his good relations with bankers and Morrison, lord president of the council, leader of the House of Commons and deputy prime minister, was alarmed when his backbenchers sang the Labour Party anthem "The Red Flag" in the House of Commons. "The brief performance horrified some of the Tories and I must admit that it mildly disturbed me. These youngsters still had to absorb the atmosphere of the House."[15]

To the personalities of the Labour leadership must be added the inexperience of large numbers of Labour MPs. Many of them were happy to accept at least initially their leaders' conviction that a majority Labour government was itself a revolution. The early breach with the Soviet Union and Labour's alliance with the United States also discouraged MPs, unless they were unusually independent-minded, from moving to the left. But more important than these factors was the response of the party to its working-class electorate: "Speculations as to the future activities of Stan Matthews and Bruce Woodcock", wrote a contributor to the *New Statesman*, "are much more attractive to the mind of the average factory worker than speculations as to the future activities of Marshal Tito and Ho Chi Minh."[16] This comment, which now seems a statement of the obvious, was thought necessary to explain to a middle-class readership workers' lack of interest in higher productivity as a means of building socialism. What was sought was higher wages, full employment and more houses, "job, family and home" as Nick Tiratsoo puts it. The egalitarian sentiments of 1945 had dissipated quickly and "only a tiny minority wished the government to pursue further socialist advances".[17] There was little discernible working-class demand to abolish the public schools, nationalize the joint stock banks or, more generally, level social classes.

Steven Fielding and his colleagues comment that building a socialist society, which had seemed to many in the Labour Party a practical objective in 1945, faltered on the rock of working-class concern with protecting independence, combating poverty and "keep[ing] interfering authorities as much at arm's length as possible". The Labour Party aims of promoting socialism or community values were not shared by the majority of the population. "Most ordinary people continued to be preoccupied with their own lives, together with those of family, kin and friends."[18] As the historian Jim Tomlinson points out, there was little popular enthusiasm for economic reconstruction to sustain the Attlee government against the opposition which it faced from private industry.

Within its own terms of reference the Attlee government of 1945 was highly successful except in securing another term of office with an adequate majority. Economic problems necessarily received special attention from the government. The economist and civil servant Alec Cairncross, by no means an uncritical friend, noted that it "pointed the economy in the right direction, rode out the various crises that the years of transition almost inevitably gave rise to, and by 1951 had brought the economy near to eventual balance".[19] It encouraged greater productivity, Cairncross pointed out, increased exports and kept inflation relatively low.

In social terms the Attlee administration was unusual amongst British governments in having an ambitious programme of reforms and actually carrying it out. Full employment was maintained. Coal, electricity and gas, railways, civil aviation, canals and road freight, iron and steel and the Bank of England were all taken into public ownership. The National Health Service, the government's crowning achievement, was brought into existence, covering the entire British population and many foreign visitors as well. The Beveridge Report was made law and the rates payable were more generous than Beveridge had suggested to allow for inflation since publication of the report in 1942. Family allowances and a higher school leaving age were introduced. Planning legislation was extended and strengthened, national parks were created and a system for protecting public footpaths and allowing access to the countryside enacted. Plural voting and university seats were abolished, the delaying powers of the House of Lords reduced and the requirement for contracting in to the political levy, enacted in 1927 in the wake of the general strike, was reversed so that members of unions affiliated to the Labour Party had to contract out if they did not wish to pay the levy. (Affiliated trade union membership of the Labour Party rose by over 50 per cent within a year, in the case of cotton union branches cited by Martin Harrison, from 27 to 100 per cent in three months.)

The historian James Cronin, writing in the early 1980s before the Thatcher government had enacted its full programme, commented that the policies of the years 1945–8 "probably represented the most successful effort to restructure British society ever attempted".[20] Although Labour had an overwhelming majority which could have been used to enact controversial proposals, its measures were generally accepted by the parliamentary opposition in principle or after compromise had been reached. The government's nationalization programme, its efforts to redistribute power and wealth, its attempts at planning and controls have not surprisingly been characterized by later historians as modest. The absence of bitter disputes on matters of principle was the result of the conditions of postwar reconstruction, the decision of the Conservatives to support a social programme and the nature and history of the Labour Party itself.

The Conservatives understood that most of the industries nationalized by Labour could not be saved for private enterprise, and the terms of nationalization and the prospect of government investment were relatively easy for them to swallow. Some of the industries like coal and railways were in poor condition, and others like electricity and gas were already in municipal hands, hence in the public domain. With regard to the railways, for example, much of the Conservative case centred on the scale of compensation, which was more generous than many had hoped or feared. Nor did Conservatives criticize the nationalization of coal with much conviction. The Bank of England too was nationalized on terms favourable to its shareholders. Difficulties arose within the nationalized industries themselves rather than from outside. The boards which managed the industries were remote from the workforce and contained few Labour supporters. Industrial democracy within the nationalized industries was seldom noticeable and raised little enthusiasm among ministers. It was not surprising that dissatisfaction was common in the nationalized industries and that unofficial strikes took place in the coal industry.

The fact that the Conservatives did not oppose most measures of nationalization on principle and that prewar and wartime reports had advocated public ownership of key industries did not mean that a Churchill peacetime government in 1945 would have followed a programme of nationalization. It should be noted, however, that the parts of the programme of public ownership which they did energetically oppose, road transport of freight and iron and steel, were the only nationalization measures to be repealed after they returned to office in 1951. Concessions were made on road haulage while the bill to nationalize it was proceeding through the Commons, and iron and steel divided the government as it had divided the party in earlier years. The steel nationalization bill was delayed until 1948 and was accompanied by a Parliament Bill which reduced the delaying powers of the House of Lords to a year. Overt opponents of nationalization included prominent civil servants, as Kenneth Morgan has shown in his detailed history of this government. The bill as passed delayed implementing nationalization of iron and steel until after another general election had taken place.

The Labour government was criticized in ensuing decades for its alleged timidity in introducing measures of public ownership and its lack of a strategy to replace capitalism. Nationalization was no doubt introduced defensively, unimaginatively and with little concern for changing power structures within industry. Jim Tomlinson argues that it was intended in part to solve problems of the 1930s like unemployment and rationalization of industry, and that expectations of transforming human relations in industry were optimistic, though Martin Francis stresses that there was also a strong strand of opinion which favoured nationalization because of its anticipated effect on redistributing wealth and power. Given the twin obstacles of financial difficulty and public concern with more urgent matters like jobs, food and homes to say nothing of trade union sensitivities, it is difficult to see how contemporary politicians could have done other than emphasize the utilitarian aspects of nationalization. As Andrew Thorpe points out, majority opinion in the Labour Party did not wish to nationalize all industries and relied instead upon the co-operation of private industry. Even had economic and social conditions been more favourable, belief in class collaboration would have made sweeping anti-capitalist measures extremely difficult if not unimaginable.

It is less easy to find major inadequacies in the National Health Service, inaugurated in 1948, for the act affected the whole population, and remains widely cherished though controversial today. Nor is it accurate to claim that a coalition government white paper advocating a health service published early in 1944 made the act consensual, for as with nationalization advocacy alone is not an act of parliament and Aneurin Bevan's bill was not identical to the coalition plans. In important aspects like the relationship between private practice and public health centres the coalition white paper was not a detailed blueprint. A plan for "a comprehensive health service" was included in the Conservative election manifesto in 1945, but hospitals were to remain divided between the voluntary sector and local authorities, which was not a feature of the Labour bill. Bevan as minister of health (then including housing), defended the decision to allow private practice to continue and to permit "pay beds" in NHS hospitals. Health centres were not aggressively developed and financial provisions were inadequately thought through. Bevan agreed that general practitioners should remain independent contractors, not salaried medical staff. He was perhaps too receptive to persuasion from the titled presidents of royal medical colleges, though as he had to win the doctors over if a health service was to become reality, these compromises were probably inevitable. Neither ministers nor the party rank and file after all could have replaced doctors if they refused *en masse* to make the new health service work.

A more serious criticism of Bevan was that he took his health responsibilities so seriously that there was too little time and energy left for housing, in the eyes of much of the public an even more important responsibility than health. When the Conservatives returned to power in 1951 they divided health and housing into separate ministries. There was a strong argument for Labour doing the same rather than combining the two functions within the same ministry as had been the case since the ministry of health was established in 1919. It was not, however, too much responsibility on one set of shoulders which led to more than 200,000 new houses being built in only one of the Labour years. Rather it was shortage of bricks, timber and building workers, division of responsibilities between ministries and between the centre and local authorities, Bevan's insistence that council houses be built to a more generous standard than the coalition government had proposed, and cuts in public investment which followed repeated balance of payments crises. In any case Labour's record on building new homes was less successful than other aspects of its policies and the failure was exploited by the Conservatives in the election of 1950.

James Griffiths, a Welsh miner and union official until his election to parliament in 1936, had become an expert on social insurance and was appointed minister of national insurance. In that capacity he set to work to make both standing Labour policy and the Beveridge Report reality. The result was the National Insurance Act of 1946 and related measures passed in the same year and in 1948. Here again the Conservatives did not offer opposition on principle. A triumphant Conservative government would undoubtedly have introduced its own welfare measures as the party promised to do in its election manifesto, though it is unlikely that it would have enacted such a comprehensive and expensive programme as Labour. In any event Griffiths introduced benefits more generous than those advocated by Beveridge several years previously, as already mentioned, though to an informed contemporary American critic as well as to posterity the rates were "decidedly grim". The same writer conceded, however: "The Labour government, all its critics and detractors to the contrary, has a justifiable right to look upon this legislation as a great and significant step in the direction of the social security objectives for which it feels that it has fought so long and against such bitter and unrelenting odds."[21] Labour had not in fact been continually associated with social insurance as a central policy, but it had certainly fought for decades for "work or maintenance" of the unemployed and against the poor law, and as pointed out above had advocated comprehensive measures of social security before the publication of the Beveridge Report.

Under the terms of the legislation the poor law was abolished and national assistance introduced, at a level of fifty shillings per week for a pensioner couple with no independent resources and paying ten shillings rent. National insurance was financed, however, by a regressive flat tax on wages and salaries, industrial assurance or "burial money" was reformed rather than abolished and means testing survived in various aspects of the new regime. Above all, if the scheme was comprehensive it was certainly not adequate in terms of benefits. Supporters of the government boasted that it had abolished poverty and so it had by the restricted criteria of the 1940s, but not by any more generous estimate of the needs of the old, the disabled and the unemployed. It was fortunate for the government, which naturally appropriated the credit to itself, that the postwar boom did not collapse as it had done after 1918 and that full employment therefore endured. It was less eager to point out that world economic conditions and the buoyant American economy deserved much of the credit. And it should be remembered that there has been severe and influential criticism of this government by the historian Correlli Barnett for devoting money to social purposes which should allegedly have been spent on rehabilitating and modernizing industry.

There has been much controversy about Labour's education policies, particularly over the failure of Labour ministers to introduce a policy of comprehensive secondary schools. More recently comprehensive schools have themselves come under fire, their supposed contribution to higher educational attainment and a more equal society being treated with scepticism or disbelief. It is perhaps unjust to Labour ministers to have expected them to see in the grammar school anything other than the road to success for working-class children, more particularly boys. The grammar school was the route which many had taken to the middle class and which Labour politicians had worked hard to foster in local government. The possibility of introducing comprehensive (then usually called multilateral) schools was included in the coalition government's Education Act in 1944, for types of secondary school were unmentioned in the act and both the Conservative minister R. A. Butler and his Labour deputy Chuter Ede, who faced relatively little pressure on the point, conceded that experiments with multilateral education were possible under its terms. For most children, however, selection for different schools and thus for different careers took place at ages ten or eleven and meant that the majority would attend a renamed senior school or in some cases the same all-age school as before.

A few Labour local authorities, of which the London County Council was much the most important, wanted to introduce comprehensive schools after the war, but they met opposition from Labour ministers. The solution of Ellen Wilkinson, Labour's first minister of education, was to urge the abolition of social classes rather than the abolition of the grammar schools which contained a disproportionate number of middle-class pupils and her successor, George Tomlinson, followed a similar approach. Fees were abolished in secondary schools after 1944, Labour ministers in conditions of extreme economic difficulty bravely raised the school leaving age from 14 to 15 in 1947. In addition war-damaged schools, numbering over a thousand in London alone, were repaired and some new building was undertaken, usually by prefabrication. But the chance was lost to strike a blow for equality in education after 1945. The reasons for this hesitation included the damage or destruction which so many schools had suffered and the lack of enthusiasm for change within the Ministry of Education. Ministers were also aware of the popularity of the grammar schools and the government was under insufficient pressure within and without the Labour Party to press for a new system. It was to take a good deal of advocacy, the experience of the early comprehensive schools, denigration of the supposedly old-fashioned curricula and inadequate equipment of grammar schools, and research findings which showed over and over again that the working class did badly in the secondary education system, before Labour politicians finally decided in the 1960s that selection at 11 was more unpopular than the loss of grammar schools.

The pattern of Labour reforms which made important changes in British society but disappointed socialist enthusiasts was followed in other fields as well as those outlined above. In retrospect the reforms themselves impress the student as much or more than their inadequacy, especially as heavy pressures were exerted on ministers to curb innovations rather than to extend them. "More socialism" was a rallying cry which appealed to activists but it meant little without detailed proposals. By 1949 there was a certain air of discouragement within socialist circles and a greater understanding that the mass of the public was concerned with bread and butter issues rather than with ideological ones. Edmund Dell was a disillusioned former Labour minister who had left the Labour Party before he wrote a history of democratic socialism in Britain, but it is not unreasonable to claim as he does that Labour had lost confidence in socialist ideas by this time: "Having lost its original purpose, it was seeking desperately for a new one which would justify its continued existence."[22]

Like other Labour governments before 1997, this one faced conditions of extreme difficulty, "a gigantic economic problem" in the words of the historian James Hinton,[23] by no means an apologist for the government. The components of the problem included the need to change rapidly from production for war to production for exports, an acute shortage of dollars exacerbated by American policy and the conundrum of how to increase output while simultaneously introducing the promised social reforms. Indeed, no British government in peacetime had ever faced such difficult conditions and the Attlee government had an ambitious and expensive programme of social reforms to finance as well as a determination to rearm the country against the threat of international communism. Rationing, shortages and austerity followed six years of war, limiting the patience of the sore-pressed electorate. Without financial assistance from the United States austerity would been even more severe. Hugh Dalton wrote in his memoirs that failure to secure an American loan in 1946 would have meant

> [l]ess food, except for bread and potatoes . . . in particular less meat and sugar. Little cotton, and, therefore, less clothes and less exports. Heavy and growing unemployment in many industries. Worst of all, from the point of view of public morale, practically no smokes, since eighty per cent of our tobacco cost dollars . . . Our feet would soon be on the downward slope, leading towards sure defeat at the next election.[24]

It is fair to point to the fact that Britain's overseas commitments, combating communism, managing the colonies and maintaining great power status, cost more than was gained from the American loan. It is also fair to point out that the obsession with securing the loan even under adverse conditions resulted from an unnecessary determination to maintain Britain's place in the world and sustain an unrealistic level of rearmament, but this is not how the situation seemed to most politicians at the time. Britain was regarded by politicians and public as a great power, it had "won" the war and it was unwilling to abandon the empire and a world role because of economic difficulties. This was particularly true of a Labour government which was determined to give its enemies no opportunity to accuse it of lack of patriotism. To imagine otherwise is to examine the conditions of 1945–51 with the spectacles of later years, though there were heartsearchings and agony within the Labour Party about the terms of the American loan. And the prospect of "no smokes", however comic it may seem to some readers decades later, was no joke at the time when cigarettes seemed essential to the well-being of many millions of people.

The American loan might have been an easier pill for the Labour left to swallow had many of its members not been opposed to the foreign policy of the United States. The Cold War, however, had begun almost immediately after the end of the Second World War in 1945. The Attlee government took the side of the United States and in some respects was even more hostile to the Soviet Union than were the Americans. The close alliance with the United States dismayed those socialists who had hoped that "left could speak to left" or Britain position itself between the two superpowers, friendly with both but allied to neither. The Stalinist Soviet Union, however defensive its actions may in fact have been, was not difficult to perceive as aggressive and hostile. The Labour government, following its coalition predecessor, strongly opposed postwar left-wing insurgency in Greece, committing troops and equipment to its suppression. In 1946 the Americans intervened in the affair, sending military aid to Greece and Turkey and constituting a barrier against expected Soviet aggression wherever it might take place.

The Labour government faced down or outmanoeuvred parliamentary rebellions over its pro-American foreign policy and the introduction and extension of conscription. It decided from an early date to develop a British nuclear weapons programme, kept secret from most of the cabinet and from parliament. Although the project was complicated, expensive and led to a degree of friction with the Americans, it was an irrevocable decision to arm against the Soviet Union in alliance with the United States. The communist takeover of Czechoslovakia, the Berlin airlift in 1948 and the formation of the North Atlantic Treaty Organization in 1949 were further developments which helped to cement the American alliance. Although Labour's domestic programme was not explicitly affected, its foreign policy seemed to some supporters and some opponents alike to be inconsistent with its socialist aims at home. How could the party consistently advocate socialism at home and collaborate with a strongly capitalist ally abroad?

In other aspects of foreign policy Britain was by no means at one with the Americans. This was particularly true of Palestine, a British mandate since 1920, where Jewish pressure for a homeland agreed under the Balfour Declaration in 1917 had been transformed by Hitler's wartime massacres into demands for a Jewish state, but where Britain still hoped to preserve good relations with the Arabs. It quickly became evident that it was not possible to placate both militant Zionists and resentful Arabs, to say nothing of the pro-Zionist American government. The situation became critical when the King David Hotel in Jerusalem was blown up in July 1946 by Jewish militants with heavy loss of life. In 1947 the mandate was surrendered and British troops withdrew from Palestine the following year. The story was starkly tragic: death and mass dislocation in Palestine itself, a short lived anti-Semitic outburst in Britain, American opposition to British policy, an enduring legacy of hatred between Arabs and the new State of Israel. The probability that any British government would have failed to resolve the Middle East problem could not disguise the fact that it was a Labour government which had been responsible for the débâcle.

The foreign development which has been most generally approved by posterity was the independence of the various parts of the Indian sub-continent in 1947. From the British point of view this was a success, although the decision to withdraw was judged precipitous by some sections of contemporary opinion. Labour as a party had never been an advocate of immediate Indian independence. As late as 1942 a Labour statement was vague about the future of the country and Attlee himself endorsed the imprisonment of Indian nationalist leaders in the same year. Jawaharlal Nehru, one of the imprisoned and soon to be the first prime minister of independent India, wrote bitterly in 1944: "[T]hat curious group which has no fixed standards or principles or much knowledge of the outside world, the leaders of the British Labour Party, have usually been the staunchest supporters of the existing order in India."[25] Even the election manifesto in 1945 went no further than support for a brief and unspecific "advancement of India to responsible self-government". The war and its aftermath, however, had introduced a more urgent need to resolve the problem. It was Attlee himself who decided that independence would have to come quickly, and he who pushed for it to take place as early as August 1947.

There has been much self-congratulation in Britain that India emerged from its colonial status without war. To Indians the story seems different. Independence was conceded belatedly under extreme pressure, the division of the country into two states was the result of years of British attempts to "divide and rule", Lord Mountbatten, the last British viceroy, was guilty of "rushing India to an Independence drenched in [the] blood" of inter-communal violence in the words of a recent biographer of Nehru.[26] There is no doubt that the decision to withdraw was taken in the knowledge that India could not in straitened times be held down by force of arms, that the birth of independent India and Pakistan was accompanied by tragic massacres of huge numbers of people and that previous British policies contributed significantly to the massacres. On the other hand, India, Pakistan, Ceylon and Burma became independent and remained relatively friendly to Britain, and, to the satisfaction of the British government, the remainder of the empire seemed to have been preserved. It should also be noted that however unwise or misguided British foreign policy may have been over a prolonged period, Hindu–Muslim hostility was not the invention of the Attlee government nor inter-communal violence its intention.

☆ ☆ ☆

It was not only in 1945 that economic pressures affected the Labour government. The winter of early 1947 was unprecedentedly bitter and was exacerbated by a shortage of coal. The following May Herbert Morrison told the party conference: "In Britain today the battle for Socialism is the battle for production",[27] in context a highly understandable declaration, but one unlikely to enthuse for long the rank and file membership of the party. Convertibility of the pound into the dollar, introduced in July 1947 under the terms of the American loan of 1946, led to a run on the pound and had to be suspended in August. Dalton was compelled to resign in November following an indiscretion which led to details of his fourth budget being published in an evening paper before they were announced in the House of Commons. He was replaced by Stafford Cripps who had been made minister of economic affairs in September and was hence Dalton's equal or even his superior. Cripps was by this time a person of considerable stature, as Harold Nicolson, who had recently and reluctantly joined the Labour Party, told his diary in early October: "It is extraordinary how much respect Cripps arouses. He is really the leading figure in the country today."[28]

The economy under Cripps had a different emphasis from Dalton's concern for cheap money and social reform. Cripps introduced a wage freeze in 1948 which led to the use of troops in unofficial industrial disputes, balanced unevenly by a voluntary and ineffective curb on profits. He was associated, not always fairly, with fondness for austerity as an end in itself, his personally frugal lifestyle encouraging the association. It is undoubtedly true that he was more concerned to curb inflation and to reduce controls on private business than Dalton had been. Economic historians and others have pointed out that under Cripps the focus of economic policy shifted from Daltonian physical planning and professedly socialist measures to indicative planning within a market economy, "incremental reformism" and, where possible, reducing taxes. Cripps's ideological shift from Marxist to Keynesian reformist, his biographer Peter Clarke asserts, was complete, though other recent historians are less willing to accept that the change from Dalton marked an important shift in the economic theory which determined policy. But Cripps's policies were in the view of the historian Kenneth Morgan generally popular with the Labour-voting working class and he was widely regarded as the strong man of the cabinet.

The balance of payments improved sharply during 1948 partly as a result of putting exports before home consumption and partly from easier economic conditions stimulated by American aid under the Marshall programme, but the dollar gap, always worrying, became intractable in 1949. The pound was devalued by about 30 per cent in September, a defeat for Cripps and the government and a gift to the Conservative opposition. Dalton had maintained high wartime taxation and introduced other egalitarian measures into the tax system, but Cripps was more concerned to use taxes to restrain domestic expenditure, unnecessarily severely in the view of his ministerial colleague Douglas Jay and others, than to foster redistribution. The upshot was that taxation was not used as a weapon to reduce inequality, at least not after the budget in April 1948 had introduced a modest capital levy. The budget in April 1949 reduced food subsidies, foreshadowed charges on the National Health Service and, significantly, insisted that there was little possibility of redistributing income in the immediate future by increasing taxation. But given the hostility of the press and Conservatives to high direct taxes, the lack of sufficient countervailing pressure within the party and electorate, and the exaggerated claims made in various parts of the political spectrum for Labour redistribution of wealth and income, it is probably fair to say that the government maintained as egalitarian a stance as it could have done. In any case during the Labour years economic inequality did decline because of conscious acts of government policy. Not all Labour governments have followed the same road.

The Labour Party had from the start of the 1945 government been divided about the speed at which it should proceed towards socialist ends. Those who were concerned not to frighten any possible Labour voters, specially among the middle class, were led by Herbert Morrison, who developed a doctrine of "consolidation" which he urged on the party, particularly in the later years of this government. As early as May 1947 he was expressing concern for the plight of the middle class, oppressed by shortages and an alleged decline in their living standards. Later in the same year he devised the concept of "the useful people", in particular those potentially sympathetic middle-class voters on whom a future Labour majority would be likely to depend. He put the case for the floating voter whom the party should not frighten. At about the same time, it will be recalled, the replacement of Hugh Dalton by Stafford Cripps seemed to suggest that direct planning controls were losing favour with party leaders in favour of Keynesian policies which were more acceptable to private business.

It would be a mistake to dismiss Morrison simply as a man who had retreated from the ardent socialism of his youth, though it is common enough to become less radical with advancing age. Morrison was above all the party manager, concerned to win elections. It is hardly surprising that he would want to maximize possible support at the expense of the party programme. Moreover, he had been a Labour leader for over twenty years. Such a person, at the centre of affairs, was almost bound to be more concerned with what would appeal to the middle-class electorate than with any remaining socialist ambitions of his own.

Early in 1949 the party executive reached agreement on a programme called *Labour Believes in Britain*, which Morrison had been deeply involved in drafting and on which the 1950 election manifesto was based. Although it reminded its readers that socialism was "our ultimate goal", it declared that the party was motivated by "the British spirit – the effort to find practical solutions of practical problems" while aiming at "a high and comprehensive purpose". Proposals for nationalization were scattered throughout the document despite Morrison's opposition, but there were qualifications such as "which cannot be dealt with in other ways" and "[i]f it should prove necessary". New public enterprises competing with private industry on equal terms, a policy of which more was to be heard in the 1950s, were also suggested where companies were for sale or a need could be clearly shown. The desire to overcome private monopoly was proclaimed as an important reason for new public ownership and the electorate was assured of Labour's intention to "continue and extend the fruitful partnership between private and public industry and the State". When Morrison presented the policy statement to the Labour Party conference in June 1949 he emphasised that in considering proposals for public ownership the party was "not concerned with applying abstract dogmatic theories or beliefs . . . We are willing to judge and willing to argue each step on the merits of the case." During the lengthy debate the statement found widespread acceptance and in replying Morrison again appealed for the support of the middle class and "the useful people".[29]

The general election took place in February 1950, several months before it was due. Ministers were divided over the best date for the election. Morrison feared that bad winter weather would affect the Labour vote, but majority opinion in the cabinet led by Cripps was in favour of an early poll. Redistribution of parliamentary constituencies, leaving only eighty seats out of 625 untouched, cost Labour anything from 20 to 40 seats, a third or more of its 1945 majority, to Hugh Dalton's fury. He later claimed that by a speech in Parliament he had saved a number of Labour seats. He poured obloquy on Chuter Ede, the home secretary who was determined to see the bill through despite the electoral consequences. To Dalton, Ede was "puritanical in outlook and habits . . . rather self-important and didactic . . . an upright Free Churchman . . . [T]his Bill, so conscientiously fabricated by Ede, was a gravedigger's spade".[30]

There were of course other reasons for Labour's decline to an overall majority of five seats. One was the fact that Attlee, his senior ministers and many of his MPs were ageing, weary after what had been for some of them ten continuous years in office, their programme fulfilled. The Labour front bench had become by this time an example of the "exhausted volcanoes" whom Disraeli had discerned among the Liberals and derided nearly eighty years earlier. Bevin and Cripps were both seriously ill, though the critical seriousness of their illnesses was not apparent to the public at the time. In addition, as Richard Crossman pointed out later with an element of paying off old scores, once the initial programme had been enacted, "the leadership was . . . obviously at a loss for what to do next . . . [T]here was no programme for a second stage of socialism on which the appeal to the country could be made".[31]

The election manifesto, while emphasizing recovery, full employment and social security, contained some proposals for public ownership which in Hugh Dalton's view "had more strong opponents than strong supporters. All probably, therefore, lost us votes."[32] In the campaign itself nationalization was not emphasized. Some of Dalton's colleagues including Attlee thought that a speech by Aneurin Bevan in July 1948, accusing the Conservatives who had introduced the inter-war means test of being "lower than vermin", cost the party dearly. But the principal reason for near-defeat lay in the long years of austerity and hardship, though in the later view of such an authority as Alec Cairncross "rationing and other controls were inevitable"[33] in postwar conditions without taking into account the desire to redistribute income. The Conservatives promised to reduce government expenditure and taxation, and to abolish rationing as soon as possible. Controls too would be "reduced to the minimum necessary as the supply situation improves". Labour's housing programme was attacked and the Conservatives promised to build more houses both to rent and to buy. "A true property-owning democracy must be based upon the wide distribution of private property". As Ina Zweiniger-Bargielowska, the historian of *Austerity in Britain* points out, despite the maintenance of full employment and the creation of the welfare state, continued controls alienated many voters, including Labour supporters. Once the war was over party consensus on the subject no longer applied and continued rationing and controls were bound to help the Conservatives, especially as there was widespread suspicion that controls were what the Labour Party liked best.

Labour did not do badly in the election, but as turnout rose to nearly 84 per cent, an unprecedented percentage since the introduction of universal suffrage and only once exceeded since 1900, and nearly 3.7 million more votes were recorded than in 1945, its larger vote is not surprising. The party had over thirteen million votes, an increase of more than one and a half million since 1945, but the Conservative vote rose by even more and included increased support from both the working and middle class. The Tories now had 298 seats against Labour's 315. The second Attlee government entered uncharted and stormy waters with a nebulous programme and against the jubilant and aggressive Conservatives. In the event its period of office was to be marked by illness, external problems and internal division.

Cripps and Bevin were forced by illness and death to leave the government in October 1950 and April 1951 respectively, at a time when they were most needed. Hugh Gaitskell, another product of Winchester replaced Cripps as chancellor, a position for which he had been groomed by Dalton for some time, though he had been an MP for only five years and at 44 was not only considerably younger than Bevan but younger than Bevan had been in 1945. Gaitskell and Bevan lacked the warm personal relations which Bevan had enjoyed with Cripps, though they were on cordial terms while Cripps remained active. Gaitskell had in addition to cope with the demand for a much enlarged British expenditure on rearmament in the wake of the Korean War which broke out in June 1950, four months after the election. It should be noted that Gaitskell, even before assuming his new role, was convinced that expenditure on health had to be restrained, that Cripps in his last budget in April 1950 had made the same point and had foreshadowed charges on the health service, as seen above, a year earlier. Bevin was replaced a few weeks before his death by his arch-enemy Herbert Morrison, who was regarded both by contemporaries and historians as an incompetent foreign secretary.

With Bevan transferred to the ministry of labour and the Korean War raging the 1951 budget was an opportune moment for Gaitskell to curb health spending. A charge on prescriptions was warded off but Gaitskell insisted that recipients should pay half the cost of NHS dentures and spectacles, believing that the policy was just though the announced sum to be raised, about £25 million in a full year, was small and his officials would have been content to raise the money through other means. It was, Gaitskell told Dalton, "'a fight for the soul of the Labour Party' . . . I am afraid that if Bevan [wins] we shall be out of power for years and years."[34]

Bevan resigned a fraught few days later, followed by Harold Wilson from the Board of Trade and John Freeman, a junior minister. Bevan had earlier defended the government's rearmament programme, though not so comprehensively as Gaitskell's supporters later claimed, but he had always vehemently opposed any charges being made to the public for the health service at the time of use. The previously leaderless parliamentary left now had a figure around whom to coalesce and a group of "Bevanites" sprang up. The era of internal peace in the Labour Party, not extending beyond the war years and the first Attlee government, was at an end.

With the great health service–rearmament debate and other difficulties, above all his tiny majority, it is not surprising that Attlee thought of a dissolution. In his memoirs he attributed the decision to the strain put on his members of parliament – many of whom lived in the outer suburbs and had to travel in the late evening by public transport – by the delaying tactics of Conservatives who lived in central London. To Morrison he wrote in late May about an election after the summer holidays when there were prospects of improved meat supplies and possibly an improvement in the international situation: "Late September and early October are best for our campaigning."[35] The king was also anxious for an early election, a point which weighed with Attlee. In the event the election was scheduled for 25 October.

Relations between left and right in the party were soured by a Bevanite surge in the elections to the constituency section of the executive in early October and by quarrels over the manifesto between the moderate leadership and the resurgent left wing. There was no mention of socialism in the manifesto and no specific proposals for public ownership, nor was the subject prominent in the campaign itself. The party promised to "take over concerns which fail the nation and start new public enterprises wherever this will serve the national interest". Workers were to be associated "more closely" with the administration of public industries and services. Taxation of moderate incomes would be reduced "[a]s soon as . . . possible" and there would be "redistribution of income and of property", including dividend limitation, higher taxation of "great fortunes and large unearned incomes" and steps "to prevent large capital gains".

If "socialist" was a word missing from the Labour manifesto, it was to be found in abundance in the Conservative one, signed by Winston Churchill. Its use as a term of abuse by Conservatives and the anti-Labour press suggests that it did not appeal to much of the electorate. The Conservatives aimed to build 300,000 houses a year, an increase of about 50 per cent on what Labour was actually building, to reduce taxation and to concentrate public spending "on those who need help and not, as at present, upon all classes indiscriminately". They also poured scorn in their manifesto on devaluation as they had done in 1950 and in their campaign on the Bevanite split. They rebutted Labour claims that a Churchill-led government would increase the risk of a war with the Soviet Union, Iran or Egypt. But the main and probably decisive Conservative appeal to the electorate was to the freedom and abundance for which they claimed to stand, criticizing Labour for what they insisted were unacceptably high living costs resulting from socialist mismanagement. Only a return to the free market, they asserted, would lead to lower prices. Churchill, while admitting that in times of shortage "some controls are inevitable", proclaimed that "wartime controls in time of peace [are] a definite evil in themselves".[36]

Over half a century later the Labour defeat seems pre-ordained. The economic and political problems of 1950 were not resolved, Bevin and Cripps were gone, Morrison had received a bad press as foreign secretary, the party was badly divided with unity restored only for the election, Britain seemed to lag behind other countries in terms of prosperity and recovery from the war. Edmund Dell was probably accurate when he wrote in 2000: "The Labour party had lost its vision, and it is difficult to conceive that a narrow victory in 1951 would have recovered it."[37] In these circumstances the party did well. "It is not remarkable that Labour [lost the election]. What is surprising is that the defeat was so very narrow", writes Kenneth Morgan.[38] Steven Fielding paints a gloomy picture of an apathetic working-class electorate, uninterested in political issues, unconvinced of the case for nationalization or increased productivity, but voting Labour through fear of the consequences of a Conservative victory. This picture is plausible though perhaps influenced by the assumptions of a later period.

If indeed Labour lost at all. It could be argued that the real victor was the British election system which gave more seats to the party with fewer votes. "Only the vagaries of the electoral system robbed Labour of a third successive victory", wrote Michael Foot.[39] Thanks to the fact that the turnout was again high and the number of Liberal candidates unprecedentedly low, the Labour Party had nearly fourteen million votes, over 200,000 more than the Conservatives and more than any other party for the next forty years. Labour's votes were concentrated in mining and industrial areas, and twenty-one of the twenty-five largest majorities were cast for Labour candidates. Class loyalties remained firm. There were 321 victorious Conservatives and allies and 295 Labour MPs. With nine other MPs, six of them Liberals, the Conservatives had an overall majority of 17 and Winston Churchill became prime minister for a second time, aged nearly 77. His majority was small but workable, three times the size of Labour's in 1950–1, and the government was at the start of a new era with new ministers eager to make their mark. Attlee, Morrison, Dalton, Gaitskell, Bevan and most of their colleagues were never to hold office again.

The Labour government of 1945 was a great reforming administration, as suggested above one of the most successful reforming governments in British history. Attlee was "fiercely proud" of creating a welfare state and ensuring "a better life for ordinary people" in the words of Francis Beckett, a recent biographer, and even the reticent Attlee himself claimed that "a peaceful revolution" had taken place since 1911 with the disappearance of "[t]he great mass of abject poverty".[40] His colleagues felt the same sense of pride. The view that theirs was a great achievement has been endorsed by sympathetic historians. But the government did not advance the cause of socialism and, beset by economic difficulties and lack of public interest, it made relatively little effort to do so. It had made important measures of change and modernization, but it showed the limits of the possible for a Labour government, constrained by economic, social and political reality. Future Labour electoral strategists would be cautious about making theoretical commitments which were important to party activists but less so to the electorate at large.

5 YEARS OF STRIFE

1951–1964

It was hoped or expected by many people in 1945 that Britain would be governed by Labour for years to come. By the end of the 1950s it began to look, on the contrary, as though the party might never again form a government.

There was no substantial period of general harmony within the Labour Party between 1951 and 1964. The Bevanite controversy was at its height in the first half of the 1950s, and there followed the bitter struggle over nuclear disarmament which reached a peak at the beginning of the 1960s. It was not until Aneurin Bevan and Hugh Gaitskell had died in 1960 and 1963 and Gaitskell had been replaced by Harold Wilson, that the party was again, narrowly, elected to office. Psephologists and politicians alike are convinced that disunity is a crucial factor in antagonizing voters and it is certainly true that there was no new Labour electoral victory before an uneasy peace settled on the party. Decades later Barbara Castle, a prominent Bevanite, publicly accepted that the personal animosities of the period had helped to ensure that Labour remained in opposition for thirteen years, but at the time the internal party struggle seemed too important for compromise.

Two other interrelated factors adversely affected the Labour Party in the early 1950s. The first was that the Attlee governments of 1945–51 had virtually exhausted the agreed Labour programme. Proposals for a further instalment of public ownership, including land and the joint stock banks, heavier taxes on the wealthy, abolition of public schools and the stock exchange would not only have antagonized the holders of social and economic power in the country but deeply divided the Labour Party itself. For the party was first and foremost dedicated to improving the living standards of the great mass of the British people, Herbert Morrison's "useful people", not to waging war between social classes or instituting large-scale social upheaval. Hugh Gaitskell, the obvious coming man, wrote in the mid-1950s that he and the friends of his youth believed in democracy and opposed "class hatred . . . understood the need for compromise . . . were for the rational and practical, and suspicious of large general ideas which on examination turned out to have no precise content . . . [We] wanted to get results." These convictions remained for Gaitskell valid until the end of his life and he had many supporters. The Campaign for Democratic Socialism, formed in 1960 to campaign for Gaitskellite policies within the Labour Party, believed, in the words of the well-informed author Stephen Haseler, that "democratic socialism . . . should work with the context of the political, economic and social situation in which it finds itself and not engage in a revolutionary upheaval of that system."[1]

This group had majority support in the Labour Party, allowing for the fact that the majority was largely composed of trade union bloc votes at the party conference and that these votes were at the disposal of a small number of officials. The left in consequence was alienated from the bulk of the unions, the institutions which were the main representative body of the organized working class. Constituency party management committees, which during the period were often dominated by left-wingers, were tarred by Gaitskell in a speech at Stalybridge in October 1952 with the brush of communism or communist influence. The speech aroused much resentment, but it was certainly not a unique view. Clement Attlee made a similar comment privately to his brother on the same day. "Gaitskell said in public these things which others were merely whispering", Roy Jenkins commented later.[2] If the organized working class affiliated to the party could plausibly be charged with following unrepresentative autocrats and the rank and file membership was influenced by communists it is not surprising that the Conservatives should have made headway with uncommitted voters. Amidst the allegations and recriminations, what was clear was the hostility which had developed within the party by the early 1950s.

The second factor was that the appeal of the socialist commonwealth to the British people was at best limited. Bevan wrote in a book published in 1952: "There is no test for progress other than its impact on the individual." Democratic socialism, he added, sought "to universalize the consumption of the best that society can afford".[3] Collective action in this view was not only fairer but more efficient than individualism in raising living standards. It was easy to allege, however, as Bevan admitted, that Labour's socialism seemed to be closely linked to rationing, a negative version of "fair shares", scarcity and dullness. In the early 1950s the British people began to enjoy the end of rationing and the first fruits of incipient affluence. "More socialism" was not a slogan which appealed to many people outside the ranks of Labour activists. Higher incomes and consumer durables were wanted, not increased communal life. People wished to become owner-occupiers, as Bevan's biographer John Campbell points out, preferring individual home ownership to the most attractive of council estates. The Conservatives understood better than Labour the desire of individuals for social mobility; the impetus to rise with one's class began to yield to the attractions of rising from one's class. This attitude was more realistic than Bevan's hope that socialist equality would prove popular with the electorate.

Bevanism was the most newsworthy feature of the Labour Party for several years after Bevan resigned from office in the Attlee government in 1951. As Roy Jenkins much later recalled, "the degree of separation and bitterness . . . was dramatic." The resignation, comments the historian Geoffrey Foote, allowed the leaderless Labour left to spring into full life and become a vehicle for Bevan's "style and ideas . . . basically a restatement of Labour Marxism, but presented in a manner appealing to the emotions of labourism". Half a century later the Bevanites can be seen as doomed to failure, a fate which some of the more astute, such as Richard Crossman, understood or feared at the time. As early as December 1951 Crossman, one of the most intellectually gifted and articulate of Bevanites concluded, in contrast to Foote's later judgment, that "the Group has no coherent analysis or policy whatsoever",[4] a harsh but understandable verdict given the fact that both Bevan and Crossman were subject to swings of mood and conviction. Crossman's comment, however, illustrates the intermittent dissatisfaction of some of the leading Bevanites. The more prominent members of the group were heavily concentrated in parliament, as Mark Jenkins, the historian of the Bevanites, points out. The best known, John Campbell adds, were middle-class professionals, often journalists and lawyers, many from public schools and Oxford, "good talkers and heavy drinkers who enjoyed one another's company"[5] at a time when social class was still important in the parliamentary party. Bevan himself was a self-made intellectual of considerable mental stature, but political philosophers, like economists, are uncommon amongst practising politicians.

It was not difficult for the leadership to attract several of the group with the carrot of possible promotion to the front bench or the stick of withdrawal of the whip or expulsion. Indeed, under the pressure of a resolution passed by the parliamentary Labour Party the group formally disbanded in autumn 1952. The nucleus continued to meet albeit with reduced effectiveness, though Bevanism remained active in the country at large. There was a strong sense of loyalty to the party in many parliamentary Bevanites; after all, they wanted to move it in the directions they advocated rather than wage an internal war. They did not want to be expelled. Trying to make the party change course was a difficult undertaking for a group many of whose members were inexperienced in political infighting, unlike the party and union bureaucrats who sought to control dissent. The leading Bevanites, moreover, had risen to prominence seeking political advancement not obloquy; Woodrow Wyatt was not the only anti-Bevanite MP who asserted that the split was "not ideological. It sprang from personal vanity and ambition."[6] Relatively few members sought to challenge the power structure not only of the party but of the country, a challenge implied by their programme but not easy to achieve by democratic means. Almost all of the press was strongly, even vitriolically opposed to Bevan and Bevanism, the liberal-minded *Manchester Guardian* as much as any other paper.

Crossman noted even at this early period that Bevan suffered from inability to lead a systematic campaign. He was concerned, Crossman thought, to become party leader rather than to formulate left-wing policy. Ian Mikardo, the chief organizer of the group, later portrayed Bevan as erratic, lacking "the patience, the self-restraint, the self-abnegation that teamwork demands".[7] Bevan's book *In Place of Fear* was, the most critical of his biographers asserts, "disappointingly woolly and backward-looking", his ideas a mixture of "confident neo-Marxism [and] naïve idealism",[8] which found relatively little response in the electorate as a whole. The book has been more generously and perhaps more accurately described as "a sweeping, emotive, blurred canvas with some sharply penetrating insights",[9] but it was not intended to contain a detailed programme around which supporters could unite. What was surprising in these circumstances was not that Bevanism remained a minority within the party but that the group was as prominent and influential as it was.

Despite the derogatory language directed against the Bevanites from all sides, their strength amongst the individual membership of the Labour Party was enormous. It was impossible for the press to attack the group without giving it publicity, and the result was that Bevanism enjoyed a long period of prominence. "Brains trusts" were organised under the banner of the Bevanite weekly *Tribune*, in imitation of the popular radio programme begun during the war. From the start they were a vehicle for the Bevanites. They were described by Ian Mikardo, a highly successful chairman, as "a runaway success", with huge and enthusiastic crowds and a relay of over twenty participants, all parliamentarians. Peggy Duff, *Tribune*'s business manager, recalled a "hard core" of nearly thirty names, most of whom were also on Mikardo's list.[10] She too remembered enormous popularity and four or five meetings in a single weekend. One hundred and fifty brains trusts had been held by the start of 1954.

A series of *Tribune* pamphlets was also published, of which the best known were *One Way Only* and *Going Our Way?*, published soon after Bevan's resignation in 1951. Pamphlets could not be as exciting as individual speakers but they sold widely and their effects were probably longer-lasting than those of ephemeral meetings. Bevan himself, now much the most celebrated and controversial Labour politician, drew enormous crowds. The Labour Party increased its individual membership by over 15 per cent in 1952, though by 1955 the increase had disappeared and membership was below the 1950 level. How much of the fall may have been due to the hostility of the party leadership to Bevanism and consequent disillusion amongst the membership is a matter for speculation.

Bevanite policy was concentrated on foreign affairs, partly because the left within the party appeared to have reached an impasse in suggesting domestic policies which would spearhead a new drive towards socialism, but chiefly because in the early 1950s as in later years it was foreign policy which aroused most controversy and passion and to which party leaders themselves devoted most attention. The Bevanites "wanted to deter the Russians, restrain the Americans, and allow the peaceful evolution of a social democratic Europe in alliance with [a] third world saved from Communism by the provision of a massive aid programme, which would establish the 'principle of fair shares between nations'".[11] Although they remained nominal adherents of the American alliance their opposition to heavy military expenditure, the South-East Asia Treaty Organization (SEATO) and, above all, German rearmament made them seem highly unreliable, even hostile in American eyes. To some at least of the Bevanites it was the United States which was the greatest menace to world peace. Denis Healey, who had strong pro-American sympathies, wrote much later that it was his "deliberate exploitation of the anti-Americanism always latent in the Labour Party" and his "irresponsibility about defence" which he found most infuriating about Bevan.[12]

Less attention was given to domestic policy, where the charge of lacking clear policies was more justified; opposition to the Cold War was "no substitute for a genuine policy of social reform at home", as James Cronin comments. The Bevanites rallied, however, to policies of extended public ownership and social and economic equality. Freed from the cares and compromises of office Bevan moved perceptibly to the left. "[T]o the Socialist" he wrote,

> Parliamentary power is to be used progressively until the main streams of economic activity are brought under public direction . . . [The socialist] asserts the efficacy of State action and of collective policies . . . [I]n order to be able to reduce inequalities in income we should institute a far-reaching capital levy . . . [I]t is a requisite of social stability that one type of property ownership should dominate. In the society of the future it should be public property.[13]

These were not views which the political or industrial leaders of the labour movement were prepared to endorse.

Bevanite policies were accompanied by the attempts of their advocates to reach places of power within the Labour Party. New policies, Bevanites hoped, would be adopted by people who believed in them and the party would be captured by more militant leaders. Bevan, who habitually came top of the poll for the seven-strong constituency section of the national executive, was joined by Barbara Castle and Ian Mikardo in 1951, Harold Wilson and Richard Crossman in 1952. This was sensational, but it was even more striking that such party leaders and former ministers as Emanuel Shinwell, Hugh Dalton and Herbert Morrison were dislodged. Tom Driberg having been elected to the executive at an earlier stage, six of the seven constituency representatives, all of them MPs, were now prominent Bevanites. Only James Griffiths, acceptable to all wings of the party, remained in this section of the executive as a non-Bevanite, "the sole survivor of . . . 'the old guard'" as he recalled.[14]

The constituency parties had been captured for Bevanite policies and personalities both by conviction and by shrewd organization within their ranks. But while the six Bevanite executive members were able and prominent, expert publicists and unlike the rest of the executive elected by the active members of local Labour parties, the fact that they constituted less than a quarter of the membership of the executive ensured that they would be a permanent minority in crucial policy matters, sharing responsibility for decisions they opposed. In this sense they were the prisoners of their own success.

This was not how it seemed at the time. "We had innocently contrived our own downfall . . . It became almost a rule that loyalty to the Party was a disadvantage for election", Morrison wrote of his defeat. Dalton reflected publicly in more philosophical terms about his age (65) and long service, his attempts as peacemaker, his expectation of defeat and acceptance of the fact that he and Morrison had both lost their seats. Privately he described the results as "very irritating". An indication of the atmosphere of the rowdy 1952 party conference from the anti-Bevanite point of view was given by Douglas Jay, then a youngish Gaitskellite MP and later a cabinet minister, who recalled its worst aspects as "hideous", and "extremists" in the gallery as full of hatred. "The hatred had a totalitarian ring." For James Griffiths, as a party loyalist, the 1952 conference was "the low-water mark in the morale of the movement".[15] The contentious nature of this conference was in glaringly sharp contrast to the relative quiescence of their predecessors during the years of the postwar labour government.

When the electorate was limited to members of parliament or expanded to include the trade unions and their bloc votes, the results were sharply different. Bevan was heavily defeated by Herbert Morrison in the parliamentary election for the deputy leadership of the party in both 1952 and 1953, though in both elections his vote was considerably greater than the number of Bevanite MPs would have produced. In 1954 he lost the conference-wide vote for the party treasurership to Hugh Gaitskell by a large majority, a result which was confirmed by an enormous landslide for

Gaitskell in a second election a year later. The unions had had their revenge and some constituency parties had also by this time deserted Bevan.

The ability of the central organization to ignore the Bevanite dominance in the constituency parties illustrated the fact that power in the Labour Party rested in the hands of the allied parliamentary and trade union leadership. Relations between the six Bevanites on the national executive and many of their colleagues were poisoned and hatred was not a sentiment limited to the gallery. Ian Mikardo referred to Edith Summerskill, one of the anti-Bevan women's section members and a parliamentary colleague, as "the undisputed world heavyweight champion hater". (Less colourfully Summerskill recalled that Mikardo's "persistent and consistent opposition to certain aspects of Labour Policy irked me."[16]) Both sides bore responsibility for the altercations which took place, but Bevan had a gift for antagonizing people whose views differed from his own (and, at times, his friends too), and bad relations were personal as well as political.

The most notable Bevanite parliamentary rebellion took place in March 1952, when 57 Labour members defied their own whips, voted against government defence estimates and abstained on an amendment put forward by the Labour leadership. "When the figure was read out the explosion was immediate", wrote Michael Foot: "57 varieties of Bevanites, pacifists and long-standing critics of the Party leadership, a much larger number than anyone had expected".[17] The figure was higher than Richard Crossman's highest estimate, though some expected supporters finally voted with the leadership, but the disparate "fifty-seven varieties" may be regarded as the high-water mark of Bevanism within the parliamentary Labour party.

One other controversy may be mentioned here. The Bevanites were of course at their strongest when they could work with other groups in the party and this they could do over the thorny issue of German rearmament, which was advocated both by the Americans who wanted armed allies against the Soviet Union and most of the British political establishment which was firmly supportive of the American alliance. As Brian Brivati, Hugh Gaitskell's most recent biographer points out, the Bevanites opposed German rearmament because of the impact of the Cold War on the British economy and what they regarded as the mistaken emphasis on containment of communism. Hugh Dalton, still an influential figure who had feared and disliked Germany for much of his adult life, was against rearmament because it was Germans who were to rearm. James Callaghan and Chuter Ede were other well-known Labour moderates who opposed German rearmament, a sentiment shared by many others who dreaded the possibility of a third European war in forty years.

The issue had been vigorously debated for several years when it finally came before the Labour Party conference held at Scarborough late in September 1954. The critical motion, which Richard Crossman found "wholly impracticable . . . wholly negative", condemned "all proposals for German rearmament" and called for "a peace treaty that will bring about a united, democratic Germany". It was moved by Roland Casasola of the foundry workers and opposed by Herbert Morrison in his role as deputy party leader and member of the national executive. Though he had lost his place as a constituency representative on the executive, Morrison had lost none of his cunning. He made a conciliatory speech, in the course of which he referred to his opponent as "Casanova". The *Manchester Guardian* reported on 29 September: "[T]he delegates burst into laughter and the mood . . . suddenly changed . . . Mr Morrison handled it beautifully." The Casasola motion was narrowly defeated after the woodworkers' union changed its vote, and the executive's own resolution accepting that Germany should "contribute to collective security" was passed, also by a small margin. Crossman and Bevan, who had left the platform during Morrison's speech, agreed according to Crossman's diary that "it would be better for the Executive to win",[18] given the nature of the anti-rearmament resolution, and Crossman expressed private satisfaction with the result. The most formidable Bevanite challenge, which took place it should be remembered two years after the group had formally disbanded, had been defeated.

It is now time to leave the Bevanites, though the attention given to them is justified by the fact that they were the greatest threat to the leadership in the entire history of the Labour Party. In retrospect the challenge of the disunited Bevanites (Crossman and Wilson, the two most prominent members of the group apart from Bevan himself, were ambitious and "pragmatic") seems less significant than it was at the time, but the fact that the dissidents had a charismatic standard-bearer whose abilities as an orator were rivalled only by Churchill and enjoyed the support of constituency activists gave Bevanism an almost mythical character. This was an important example of the crucial importance of the individual in public life. "Nye was the only one amongst us who was totally indispensable to our common effort", wrote Ian Mikardo. "[I]n spite of our considerable array of talent, without him we wouldn't be a force to be taken seriously." He was, his centre-left colleague George Wigg recalled, "a giant among men. A mighty tribune of Socialism".[19]

The inactivity of Attlee, who turned 70 at the start of 1953 and was concerned above all that the party should not break into pieces, was another factor which allowed internal strife to continue. The party whip was withdrawn from Bevan following an outburst of parliamentary indiscipline over nuclear weapons in March 1955. It was followed by an attempt to expel him from the party, an attempt opposed by Attlee but defeated in the party executive by only a single vote. There was unexpected support for Bevan from Jean Mann, a member of the executive and "a reliable and implacable anti-Bevanite",[20] and from Mikardo, who rushed back to London from his daughter's wedding in Israel at the last minute. There was also support from rank and file members, who wrote to Attlee and party headquarters in large numbers protesting against the proposed expulsion. Attlee, in the words of Harold Macmillan "an exceptionally gifted Party leader",[21] worked tardily but effectively to ensure that just before a general election his most famous and talented lieutenant was not expelled from the party.

Attlee may not have realised just how close that general election was. Churchill, who had turned 80 shortly before the end of 1954, finally retired in early April 1955 and Anthony Eden, the new prime minister, called an election for 26 May within a few days of taking office. His official reason was that a new prime minister required a new mandate, but it was widely acknowledged that it would have been foolish for him not to have taken advantage of the disarray in the opposition ranks. The Labour Party's four-page manifesto, entitled *Forward with Labour*, was internally relatively uncontroversial and inevitably insubstantial compared to the sizeable illustrated booklets which all parties adopted in later years. It avoided thorny questions like German rearmament but laid emphasis on peace and disarmament and keeping steady the cost of living without reintroducing rationing. It promised to renationalize steel and road haulage, privatized by the Conservatives, and to bring into public ownership water and "sections of the chemical and machine tools industries". "Where necessary", it stated, new public enterprises would be started. It promised, in addition, to remove all charges on the health service and to encourage comprehensive secondary schools. The word "socialism" was missing from the manifesto, though social equality and social justice were advocated.

Such a manifesto was inadequate ammunition against the Conservatives, who appeared to be united under a new leader. It was hardly possible to deny that rationing had ended, living standards had risen, a large-scale housing drive had taken place and full employment had been maintained. Apathy amongst voters was widespread, as some politicians noted. Dalton found the campaign "the most tedious, apathetic, uninteresting and . . . worst organized" of his twelve parliamentary elections, though he was perhaps jaundiced by no longer being at the centre of events. Turn-out declined from over 82 to under 77 per cent, low compared to 1950 and 1951, but high compared to elections in later years. Attlee demonstrated his lack of understanding of the new consumerist world by praising the co-operative movement as an example of a real "property-owning democracy", a Conservative slogan long identified with Eden and popular with voters who wished to own their own homes. "Fair shares" was a subject stressed in the Labour manifesto and the election campaign, but as the journalist Harry Hopkins wrote a few years later, it "began to appear pedantic beside the delicious and ever-present prospect of 'Shares for All'",[22] though that prospect was still distant in 1955.

Given the circumstances of Conservative prosperity, a new prime minister and Labour disunity, it was perhaps surprising that the election was not more decisive. Labour lost over a million and a half votes and eighteen seats while the Conservatives, who lost over 400,000 votes, gained 24 seats. They achieved a higher percentage than they had had for twenty years and their majority over other parties rose from 17 to sixty. The future seemed set fair for them in contrast to the ominous outlook for the quarrelsome Labour Party.

Attlee's remaining political ambition appears to have been to ensure that he was not succeeded by Morrison, exactly five years his junior. By the autumn of 1955 if not before he was convinced that Gaitskell was the best person to replace him, despite the latter's unequivocal identification with the party's right wing. In October Gaitskell made a speech at the Labour Party conference in Margate in which he expounded his socialist convictions and pointed out that he had been a socialist for thirty years. Even the arch-Bevanite Michel Foot recalled it as "a superbly delivered peroration"[23] and it took the conference by storm. It was beyond any doubt the speech of the week and was an enormous boost to Gaitskell's status within the wider party. Never had he seemed less like a "desiccated calculating machine", the phrase which Bevan had used a year before supposedly in reference to Gaitskell. (He denied strongly that he had had Gaitskell in mind.) Later the same month Gaitskell made a strong attack on the autumn budget presented by R. A. Butler, destroying in the eyes of the press the image of "Mr Butskell" which had been much talked about since its invention by *The Economist* a few years previously.

Attlee announced his retirement in December 1955 and the vote for his successor was held a week later. He said later that he had previously wanted to be succeeded by Bevan, but if the statement had once been true it was no longer. The vote of the parliamentary party, which then and for long afterwards elected its leader without wider party participation, was as follows: Gaitskell, 157, Bevan 70, Morrison 40. It was a bitter moment for the two losers, both of whom knew that as older men they would not have another chance of becoming leader. Bevan thought Gaitskell incapable of leading the party successfully while Morrison had made periodic attempts to replace Attlee over the previous twenty years. He had now been overwhelmingly defeated in the contest for the succession, though he was presumably aware that some of his promised supporters had voted for Gaitskell mainly to stop Bevan and to ensure that there would be no rerun of the contest in later years. Morrison refused to continue as deputy leader and retired to the back benches.

It was the end of the "big five" and indeed of Labour's second generation of leaders. Cripps and Bevin were dead, Attlee a peer, Dalton and Morrison backbenchers who left the House of Commons in 1959 and joined Attlee in the House of Lords. Even Bevan at nearly sixty was to be unexpectedly willing to work with the new leader and, in some moods, to assume the role of elder statesman. After thirty or more years of serving the party and over twenty in leading roles the old guard had almost left the scene and a new age loomed.

Gaitskell, still under fifty, seemed to have the world at his feet. He had triumphed over the left and was in unchallenged control of the right and centre within the party. He enjoyed the luxury of a talented group of personal and political friends prepared to follow him "through thick and thin"[24] as one of them, Denis Howell MP, wrote later. He and his group were not enthusiasts for sweeping new measures of public ownership and his foreign policy was dominated by what he and many others regarded as the need to contain the threat of the Soviet Union. He was under no illusion that his leadership would be free from controversy, but he could reasonably have anticipated that internal strife would gradually decline and that he would be prime minister within a measurable period. In the event party harmony did not last and the hope of office failed to materialize.

With Gaitskell the Labour Party continued to be led by an Oxford graduate who had attended fee-paying schools as it had been under Attlee and would be under Michael Foot and Tony Blair. This did Gaitskell no harm on the Labour right and at least in one case smoothed his passage with the left. Richard Crossman, who had followed Gaitskell to Winchester and New College Oxford and who, like Wilson, had decided to support Gaitskell in the leadership contest, wrote in his diary:

> I am regarded as somebody who is much more personally and intimately acquainted with Gaitskell than I really am, and, as every paper has been publishing accounts of our being at school together, this was really felt to be an Old School Tie collaboration. Moreover, in a sense it is. I do know Gaitskell better than most people and realize how wrong people get him.[25]

It is a curious fact that in the class-divided British society of 1918 to the 1970s former public school pupils made their way to positions of prominence apparently without difficulty if their politics were sympathetic to the Labour Party's trade union power base, while in the more homogeneous society of the late nineties such persons were fewer and less important with the major exception of the leader himself.

Crossman was not a member of the parliamentary Labour Party's executive, the shadow cabinet, but Wilson and Bevan were, and although the latter was defeated by Jim Griffiths for the deputy leadership the result was relatively close and the icy atmosphere between the various factions in the party began to break up. Bevan was finally elected to the party treasurership over George Brown at the party conference in the autumn of 1956, though the margin was narrow and Bevan still deeply suspect in the eyes of many trade union leaders. Gaitskell too had reservations but Bevan's victory was in the interests of the party leader, perhaps more so than of Bevan himself. An important development that year was the election to the general secretaryship of the Transport and General Workers of the left-winger Frank Cousins, an event which appeared initially to be significant mainly because it presaged better relations between the unions and constituency members. It was into this changing political situation that the Suez bombshell, which had been fizzing since late July, finally exploded.

Egyptian nationalism was a subject which British politicians had had to confront for some years and the sudden nationalization of the Suez Canal in the summer of 1956 brought about a major crisis. Both Gaitskell and Bevan criticized the Egyptian action but neither wanted war and both moved vehemently as the weeks passed to oppose the bellicose line of the Eden government. Anglo-French military action began at the end of October ostensibly to separate the Israeli–Egyptian combatants but actually as an attempt to overthrow the Egyptian government led by Gamal Abdul Nasser. Gaitskell made a strongly-worded broadcast on 4 November calling for Eden's resignation and Bevan was the star of an enormous anti-war rally held on the same day in Trafalgar Square. This division of function seemed to summarize the complementary strengths of the two men: Gaitskell speaking to an unseen audience in the relative calm of a BBC studio and Bevan addressing passionately the enthusiastic crowd in the open air. The division should not be pressed too far, for Gaitskell was an excellent platform speaker and Bevan was well accustomed to address audiences of all kinds.

If Eden had made real efforts to pursue a bipartisan foreign policy he might have taken Gaitskell with him. In the absence of such efforts both Gaitskell and Bevan may have trimmed their sails somewhat to the prevailing anti-war wind which swept through the Labour Party. In any event both men spoke out strongly against war, they were heroes within their own party and they had shown that joint action on their part was both possible and effective. Whatever the effect of the crisis on the British public, it seemed initially to be highly beneficial for Labour. It was the most controversial issue in British politics since 1945 and the great mass of the Labour Party, despite the internal war which had raged for much of the period since 1951, united behind its leaders. The effects of the Suez episode, however, were surprisingly short-lived except for the unfortunate Eden, who resigned early in 1957 and was replaced by Harold Macmillan.

Perhaps the most significant event in the longer term for the Labour Party in 1956 was neither the growing rapprochement between Gaitskell and Bevan nor the Suez imbroglio, but the publication of Anthony Crosland's book *The Future of Socialism*. This was not because it changed minds, for books seldom do so, though it is difficult to dissent from Hugh Dalton's view that it was at the time "by far the most considerable book on Socialism in English since the war".[26] It was rather that it demonstrated that the intellectual ascendancy or at least initiative in the Labour Party was passing from left to right. The right was in firm bureaucratic control of the party and now it was arguably in ideological control as well.

Crosland was one of the youngest of the right-wing Labour public schoolboys and Oxford graduates who were given active support by Dalton. Born in 1918 he was a close associate of Gaitskell, though he had lost his place in parliament in 1955 after sitting for South Gloucestershire since 1950. He was returned for Grimsby in 1959 and held the seat until his death in 1977.

His book was by no means the first example of Labour revisionist thinking since 1945, and many of his arguments and proposals were not new. *New Fabian Essays* was an earlier example. Edited by Richard Crossman and with contributions from Crosland, Roy Jenkins, Denis Healey and others, it had been published four years previously. The publication of *The Future of Socialism*, however, was a much more important event. In over five hundred pages Crosland claimed that remaining poverty was in large part due to maldistribution of income within families (p. 149), that a large capital levy should be resisted for fear of interfering with the "organic unity" of society (p. 314), that socialists should seek to increase the lowest incomes rather than attack the highest (p. 213), that capitalism had been transformed beyond recognition (ch. 3) and that public ownership should be approached sceptically: "Indeed it was a common saying that the Government had less power over Lord Citrine [the former general secretary of the TUC, subsequently chairman of the publicly-owned Central Electricity Authority] than over [the privately owned] ICI" (pp. 466–7). Nationalized industries after the war were largely uncontrolled by government as in the Citrine case, Crosland asserted, investment was unco-ordinated, planning had failed, pricing policy was unclear. Public ownership had not contributed to greater equality of income or property and in future should be supplemented by competitive public enterprise, challenging private industry on "scrupulously fair" terms. (As seen above, the party had already concluded that it was unnecessary to nationalize entire industries.) The ideal was a mixed economy in which public and private industry would both play their part. "The objective is not wholly to destroy private ownership, but to alter its distribution" (chs 22–3; quotation p. 496). Crosland was, however, in no doubt of the ethical case for socialism, which he claimed would "appreciably increase personal freedom, social contentment, and justice" (p. 116).

The book, one of the intellectual forebears of New Labour thinking, had an important impact. "It became the political bible of a host of younger Labour men and women", *The Guardian* wrote when Crosland died: "undoubtedly the seminal work of the post-war period", added its columnist Peter Jenkins. Twenty years later Gordon Brown's judgment was similar: "No other postwar contribution to Labour thinking has had such an impact."[27] Crosland said before his death that *The Future of Socialism* was dated, but if this was so it did not reduce its impact in the Gaitskell period. The time of publication, after a majority Labour government had served a full term and during a period when the party right was seeking a new synthesis, was fortunate for its success. Revisionism's hour had come and Crosland's book was more influential than Evan Durbin's *The Politics of Democratic Socialism* (1940), an earlier revisionist work. The left-wing Bevanite remedies now began to look old-fashioned.

In July 1957 the policy document *Industry and Society* appeared, the draft being belatedly revised by Tony Crosland. It was a curious document, radical in its diagnosis, conservative in its prescriptions, but though it was denounced on the left and elsewhere, Bevan, Mikardo and Barbara Castle had all been members of the drafting committee and were at least in theory committed to the advocacy of buying shares in private industry to supplement what Harold Wilson told the Labour Party conference "is being called 'old-fashioned nationalization'". Gaitskell, while accepting the commitments to renationalize steel and road haulage, reorganize water as a wholly publicly-owned industry and municipalize rent-controlled private housing, resisted demands to nationalize more industries as part of a general plan to move towards socialism. Each act of nationalization had to be "relevant to the actual problems of today", not undertaken in pursuit of "some distant ideal".[28]

Industry and Society resulted in a somewhat confused row before and during the Labour Party conference of 1957 at which the veterans Morrison and Shinwell joined the left in denunciation of share purchasing. Morrison's "enthusiasm for nationalization had waned when he was making Labour's policy but reappeared once Gaitskell was doing so",[29] Gaitskell's biographer Philip Williams commented acerbically. Insiders knew by this time that both Crossman and Harold Wilson had abandoned such beliefs as they had ever had in a new programme of nationalization.

Despite the row over *Industry and Society*, the old wounds in the party were being healed throughout 1957. This was the result not only of weariness with internal strife and former dissidents making their peace with the leadership. It was due also to the fact that Gaitskell and Bevan (shadow foreign secretary from the end of 1956) had buried the hatchet and were working as a team, politically if not socially. This new partnership came to a head at the 1957 conference, when Bevan abandoned many of his most ardent followers and accepted the case for British retention of nuclear weapons until such time as they were bargained away by multi-lateral negotiations. He called the desire to repudiate nuclear weapons unilaterally "an emotional spasm" and in one of his most celebrated and excoriated phrases declared: "[I]f you carry this resolution and follow out all its implications and do not run away from it you will send a Foreign Secretary, whoever he may be, naked into the conference chamber."[30] The motion to pledge the next Labour government to ban the testing, manu-facture and use of nuclear weapons was defeated by a huge majority, but many of the constituency parties supported the motion and its defeat left the Labour Party as internally divided as in the first Bevanite days over an issue which was as stark as any of the earlier causes. The left had lost its leader though it did not disintegrate as some observers thought or hoped it would do.

Why did he do it? Why did Aneurin Bevan break with his own past by publicly allying himself with Labour Party leaders and incur the wrath of his supporters on the left? Why had the rebel become a statesman or Bevan become Bevin as the *Daily Telegraph* put it? It is not easy to provide a definitive answer, though many colleagues, journalists and historians have struggled to do so. The more cynical have blamed Sam Watson, the Durham miners' leader, for plying Bevan with whisky and soft-soap, or Bevan's desire to become foreign secretary. Others have suggested that Bevan had accepted that he was now subordinate to the elected leader, that he wanted to play a positive role in a united party in helping to bring about a negotiated world peace rather than a negative one from outside, that he was weary of constant rebellion and wanted to work with his prin-cipal colleagues rather than against them. His wife Jennie Lee wrote a few years later that refusal to work with Gaitskell at a time when Bevan believed that "mankind was again and again within a hair's-breadth of nuclear war"[31] would in his view have been irresponsible. Personal and political factors probably both played their part, and it should also be noted that battle lines over nuclear disarmament were not in September 1957 as firmly drawn as they were to become soon afterwards. But Bevan's gift for the wounding phrase, his capacity for what Richard Crossman called "intellectual emotional somersaults"[32] (a charge also made against Crossman himself) since he had been understood to be an unqualified opponent of nuclear weapons, deepened the division within the party and ensured that the effect of his speech would be immense. He may not have realized that the controversy over nuclear armament and disarmament would lead to bitter rancour whichever line he took.

The turbulence of 1956–7 was, however, followed by a quieter period in the run-up to the election of 1959. Bevan pursued the role of shadow foreign secretary, making numerous trips abroad, while Gaitskell worked hard at domestic policies and foreign relations without succeeding in ending all discontent with his leadership. In 1958 the party published a policy pamphlet called *The Future Labour Offers You*. In a preface Gaitskell commended the plans in the pamphlet as "democratic Socialism in action", but further nationalization was to be limited to steel and road haulage and "other industries [which] are found to be failing the nation . . . [P]ublic control" would be extended to the "fewer than 600" firms which dominated "the private sector of Britain's economy". Other proposals were intended to be firmly practical including "overcoming the evils of segregation [in secondary schools] at 11" though not abolishing grammar school education, improving the welfare state and keeping prices stable "without raising the general level of taxation".[33]

The general election was called for October 1959. Labour struggled against the political genius of Harold Macmillan, whose affable cynicism seemed to suit the electorate better than Gaitskell's tense earnestness, and also against the growth of what was already being referred to, following the publication of a book by the American economist J. K. Galbraith in 1958, as an "affluent society". Macmillan had been an unexpected choice to replace Eden, but he soon grew into the job and was probably more successful than R. A. Butler, the more obvious candidate for the job, would have been. As a progressive Conservative of pre-war vintage, he understood the "wind of change" blowing through not only Africa, to which he applied the phrase in 1960, but also his own country. He also understood the need to present a persona attractive to the public; thus he adopted a fur hat on a well publicized visit to the Soviet Union and cultivated an image as the "unflappable" and apparently unbeatable prime minister who could talk in a language the voters understood.

The French historian François Bédarida has described a cartoon in which Macmillan thanked four of his "election agents" of 1959 for their successful work. They were a refrigerator, a motor-car, a television set and a washing machine. Though "affluence" was in its early stages the transformation of Britain had begun and already seemed to some observers to have brought about radical changes. The bulk of the workforce still consisted of manual workers but they were in relative terms a declining force. There were about 2¼ million motor cars in use in 1950, 5½ million in 1960. Eight per cent of homes had refrigerators in 1956, 33 per cent in 1962. Real, post-tax income rose steadily throughout the 1950s. Home ownership rose from under 30 to 40 per cent between 1951 and 1961. In 1951 under 10 per cent of households had black and white television sets; by 1961 the percentage had risen to 75. There were just over 70,000 full-time undergraduates at British universities in 1953/4, nearly 100,000 in 1961/2 as the Conservative-inspired leap in student numbers began. Above all, though the end of social classes and social ideologies was hailed prematurely, as Bédarida puts it by the beginning of the 1960s "boundaries between social groups had become hazier and less easy to define".[34] It was not surprising that Macmillan should claim flamboyantly in 1957: "most of our people have never had it so good", nor that the electorate rewarded him in 1959. For a period, as David Cannadine points out in his study of *Class in Britain*, the Tories seemed destined to reap rich and permanent rewards from the new affluence, the growth of the middle class and the proclaimed ending of the class war. Part of this development was seen in the fact that a sizeable segment of society now rejected the notion of social categories as applying to themselves.

In retrospect the election of 1959 was an election which Labour could not win. Suez had been forgotten by most of the electorate, national service was being phased out, Macmillan the old showman was at the helm, affluence had either arrived or seemed to be round the corner. Labour promised peace and prosperity, but it seemed to be the party of the working class and the underprivileged, groups which many voters thought or hoped that they had left behind. "[T]he Socialist belief in the equal value of every human being . . . the belief which inspired the pioneers of Socialism" extolled in its election manifesto evidently did not appeal to enough voters to return Labour to power, nor did the formulation enunciated by Roy Jenkins, who in a campaign book published shortly before the election wrote that Labour was a "socialist party [which] looks forward to a society in which class barriers will disappear, in which rewards will be equated with service . . . At the same time it is a practical party . . . quite as much concerned with immediate reforms as with ultimate purposes." He pointed out in an accurate later comment that the "moderate section of the party . . . particularly as elections approach, almost always triumphs",[35] and Labour said little during the campaign about wishing to create a socialist society.

It should be added that though foreign policy was the special interest of the Labour left the whole party was pledged to ameliorate the arms race, end nuclear tests and conclude a comprehensive disarmament treaty, commitments contained in its election manifesto. These policies were not necessarily popular with the electorate at large. Many voters were probably, and most of the press was certainly, more concerned to support the United States and to demonstrate Britain's great power status by developing its nuclear arsenal than to endorse peace proposals. It was easy to stress one's patriotism by military preparations; proposals for disarmament could be represented as weakness. Labour could not easily claim to be as patriotic as the Conservatives, whose long association with the empire and the armed forces gave them a latitude in terms of foreign policy which was denied to their opponents.

Part of the reason for Labour's defeat was said to be Gaitskell's promise not to raise income tax in "normal peacetime conditions"[36] in a speech delivered ten days before the election. So much was made of this pledge as an alleged electoral bribe by Conservative politicians and the press that it is difficult to conclude that it was not a blunder, but in fact Gaitskell said little or nothing new. In *The Future Labour Offers You* the party had as seen above pledged to carry through its programme "without raising the general level of taxation", and the pledge was repeated in its election manifesto. Harold Wilson, the shadow chancellor, had long been making the same point. But the fact that both contemporaries and later historians concluded that the speech gave the Conservatives an unassailable lead shows how important the question of income tax, which since the war affected far more voters than previously, had now become.

It means little to say that Labour had a higher share of the poll in 1959 than in its landslide victories in 1997 and 2001 because of the different distribution of the votes between parties. In fact, the Conservative percentage in 1959 declined very slightly compared with 1955 as the Liberal share rose, but the Labour percentage dropped by considerably more and the party lost another nineteen seats. The Conservatives gained 20 and now had a majority of one hundred over other parties. The Liberals returned six members, the same figure as in 1951 and 1955, though their number of candidates nearly doubled and their percentage of the poll rose by even more. The Conservatives had not enjoyed a crushing victory in any of their three election successes in the 1950s, but their majorities had continued to rise and their number of seats was now within sight of Labour's triumph in 1945. A united party with an unchallenged leader was no substitute for the victory which opinion polls had suggested was possible and Gaitskell had come to expect. His disappointment and shock were in consequence all the greater.

The mood of unity in which the election had been fought did not last. A meeting of Gaitskell's right-wing Labour MP friends, mainly journalists and Oxford graduates (and Dalton who had attended Cambridge) was held at his home in Hampstead a few days after the election. Patrick Gordon Walker MP, who was present, recorded: "The broad feeling was that unless we changed our policies in order to appeal to the people we should be out permanently, but for an economic depression."[37] Douglas Jay wrote an article for the Gaitskellite periodical *Forward* soon after the election, arguing against Labour's identification with the allegedly disappearing working class and with nationalization in the form of state monopoly. The party name, he suggested, should be amended to add the word "radical" or "reform". It is true that he did not advocate abandoning the word "Labour" or jettison all forms of social ownership. But his private views were thought to be more sweeping, including a wish to break the party's ties with the trade unions and, conversely, to work if possible with the Liberals. It was also easy to believe that he spoke for Gaitskell, who shared some of the same sentiments but was more cautious in expressing them in the immediate wake of election defeat. Christopher Mayhew and Roy Jenkins, prominent figures on the Labour right, spoke in similar terms in subsequent days, without receiving the degree of publicity given to Jay.

At the end of the next month the Labour Party conference met for a weekend in Blackpool. It was inevitable but unfortunate for party unity that the two days should have been devoted to an inquest on the election, for in the context of Jay's article and rumours of right-wing intrigue the prolonged debate could only be damaging. Gaitskell followed Barbara Castle's passionate socialist speech from the chair by urging the abandonment of Clause Four, section 4 of the party constitution, which proclaimed belief in "the common ownership of the means of production, distribution and exchange". This commitment implied to Gaitskell not only an unnecessary increase in state control of the economy but an extension of the number and power of the large public monopolies which were a popular target of Conservatives and much of the press. In his enthusiasm he neglected the views of his trade union supporters, many of whom opposed him. As his sympathetic biographer Philip Williams admitted: "Gaitskell lost the Clause Four battle, and endangered his leadership, by driving most of the trade union centre for the first time into the arms of the Left." It was "one of his occasional infelicities", wrote Michael Stewart, a future foreign secretary, in a generally bland autobiography: "he had not realised how much sentiment and tradition he would outrage".[38]

After a passionate debate, distinguished by speeches putting opposing points of view by the young Shirley Williams, Denis Healey and Michael Foot among many others, Aneurin Bevan, now deputy leader of the party, rose to conciliate the opposing points of view. He did it by what his biographer John Campbell termed "a virtuoso fudge",[39] insisting that as both Castle and Gaitskell had quoted the same passage from one of his speeches they were equal to him and hence to each other. It was not an heroic manoeuvre but it was effective, and the delegates probably left Blackpool in a happier mood than when they arrived. Bevan, who also criticized relatively mildly as "a mistake"[40] the attempt to alter party policy after the election defeat, was the acknowledged hero of the conference. As for Clause Four, it was supplemented in 1960 by a form of words which did little to disguise the fact that Gaitskell's attempt to abandon it had failed.

Aneurin Bevan could no longer challenge or protect Gaitskell. He entered hospital at the end of 1959 for an operation on a stomach ulcer which was found to be cancer. He died in July 1960. The obituaries were prominent, lengthy and surprisingly favourable. They reflected the fact that at 62 Bevan had died young for a public man, and that though he had never held any of the great offices of state and had a gift for antagonizing both friends and political enemies, he was still idolized within the Labour Party and the outstanding political figure of his generation. His ability as an orator was the subject of special mention. But as John Campbell has pointed out: "In his life, Bevan proved to be mistaken in his confident anticipation of the course of history. He was unable to persuade his fellow-countrymen, even in his own party, to share his vision of the right way forward for Britain and the world." His early belief that the working class would triumph and that the upper-middle class was "on the down",[41] as he told R. A. Butler in 1930, was ultimately to prove mistaken, though the emergence of a new society was not fully understood in 1960. It subsequently became apparent that with Bevan's death, hope for a socialist transformation through a Labour government was no longer realistic.

Meanwhile, Gaitskell remained embattled, though he recovered from the self-inflicted wounds which the Clause Four struggle had caused. The nuclear armaments issue, the source of such bitterness and distress in 1957, had not disappeared. The first Campaign for Nuclear Disarmament march from London to Aldermaston took place in 1958 and for a period the annual Easter march, whose direction was subsequently reversed, was larger year by year. The nuclear disarmers were easily defeated at the party conference in 1958 and the truncated conference of 1959 did not discuss the subject, but in 1960 the left gained greatly in numbers, partly because with the influence of Frank Cousins the giant Transport and General Workers Union was now on the unilateralist side. Gaitskell, who had been involved that year in complicated and unsuccessful attempts at compromise over the issue, had the support of most of the parliamentary Labour Party and the national executive but much opinion opposed him in the wider party and his position in the summer of 1960 appeared to be shaky. At the party conference in October he made a stirring speech against unilateralism, marred by reference to his opponents as "pacifists, neutralists and fellow-travellers". (He had been persuaded not to add the words "and Communists".) He declared: "There are some of us, Mr. Chairman [the trade unionist George Brinham], who will fight and fight and fight again to save the Party we love . . . so that our Party with its great past may retain its glory and its greatness."[42]

He narrowly lost the vote, but despite complaints that he was unduly inflexible his personal position in the party remained strong, primarily because the nuclear disarmers had overreached themselves. How far their weakness was due to the hostility of the press is hardly relevant; though nuclear disarmament had passionate supporters they were a minority in the country and probably among Labour voters as well. Gaitskell's friends worked hard to fight back, making use of paid organizers to recruit support. He defeated the unilateralists the next year by a far larger majority than the margin of his own defeat in 1960.

His problems, however, had not ended. Harold Wilson stood for the party leadership in the autumn of 1960 as a self-proclaimed "unity" candidate and secured nearly a third of the votes of the parliamentary party. Gaitskell's leadership was thereafter secure, but in 1962 the question of Britain's adhesion to the European Common Market had to be faced since the Macmillan government had decided in the summer of 1961 to apply for membership. Gaitskell was, says his biographer Brian Brivati, agnostic on the matter: "his faith in the Commonwealth and belief in Britain's global role conflicted with his loyalty to his supporters and an instinct that the British bid would in any case be rejected."[43] He was a convinced believer in the American alliance, much less sympathetic to the spokesmen of the six nations which then formed the Common Market and his scepticism grew stronger with time. His long speech to the Labour Party conference in October 1962 opposing entry to the market on the terms then proposed distressed or angered many of his supporters. They included George Brown, now the party's deputy leader, whom the speech put into "an absolutely raging temper".[44] It produced elation on the party left, most of whom were then passionate anti-marketeers, though by no means for the same reasons as Gaitskell.

It was at this point, late in 1962, when he had gained control of his party, overtaken Macmillan in opinion polls and appeared to be not far from a triumphant election victory that Hugh Gaitskell went into hospital. He died of lupus erythematosus, a rare disease of the immune system on 18 January 1963, wholly unexpectedly so far as the public was concerned. His death was a huge blow to the party, because of its suddenness, because he had become the unchallenged party leader and because of the death of Nye Bevan less than three years earlier. Harold Macmillan said that his death was "a grievous loss to the whole nation", words repeated almost verbatim by *The Times*. The Conservative *Daily Telegraph* wrote that he would be "deeply mourned" and hinted that he would soon have become prime minister, *The Guardian* that his death was "a personal, political, and national tragedy". It called him "a man of immense courage and integrity", a sentiment often repeated. Even Michael Foot in *Tribune*, in a notice by no means free of criticism, acknowledged that "he had the leadership [of the Labour Party] in his hands on his own terms. The likelihood that he would be the next Prime Minister of Britain was every week becoming more of a certainty." John Freeman, the former Bevanite rebel who now edited the left-wing *New Statesman*, wrote of Gaitskell's alleged defects: his "alarmingly non-socialist" reaction to events, his "bad political company" among right-wing trade union leaders and his "personal resentment of purely political criticism". But among his friends and sympathetic opinion in the Labour Party he was felt to be, in Douglas Jay's words, "probably better fitted to be prime minister than any other party leader of this century", that is between 1900 and his death in 1963.[45]

Politicians like journalists are an unsentimental crew and their close knowledge of their fellows often inhibits generous emotions. Certainly little sentiment was wasted by those who wanted to become leader and those who surrounded them, and in any case it would have been no tribute to Gaitskell to leave the party leaderless. George Brown was backed in his leadership bid by most of the party right and trade unionists, although what Roy Jenkins recalled as his "appalling faults" – his over-indulgence in alcoholic drink, volatility and aggressiveness, and in some cases his support for the Common Market – aroused opposition. (Michael Foot, however, who later pointed out that Brown could be a "boorish bully", also remembered "another George, a man of good courage, zeal and willpower, and genuine streaks of imagination".) Wilson, former shadow chancellor and now shadow foreign secretary, had become a man of the centre and was wisely accused of deviousness, but still gathered support from those who remembered him as an early Bevanite. James Callaghan, the third candidate, recalled succinctly: "Harold automatically got the vote of the left and George scored heavily with the right, while I secured only the votes of those who preferred neither candidate. This was not a very solid base and I came bottom of the poll." In the event Callaghan's intervention seems to have been decisive and Wilson was elected on the second ballot by a majority of 41. "It was", Brown recalled, "not a nice election."[46]

Wilson was lucky, a quality often cited as essential for success in politics and one notably lacking in Gaitskell. He was born in March 1916 so that he had unexpectedly become party leader at the age of only 47, younger than Gaitskell had been in 1955 and with a better chance of becoming prime minister at an early date. He had followed leaders whose deaths had been unexpected; had they lived his own succession would have been long delayed. Macmillan had sacked a third of his cabinet in July 1962 in an unsuccessful attempt to revive the fortunes of his government. Following the Vassall spy affair in October 1962, the Profumo scandal the following summer horrified and entertained much of the public, doing incalculable damage to the myth of unflappability and effortless superiority which Macmillan had cultivated. At best he seemed not to know what was happening in his own government, at worst to have jeopardized national security.

Early in January 1963 the British application to join the Common Market was rejected by the French government, a major policy defeat for the Conservatives. At the start of the following October Macmillan went into hospital for a prostate operation, an event whose seriousness was exaggerated, for he recovered and lived until the end of 1986. He soon resigned and his successor, the Earl of Home (who renounced his peerage once he had become prime minister), seemed a nonentity, pushed into the highest office by an old Etonian cabal and "railroading by Macmillan",[47] as Lady Butler, whose husband R. A. seemed the more obvious candidate and was now passed over for the second time, believed over the decades. These developments, which showed that the Conservatives, like Labour, were vulnerable to the tyranny of "events", were of enormous benefit to Wilson.

A successful politician must not only be lucky but know how to use good fortune. Wilson was well equipped to do this. He made the most of his relatively ordinary origins, simple tastes and northern accent: "I don't do much socializing and my tastes are simple', he said in November 1962. "If I had the choice between smoked salmon and tinned salmon I'd have it tinned. With vinegar. I prefer beer to champagne".[48] This kind of statement, though in some respects misleading, was popular in the 1960s when deferential attitudes were declining.

Ben Pimlott, Wilson's most authoritative biographer, says that while Macmillan looked on Gaitskell as "tiresomely self-righteous and pompous", he respected Wilson's professionalism and ability as a political manager. Stephen Haseler is less charitable to Wilson: "Gaitskell was a leader whereas Wilson was a party manager."[49] Woodrow Wyatt, for long a parliamentary colleague of both men, thought that Macmillan and Wilson liked each other because both were cynics. Wilson was undoubtedly an astute politician on whom political principle seemed to hang loosely. The period between his election as party leader in February 1963 and the general election in October 1964 was carefully used to rally support for Labour. Since the public was clearly unimpressed by the traditional appeal of the party to collective and community action, it had to be attracted by non-ideological appeals. Central to this strategy was the theme of modernization, not least because the Conservatives were led by an old Etonian aristocrat replacing an old Etonian quasi-aristocrat, both born long before Wilson. The Labour leader was a trained economist, the Conservative prime minister worked out economic problems with, he admitted, the aid of matchsticks. At the Labour Party conference in 1963, Wilson's only conference as leader before the general election, he spoke of technology and science and appealed to both workers and management, not to producers alone: "[I]n all our plans for the future, we are re-defining and we are re-stating our Socialism in terms of the scientific revolution . . . The Britain that is going to be forged in the white heat of this revolution will be no place for restrictive practices or for outdated methods on either side of industry." The young Paul Foot, a political opponent, wrote not long afterwards: "The long standing ovation was spontaneous and genuine."[50]

The general election was held in October 1964, a full five years after its predecessor. Labour's manifesto was more substantial than previous versions and it was intended not to antagonize the voters. The word socialism was not mentioned and new ventures in public ownership were to be limited to steel, first nationalized in 1948–50 and water, already mostly in public hands. There were ambitious proposals to integrate the public schools into the state system of education, raise the school-leaving age to 16, introduce a "reasonable target" of 400,000 new homes a year, restore "a completely free health service" and scrap the Conservative plan to introduce Polaris nuclear missiles. There were also promises to introduce a national economic plan but to put "the freedom of the individual first", to devise ways for "injecting modern technology into our industries" and to introduce a national incomes policy. Taxation would be made fairer by the introduction of a capital gains tax and ending "notorious avoidance and evasion devices", but there was no promise not to raise income tax.

Given the disarray of the Conservatives at the end of the Macmillan era, it is surprising that the election result should have been so close. The matchstick prime minister turned into a competent parliamentarian and party leader though not an effective election campaigner. Despite this drawback the election result was extremely close. The Labour vote actually declined marginally and its percentage rose only slightly. The Conservatives, however, fell from nearly 50 per cent of the vote to 43.4. They lost 61 MPs and 1¾ million votes. The Liberals nearly doubled both their vote and their percentage, but their number of MPs rose only from 6 to 9. Labour, now a party more inclined to tolerate dissent than in the Gaitskell years, enjoyed an absolute majority over all other parties of only four. There was satisfaction for Wilson in the fact that that he had dominated Labour's campaign and above all that he had become prime minister. He had taken away at a single election almost all the gains which the Conservatives had made in the past three. After what he and his party had unceasingly called "thirteen wasted years" there was at last to be another Labour government.

6 PROGRESS AND DECLINE

1964–1979

Ramsay MacDonald presided over a Labour Party which became an important and respectable political organization. Attlee could only have been a leader in a period before television and the full flowering of the popular press, though it should be added that he lived until middle age in a world of florid political oratory which was alien to him. Gaitskell was a man who made both friends and enemies and who was preoccupied with internal disputes. Harold Wilson, it can reasonably be said, was a leader under whose guidance the party entered the harsh world of media-dominated politics.

Wilson was a new type of leader. Like Gaitskell he was an Oxford-trained economist but there the resemblance ended. Gaitskell had enjoyed a privileged schooling at the Dragon preparatory school in Oxford and Winchester College, a leading public school also attended by Stafford Cripps, Richard Crossman and Douglas Jay. He was at home at Oxford, "moving in a fast, fashionable and predominantly homosexual set",[1] as one of his biographers writes, though the last-mentioned feature left no long-term trace. Wilson's experience was different. He had never lived away from home before going to Oxford, his college, Jesus, was widely regarded as of secondary quality, he was homesick and he did not move in a fashionable set. The differences begun in youth extended into later life. Gaitskell as leader remained at the centre of a group of close and "classy" friends within and in some cases outside the Labour Party. He was the only party leader until that time with close ties of personal friendship to a circle within the party, a situation which caused him problems as well as providing affection and support.

Wilson was less gregarious. He had few close friends amongst his political colleagues and little interest in socializing. As previously mentioned, he tried to make a virtue of his "ordinary" tastes and activities, appealing to the public through the media in a way which Gaitskell would not have been able or wished to do. Above all, though Wilson had not come from a poor family, he was a provincial and a northerner, origins of which he made careful use. The pipe which he smoked in public (a cigar was more common in private) was intended to typify the reassuring qualities which he wanted to present to the public: "self-help, energy, efficiency and hostility to upper-class pretension and privilege".[2] At a time when meritocracy was struggling to supersede the older, class-ridden society, Wilson seemed to be enough of a man of the people (though his origins and education were more privileged than those of George Brown or James Callaghan) to typify a new age. He was a supreme tactician, able to manipulate personalities and the media, but had little concern with longer term strategy. "A week is a long time in politics" was appropriately enough his best-known phrase, and he learned a good deal from Harold Macmillan, the master of political manoeuvre. His wider ambition appeared to be to use the scientific revolution of which he had spoken to the Labour Party conference in 1963 to hasten the replacement of the old class-ridden society with a new technologically-based one. This approach did not appeal to all party members.

By the time that Wilson became prime minister his political convictions seemed less relevant than the necessity to control his restless party and placate its various factions. This was in a sense the party's good fortune and led to repeated electoral success, or at least non-defeat. Wilson's failure to bestride the Labour world like a colossus, however, and his reputation for untrustworthiness were to cause him difficulties. It is probable that a leader concerned to ensure party unity was better suited to turbulent times than one who would have instantly and fatally alienated large numbers of his followers, though the former Gaitskellites in particular were suspicious or hostile. "[O]ne of the basic tenets of Gaitskellism", recalled Roy Jenkins, "was that Wilson was a tricky fellow".[3] He had a much steadier character than Brown, however, whose behaviour was highly erratic. It should be noted from the vantage point of the early twenty-first century that Wilson was a man of two worlds. He was aware that a new society was struggling to be born, but he was the product of an older world of distinct social classes and mass poverty. Close relations with the trade unions and a comprehensive welfare state were goals not easily achieved but always desired. It is not surprising that more than forty years after he formed his first government Wilson seems almost as old-fashioned a figure as Macmillan or Alec Douglas-Home.

In the eighteen-month period between the general elections of 1964 and 1966 Wilson was necessarily obsessed with party unity and ensuring that his government could perform adequately despite its tiny majority. The first aim was made easier by the second, in that party rebellion in such conditions was an unaffordable luxury. Wilson's initial cabinet was a fairly balanced affair, though he went to considerable lengths initially and later not to be accused of left-wing bias. James Griffiths, the party and Wilson loyalist, was made in old age first secretary of state for Wales, fulfilling a long-held ambition. Sir Frank Soskice, though a Labour right-winger, was the first home secretary to manifest his opposition to capital punishment while actually in office and he was to preside over its aboli-tion, initially on a temporary basis. Gerald Gardiner, a barrister who had won a reputation as a reformer, became lord chancellor and Frank Cousins was appointed to the new ministry of technology, though any expectation that he was to be as long-serving, reliable and dominant a minister as his union and government predecessor Ernest Bevin was to be disappointed, for he remained in government less than two years. Richard Crossman, Barbara Castle and Anthony Greenwood were the other cabinet ministers with a left-wing past, though Crossman like Wilson had drifted towards the centre and Greenwood was not an important political figure. Castle, like Ellen Wilkinson in 1945 and Margaret Bondfield in 1929, was the only woman cabinet minister. Wilson, Patrick Gordon-Walker, who was at first to be a member of the Wilson government for barely three months, James Griffiths and Lord Longford were survivors of the Attlee cabinets, but the new team had a more middle-class compo-sition than previous Labour governments. For the first time in Labour history more than half the cabinet members were university graduates, all but two of whom had attended Oxford. The two leading cabinet members apart from Wilson, however, George Brown and James Callaghan, had left school in their teens and did not attend university.

What was to be done with Brown and Callaghan was not immediately obvious, since neither was initially thought of as suitable for the foreign office, though both were to be foreign secretaries in later years. Each was a man who must have a major office of state. Whether the two were given posts in competition with each other, as was widely suspected, or whether Wilson really believed that planning and expanded production, and the traditional restrictive economic and financial role of the treasury should be kept apart is difficult to determine. Callaghan, the new chancellor of the exchequer, claimed subsequently to be a supporter of a department of economic affairs but that it took long negotiations to agree a "concordat" which divided responsibilities between the two departments. Wilson's recollection, however, was that the initial agreement was quickly made. Brown remembered that the division of responsibilities was never formal-ized, resulting in "an unhappy bearing on the never-ending disputes that came later between the two departments at every level".[4] In any case the decision to graft Brown's department of economic affairs on to the government structure was bound to lead to trouble, specially when the ministers involved were senior and, in Brown's case, impulsive and mercu-rial. As the two departments functioned in practice it is hard to disagree with the judgment of Douglas Jay, who had an insider's seat as president of the board of trade, that there was "persistent overlapping between departments and consequent indecision".⁵

There was another major difficulty. This was the appointment of Patrick Gordon Walker, who had gone to the foreign office. He had lost his seat in Smethwick, where he had sat since 1945 and won by a majority of about 3,500 in 1959. The seat was won by a Conservative who had profited from racial prejudice and rancour against the sitting member. Gordon Walker had opposed the Commonwealth Immigration Act of 1962, an act whose scarcely disguised aim was to restrict entry to Britain of non-white members of the Commonwealth. He was "supposed", Robert Pearce wrote in his introduction to Gordon Walker's political diaries, "to have sold his Smethwick house to West Indians; [and it was alleged that] he had personally recruited workers from the West Indies; his wife was black; his daughters had married black men; he had arranged for leper hospitals to be secretly built in the town".⁶ Wilson, who roundly termed the Conservative victor a "Parliamentary leper", appointed Gordon Walker as a demonstration of opposition to racism, but also because of his experience in foreign affairs and perhaps because he had been a prominent Gaitskellite whose support was regarded as vital. A seat was found for him at Leyton, where the local MP Reginald Sorensen had sat since 1929 with a single break after 1931. This contest Gordon Walker also lost, by a majority of 205 votes, whether due to the stigma of the Smethwick defeat, a poor campaign, racial prejudice or local resentment at Sorensen's enforced departure. Richard Crossman recorded just before the election that Gordon Walker was "doing a thoroughly dreary job of putting himself across"; Anthony Wedgwood Benn wrote just afterwards that the result of the by-election was "a terrible shock to the Government", whose majority now dropped to two.⁷ Gordon Walker at once resigned and was replaced at the foreign office by Michael Stewart, whose education post went to Tony Crosland, the author of *The Future of Socialism* (1956) and a key Gaitskell aide and friend.

It should be noted that this government was more fully chronicled by insiders than any of its predecessors. Three ministers, Benn, Barbara Castle and Crossman, kept full diaries which were published as early as 1975 in Crossman's case, but Wilson was first in the field with a lengthy account of his administration which appeared in 1971. Subsequently autobiographies were published by most of the other leading figures, a practice which was to become standard in later years. The interest of the reading public in political gossip and intrigue has perhaps been as well served by these ministerial exercises in self-justification as the cause of historical veracity, though it must be acknowledged that political memoirs are often important as well as entertaining.

In its first weeks the Wilson government picked its way with skill and good fortune through the numerous pitfalls which beset it. The most pressing problems included a huge balance of payments deficit and the threat of a white Rhodesian declaration of independence. The government was aided by the fact that it was full of ministers whose experience had been limited to opposition and were now eager to make their mark. Clive Ponting, a severe critic (as is manifested by the title of his book about the government), points out that Labour held a number of advantages, above all the political initiative. "By careful selection of issues the Government could pose a difficult choice for the Conservatives between opposing popular measures or agreeing with the government."[8] Wilson himself had already said that he wanted to emulate John Kennedy by what he called "a hundred days of dynamic action". The government made an early decision to tax all imports except for food, tobacco ("smokes" again) and raw materials, a decision strongly opposed by European trading partners who threatened retaliation. The government also warned the Rhodesian administration of Ian Smith against an early declaration of independence. Wilson and the cabinet decided to put forward a Queen's Speech and to develop policies "exactly as if we had a majority not of four but of a hundred".[9] The speech included the salient points of the Labour manifesto, including the renationalization of steel, though it was opposed by two prominent Labour backbenchers, abolition of prescription charges, higher pensions and potentially lower rents, and various measures to promote economic development. Wilson, Brown and Callaghan had already decided that devaluation of sterling should be resisted, a decision defended then and in his memoirs by their economist colleague Douglas Jay.

The balance of payments was to be the government's enduring problem, continuing until the end of the period in 1979. The problem was not new in 1964. Indeed, one of the Labour Party's principal targets in the election of that year was "stop–go" (more accurately "go–stop") economics, which it described in its election manifesto of 1964: "A continuing excess of imports over exports, with consequential balance of payments and currency crises has forced the Government, again and again to halt expansion and to squeeze and freeze the economy." Unfortunately the description was a grim forecast of the economic policies followed perforce by the Wilson and Callaghan governments of the 1960s and 1970s.

The period between the elections of 1964 and 1966 was a difficult time for the government, with wearisome parliamentary fights, attempted growth in 1965 soon followed by deflation in the classic stop–go mould ("a real panic measure",[10] Crossman noted on 26 July 1965), and a new Conservative leader in Edward Heath appearing to pose more severe problems for Labour than Douglas-Home had done. Crossman wrote in his diary in February 1965 that affluence had produced a more sophisticated Labour Party in his Coventry constituency and elsewhere, which had to be addressed in new terms. (In other places the party remained more traditional.) The government, he wrote in this early phase, "isn't getting a grip . . . we haven't grappled with our problems" and he added that Frank Cousins "may well be right"[11] in predicting its early fall from power.

In the short term, however, the government fared better than the pessimists feared. Heath proved to be an ineffective party leader in his first phase, being regularly worsted in the House of Commons by Wilson. The Conservatives were deeply divided over Rhodesia, as Heath later recalled, a section of the party having family, racial or emotional ties with the white minority. "The visible party disunity", he wrote, "did not help us at the 1966 general election."[12] Labour took pride in the continued rise in national income and the fact that more houses were built in 1965 than in any previous year. (More than half were built for private owners but by 1967 even more houses were built with a small public sector majority.) It did not escape the notice of politicians and party bureaucrats that the party was beginning to do well in opinion polls.

In late January 1966 a critical (and rowdy) by-election was won by Labour in Hull North with a majority between four and five times the size of the marginal result in the previous general election. There is evidence to suggest that Wilson had made up his mind to call a general election before the Hull result was announced, but at least he must have been reassured by the by-election that he had chosen the right date from the party point of view. Partisans of an early election breathed a sigh of relief when he did not use the by-election as a reason to continue in government with his tiny majority.

The general election of 1966 was held on 31 March. Labour's election manifesto made much of the economic crisis which it had inherited and which it claimed to have done much to ameliorate. "We are asking for a mandate to carry through the radical reconstruction of our national life which we began eighteen months ago", it asserted. The slogan of the manifesto and the campaign was "you know Labour government works." The issues of the campaign boiled down to two in the view of Wilson's biographer Ben Pimlott: the state of the economy and Harold Wilson himself. Public ownership, socialism and even the Labour Party were little in evidence in Wilson's speeches and appearances. "If it was not quite a coronation," writes Pimlott, "it had become more of a ceremonial endorsement than a contest."[13]

That it was an endorsement there is no doubt. The Labour majority at this election, its only convincing victory between 1945 and 1997, rose from four in 1964 to nearly one hundred, its majority over the Tories from 13 to 111. The party won 48 per cent of the vote compared with just over 44 per cent in 1964, and nearly 900,000 more votes, although the overall number of recorded votes fell slightly. The Conservatives, on the other hand, lost more than half a million votes and 51 parliamentary seats. This was the high point of Wilson's leadership and, as Richard Crossman recognised in the immediate aftermath of the election, "Harold's personality" was of the greatest assistance. Interestingly Crossman went on to analyse the result in class terms: "Millions of lower-middle-class people voted Labour because [Wilson] was someone of their class, someone to their taste, someone they had confidence in, leading the nation and acting like a statesman. Moreover, economically they felt all right."[14] The middle class continued to grow larger, owner-occupation and consumer durables were increasingly common, class differences had softened. An apparently classless northerner was suited to the times.

After Wilson won his great victory, Kenneth Morgan notes, "things promptly fell apart".[15] There were several reasons for the débâcle, but it must be borne in mind that if Wilson had won the election of 1970, held 4¼ years after his success in 1966, he would probably have remained one of the greatest of Labour heroes. Despite expectations, however, he did not win and it is necessary to ask why and how things went wrong in these four years. First, Wilson was a good leader when things went well but not when they went badly. As seen above he was not a statesman but a tactician, and in bad times he was blamed as in good times he was given the credit for success. Election victory, however, did not end the hostility which many leading party members felt towards him and each other. He was too preoccupied with saving his own head to be able to knock others together. Second, his foreign policy and especially his support for the American war in Vietnam, cost him dearly within his own party and made his claim that the Labour Party was "a moral crusade" seem comic or worse. The Rhodesian imbroglio was also a severe headache to the government. Third, Wilson was caught by the struggle between the old and the new Britain which had eroded old loyalties and made political allegiances fragile and unreliable. What to do about the trade unions was an important part of this dilemma. Finally, the continuing economic problems elaborated daily by the press made Wilson seem a poor manager of the country's domestic affairs, even though living standards continued to rise. He put this point somewhat differently in commenting on the result of the general election of 1970: "The improvement in our economic position, as in other ways, had not erased all the scars from the tough things we had to do to get that strong position".[16]

"Wilson's great talent", Kenneth Morgan comments, "as was popularly supposed, for political tactics and manoeuvre, became the cloven hoof of his government." He aroused distrust on both left and right by making clear that the Clause Four commitment of the Labour Party to large-scale public ownership would not be fulfilled, but manifested at the same time his desire to retain it in the party's constitution. Anthony Wedgwood Benn, before becoming the tribune of the left with an apparently more popular name, criticized his leader privately before the election of 1966 for appearing, since becoming prime minister, "to be too cunning and crafty and smart, and to be somewhat lacking in principle". Writing immediately after the election he noted "the inrush of new Members, most of them young, many of them professional, and all of them keen and eager. They will be very different from the old Left and from the solid trade union members."[17] Wilson was well aware of the changed nature of his parliamentary colleagues, who with their increased numbers and demands, created new problems for the leadership.

For Wilson to be a successful prime minister he needed to win elections, and this he had done. But dealing with politicians whose sense of loyalty depended on events as much or more than political principle he needed to win over those who had previously been hostile to him, and this he largely failed to do. Politicians are seldom motivated by gratitude or personal affection, but Wilson failed to build up enough respect, fear or trust to stand him in good stead when he needed support. Crossman, who regarded himself as Wilson's friend, though as Ben Pimlott points out a fair-weather friend, was disillusioned, telling his diary in April 1969: "There is nothing left of him as a leader and a Leftist. He is just a figure posturing there in the middle without any drive except to stay Prime Minister as long as he can." The generally sympathetic Pimlott admits that many of his colleagues found Wilson shifty and untrustworthy, a man who did not inspire loyalty. Peter Shore, formerly an aide and now one of the minority of Wilson loyalists in his cabinet, noted that he was not only under attack by the Conservative press but also suffered "the systematic denigration of many in his own Party". The American president Lyndon Johnson was informed by his secretary of state Dean Rusk that Wilson was "not a man of strong political conviction" and that he did "not inspire a feeling of trust in many people".[18]

Wilson had enjoyed good luck until 1966, as outlined above. Now he was to experience a period of sustained bad luck. An important example was having to cope with George Brown, who, having left the department of economic affairs in 1966 at a time of economic crisis and the effective abandonment of his national economic plan, had been appointed foreign secretary. Relations between him and Wilson were abysmal at a time when crucial issues required their close collaboration, and Brown was often drunk, perhaps partly through frustration with Wilson. The issues were both foreign and domestic, but what was paramount was the fact that Wilson thought that Brown was plotting to oust him while Brown felt that Wilson was deliberately keeping him in the dark over important issues. In any event Brown, having threatened or offered resignation on repeated occasions, finally went in March 1968. As Ben Pimlott points out, he was by no means without supporters. Wilson's style of government was widely criticized as "presidential", decisions being made without reference to other ministers than the ones immediately involved, and Crossman recorded when Brown resigned: "If I was ever to resign it is precisely because I can't stand the way Cabinet is being run."[19]

Foreign policy was a major issue in disillusioning party members with their leader. To many ardent party members he seemed to be more concerned to forestall the United Nations from deploying the "Red army in blue berets" as peacekeepers in Rhodesia than to put an end to the government of Ian Smith, who declared independence from Britain in November 1965. It was felt by critics that Wilson yielded to the concern of those who, often influenced by white racism, talked of "our kith and kin", and was apprehensive of the use which might be made of the issue by the Conservatives. Although he spoke of ending the rebellion "within a matter of weeks rather than months" (in fact the Smith government remained in office until 1979), he made clear even before the declaration of independence that there would be no British military action to hasten the collapse of the regime. In this attitude he had the support of important cabinet ministers, including Denis Healey, the defence minister, who later wrote: "It was far too risky an enterprise to be seriously considered."[20]

Important as Rhodesia was, it was less so than the Vietnam imbroglio, which sullied the relations of Wilson with his party rank and file throughout his period in office in the 1960s. Although the Hull North by-election in January 1966 showed that few voters in that constituency, and presumably others, were prepared to go so far as to vote for a peace candidate against the Labour government, there was huge opposition within the party to the government's policy of sympathy and tacit support for the American war. The Wilson government decided to allow only British weapons, not armed forces, to be used in Vietnam, for Wilson dared not send even a token force as he apparently wished to do. In October 1967 the Labour Party conference repudiated his approach by narrowly passing a resolution calling on Britain to "dissociate itself completely" from American policy in Vietnam. Wilson himself described a visit to Cambridge in 1967 when his car was "stopped by a yelling mob of demon-strators", a procedure which "had become a familiar routine when I was known to be visiting any town". He was in the event trusted neither within his party nor by the Americans. As the loyalist Peter Shore reflected in later years, Wilson did nothing to limit the mounting opposition to American policy and his policy "looked grubby and self-seeking . . . The seeds of cynicism and alienation from the Labour leadership were widely sown at this time."[21]

The Vietnam débâcle was Wilson's worst experience as Labour leader and the diminution of his status which resulted must have contributed to the precipitous decline in Labour's standing in the opinion polls which became apparent in 1967–8. By-elections were regularly lost as well as local authorities which had been regarded as unshakeably Labour.

Sheffield, which had had a Labour council with a single year's exception since 1926 was the most spectacular loss, but there were many other defeats in this grim period.

The 1960s were the start of an era in which old allegiances began to fall apart. It was, like most periods of modern history, a time of transition but the Labour Party did not feel that it could afford to alienate old friends. The press and parliamentary opposition made repeated demands for fewer strikes and for the power of the trade unions to be curbed, but the government was conscious that they provided both financial and electoral support to the party as well as a source of members There was also in the wider party a strong emotional bond with the unions. The middle class, though growing, was still relatively small and, crucially, seemed to have at that time little electoral potential for Labour to exploit. A government with an ambitious legislative programme, however, determined to enforce its prices and incomes policy and obsessed with potential damage to the balance of payments, was deeply concerned to prevent strikes which could inflict both economic and political damage. Wilson wrote in his history of the government that he had recognised in early 1966 that "to yield incontinently to strike threats would mean the end of any meaningful prices and incomes policy, with serious effects abroad". Later in the same year he roundly condemned the prolonged seamen's strike, and the part played in it by "this tightly knit group of politically motivated men", meaning, as he later wrote, "a small professional group of Communists or near-Communists who planned their tactics with outside help".[22]

Though trade union membership had risen gradually in the 1950s and '60s, Britain was beginning to change into a nation in which the demands of consumers had to be given precedence by the Labour Party over those of producers. Working days lost through industrial disputes were not high in comparison with other industrial nations, including Italy, France, Canada and the United States, and were lower in the period 1963–7 than previously, but this did not stop the anger caused by strikes, especially "unofficial" action which arose locally, potentially harmed exports and was waged without the sanction of the central union leadership. Such demands to curb strikes apparently enjoyed public approval, even of trade unionists themselves. Barbara Castle, who was from April 1968 secretary of state for employment and still the cabinet's only woman, wrote later: "I wanted to raise the status and rights of trade unions, but I also believed I had the right in return to ask them to accept greater responsibilities in preventing the needless disruption of the country's economic life." Her most important opponent was James Callaghan, now home secretary, and a longstanding friend of the unions. His view was that proposals to introduce legal sanctions to curb unofficial strikes "ran counter to the whole history of the trade union movement and . . . could not succeed".[23] Backbenchers though admiring Castle agreed with Callaghan, and they were also worried about the views of their constituents and union support at election time.

The Castle proposals contained in the white paper *In Place of Strife* (1969) included measures to strengthen trade unions and other reforms which did not involve using the law against them, but attention concentrated on the attempts of the government to prevent unofficial strikes. These included powers to order ballots before strikes, impose a 28-day conciliation pause or "cooling-off period" before they actually took place, and where the law was defied, fines. The proposals, though mild in the light of later legislation, stirred up a hornet's nest in the Labour Party and supporters of the white paper within the cabinet fell away as opposition increased. It was, as Callaghan recalled, "a venture bound to end in tears".[24] There was a renewed attempt to replace Wilson as leader and prime minister, an attempt which failed in part because neither of the obvious successors, James Callaghan and Roy Jenkins, now chancellor of the exchequer, was acceptable to enough of the plotters (or each other) to stage a successful coup. Neither was eager for an open challenge and rivalry between Jenkins, Tony Crosland and Denis Healey also played a part. As for the white paper, in which Wilson as well as Barbara Castle had invested so much effort, it was dropped in favour of an agreement with the Trades Union Congress that it should give a "solemn and binding" undertaking to monitor and attempt to reduce unofficial strikes. The undertaking, guyed by politicians and press as "Solomon Binding", changed little in practice, but it did mean that party and unions could abandon their war footing, at the price of ridicule and loss of status for Castle and Wilson. Months of internal struggle and plotting at last came to an end, the Labour Party, the unions and relations between them being severely damaged by an experience from which only their political enemies profited.

The Vietnamese war and the attempts to reform industrial relations aroused strong passions. Less spectacular but more immediately pressing was the continuing struggle to solve the nation's economic problems – an inescapable obsession throughout the government's term of office. The government faced a curious dilemma. During the 1940s the ravages of war, including shortages, controls and rationing, were apparent to everyone. The 1960s, however, was a period in which personal incomes and the acquisition of consumer durables rose steadily, incomes from 72 to 86 on a scale in which 1975 equalled 100. The number of privately owned homes increased by well over a third and private cars and vans licensed nearly doubled, from below 6 million to over 11½ million. How could the national finances be in dire straits, it seemed reasonable to ask, when private finances were booming and the population as a whole was unprecedentedly affluent?

A glance at the chapter titles of Sir Alec Cairncross's *Managing the*

British Economy in the 1960s leaves no doubt from the treasury point of view that the economy was in crisis. Successive chapters of this book by the then head of the government economic service deal with the exchange crises of 1965 and 1966, then with devaluation followed by "a long hard slog" and "success at last" in 1969. Throughout the period it was the balance of payments, the problem of too many imports and too few exports, which was at stake. The first half of the government's period of office was never free from worry about devaluation before it finally took place in November 1967. About 14 per cent of the value of the pound was lost, a much smaller devaluation than in 1949, but a blow for the government which occasioned Callaghan's resignation and transfer to the home office.

Like most economic issues this one was full of political implications. George Brown was convinced that devaluation was inevitable in July 1966 and came close to resignation to support his case. By late 1967, however, the issue was no longer so divisive within the cabinet because after three years of struggle devaluation was accepted as inevitable, even by Callaghan, who was forced to conclude that "[i]t would not be sensible to continue . . . to defend the existing parity of sterling . . . by means of short-term credits from other countries".[25]

For the second majority Labour government to execute a second Labour devaluation was a crushing political defeat and it was seen as such by press, political and public opinion. A broadcast by Wilson, in which he appeared to make light of the defeat was, as Pimlott points out, "a public relations disaster". Wilson knew that devaluation, like the three years of deflation which had preceded it, would hurt the poor most, and he was anxious to point out that the effects would not be immediate. But the broadcast came across as complacent and patronizing: "the pound in the pocket",[26] he insisted, had not been devalued.

Devaluation, Cairncross recalled, "got off to a bad start". Callaghan's successor Roy Jenkins determined to solve the economic crisis by a series of deflationary measures, but he had to cope with the Labour left wing, which was still influential and pressing for the burden of the crisis not to be borne by domestic consumers. Nonetheless, in January 1968 expenditure cuts of £700 million were announced, and the budget in March imposed increased taxation of over £900 million, "the most deflationary Budget ever in peacetime", Clive Ponting claims. If Labour had wanted to give an object lesson in 'stop–go' economics they could not have picked a better example; Wilson had outdone even the Conservatives, commented the sympathetic financier Nicholas Davenport. Raising of the school leaving age from 15 to 16 was postponed, occasioning the resignation of Lord Longford from the cabinet, health service and national insurance charges were increased, and defence spending was reduced. As for the budget, the emphasis was on indirect taxes on consumption, but there was also a special one-year tax on large unearned incomes and a rise in corporation tax. The combination of taxes together with the obviously critical economic situation ensured that there was no revolt on the Labour benches, and Jenkins was widely praised, though a further devaluation was considered in 1968 before the deflationary measures began to work. Consumers' expenditure remained almost stationary in 1969 before rising again in 1970. "It had been a long and anxious struggle," Cairncross later wrote, "but balance had at last been achieved, and achieved with a margin in hand."[27]

The "long hard slog" put a temporary end to the weakness of the pound and established Jenkins's reputation as an iron chancellor. The Labour election manifesto of 1970 took pride in the fact that the government had achieved a record balance of payments surplus and contrasted it with the Conservative record deficit. Making the best of the difficulties experienced in acute form over five years the manifesto claimed: "We have got out of the red in our national accounts. We are now strong and solvent and we intend to remain so." How well the years of economic crisis and crisis management had gone down with the electorate was another matter.

The foregoing pages have outlined the principal problems faced by the Wilson government in the years 1964–70, but there were others, including the fraught issue of whether to sell arms to the white South African government, a controversial immigration act, reaction to civil war in Nigeria, rejection of the renewed British bid to join the European Common Market and the outbreak of violent strife in Northern Ireland. It would be a mistake, however, to think that the record of the Wilson government was one of continuous crisis and disaster. Nor was it deserted by its electorate. Wilson and his colleagues either retained or regained support, for they were generally expected to win the general election of 1970.

The Labour government of the 1960s had considerable achievements to its credit. As pointed out above, these were years of increasing incomes and rising levels of consumer durables, only the initial Jenkins measures of retrenchment in 1968 putting a temporary halt to increasing affluence. Economic inequality declined during the government's term of office, partly because of a more progressive tax system. The nation's housing stock expanded at an unprecedented rate. The first real breakthrough for comprehensive secondary education took place through deliberate government policy, and higher education continued the expansion begun by the Conservatives after the publication of the Robbins report in late 1963. Old and new universities were encouraged to expand and the bold experiment of an "Open University" was promoted by Jennie Lee with Wilson's active support, a new departure in which both ministers took special pride. The minimum voting age was reduced from 21 to 18. Legislation was introduced to protect historic buildings and civic amenities and to encourage access by foot, horseback and bicycle to the country-side. Unemployment rose somewhat but remained low by both pre-war and later standards. Improvements were made to social service provision by more generous and novel types of benefits. Steel was renationalized. The "permissive society" and the image of the "swinging sixties" may have been in part a media construct, but a new mood was apparent in the country which was reflected in legislation. Theatre censorship was ended in 1968, a year after the laws on homosexuality and abortion were liberalized and a year before divorce was made easier to obtain. Capital punishment, mentioned earlier, was abolished by an act passed in 1965, and in 1967 an ombudsman (a Swedish innovation) was installed to investigate and, it was hoped, rectify abuses by government officials. The first race relations acts were passed in 1965 and 1968. The equal pay act of 1970 sought to end discrimination in remuneration on grounds of gender. Many of these "civilizing" statutes were no more than initial steps towards redressing inequality and discrimination, and several of them resulted from private members' initiatives, but without the acquiescence or support of ministers, notably Roy Jenkins during his period at the home office, they would not have been passed.

It is difficult to weigh accurately the achievements and failures of this government. Judgment depends on the weight given to the various aspects of policy. However, it should be pointed out that it was judged a disappointment by many of its more ardent followers who perhaps failed to appreciate that many of the lauded reforms of 1945–51 were relatively uncontroversial and who may have been guilty, as charged by Ross McKibbin, of "utopianism". Yet the disappointment was real enough; as Kevin Jefferys comments, "[t]he sense of failure . . . persists". Ben Pimlott writes of "an uneasy feeling on the Labour side that the promises of the mid-1960s had yet to be fulfilled". Denis Healey's verdict was that the government from 1966 to 1970 "was not regarded as a success even by the Labour movement . . . [I]t never appeared as the master of events, but always as their victim". Clive Ponting's harsh judgment is: "Overall the general impression of the record of the government is one of a series of lost opportunities and broken promises."[28] Between 1964 and 1970 the Labour Party lost 140,000 members, nearly 17 per cent of its previous total.

At the end of 1968 the Conservatives had enjoyed a two to one lead over Labour in opinion polls. Even in July 1969 their lead was 55 to 31 per cent. But from this point Labour's polling fortunes improved and reached near equality with the Conservatives in October, before slipping at the end of the year. As early as 5 September leading ministers met at Chequers, where Wilson told them that economy was improving and public opinion was now more favourable to Labour, though he noted in his history of the government that there was still a Conservative lead in the opinion polls until the following April. In any case the government took on a new lease of life in autumn 1969, with its industrial relations troubles behind it and its Northern Irish policies a temporary success, though Jenkins declined to produce a "give-away" budget in spring 1970. Electoral success seemed an attainable goal.

Wilson finally fixed the election date for 18 June 1970. His photograph dominated the cover of the party manifesto, but there was room for the awkward slogan: "Now Britain's strong let's make it great to live in." The manifesto gave the government full credit for the improvements in the economy and promised numerous reforms which inevitably tended to be more general than specific, such as "a fairer distribution of wealth in our community". (George Brown later called it "pretty colourless and almost totally irrelevant".) Labour's claim to be a socialist party was mentioned in passing four lines from the end of a 29-page manifesto. After having been the butt of attack from within and without the party, notably on satirical radio and television programmes from which he had previously profited, Wilson had become the unchallenged leader, the essential man. "Wherever he could, Wilson kept off politics", Pimlott notes. "His style was not so much 'presidential' as that of a stage personality who could share old jokes with his fans."[29] His behaviour in this election has been compared to the pre-war Conservative leader Stanley Baldwin; safe, non-controversial, reassuring.

Nonetheless, the election was lost, whether because of doubts about the reliability and honesty of Wilson himself, uncertainty about recovery and Labour's economic competence especially in the light of devaluation, rising prices, the history of party disunity, the fact that Edward Heath turned out to be a better campaigner than expected, inadequacies of party organization or short-term factors like an unexpected trade deficit in May or defeat in the football world cup. Perhaps the safest conclusion is that the loss of confidence which the electorate had experienced over several years could not be overcome in a few months. Ian Mikardo, writing as a left-wing back-bencher, pointed to the abstentions of Labour voters which he ascribed to disillusion with the policies of the government. George Brown criticised the party's faith in the opinion polls, which he was told on his election tour around the country were not borne out by canvassing returns, and the decision to fight a low-key campaign whose main theme was to "Trust Harold".

The defeat was real enough. The Conservatives gained nearly eighty seats and 4.5 per cent of the vote; Labour lost seventy-six and nearly 5 per cent. There was now a Conservative lead of thirty seats over all other parties, a sufficient majority without being a landslide. Among Labour's defeated candidates were the cabinet minister John Diamond, the junior minister Jennie Lee and, despite his strenuous campaign, George Brown, still the party's deputy leader. All were subsequently made peers. Brown's majority of over 4,000 turned into defeat by over 2,000 because, he wrote, new voters, mainly Conservative, had moved into his Derbyshire constituency. In any event he disappeared suddenly and permanently from the leadership and several years later resigned his party membership.

The Labour Party was in a state of shock after the election. It not unnaturally moved to the left without giving much consideration to changing policy to accommodate postwar developments in British society. These included the decline in class sentiment stimulated by the impact of television, home ownership and consumer durables, the growing unpopularity of the trade unions and the birth of the modern women's movement. Some of the changes, as Ben Pimlott suggests, especially decline in class prejudice and social deference, were encouraged by Wilson's personal style and the actions of his government. It should also be noted that public interest in politics, never as great as politicians and much of the media fondly hoped, had declined over the past two decades, a change which was bound to affect the traditional Labour Party. This decline probably also owed something to Wilson, who had "wanted to remove as many issues as possible from the political arena".[30] Sentiments apparently widespread among the public, including prejudice against ethnic and sexual minorities, and opposition to welfare payments to "scroungers", stimulated anti-Labour attitudes and, like the changes in society mentioned above, caused problems for a party obsessed by its desire to ensure an early return to government. It was difficult to placate these sections of the electorate without antagonizing party members.

Developments in industrial relations and Conservative legislation restricting trade union powers had the effect of ameliorating relations between the unions and Labour Party. In other fields such as entry to the Common Market, Conservative policy exposed the divisions in Labour's ranks, above all in October 1971 when 69 Labour MPs led by Roy Jenkins, now the party's deputy leader, defied the whip and voted for entry to the market. The Labour Party as a whole has subsequently moved in the direction of increased co-operation with other European countries, but it was then as a whole suspicious of or antagonistic to the Common Market. Jenkins and his friends made theoretically possible the favourable vote, since the 39 Conservative rebels could otherwise have inflicted defeat on their own government. Jenkins remained deputy leader until April 1972 when he resigned from the post over the continuing Common Market disagreement and his enduring distrust of Wilson. The decision to resign was important both for him and for the party. "[T]he creation of a new Centre Party was inevitable", wrote Roy Hattersley, himself a future deputy leader. "After that day, the Labour Party was never the same again."[31]

Plots against Wilson's leadership continued at least until late 1972. But at the same time Labour policies were adopted which sought to remove

Conservative controls on union activities, extend public ownership to twenty-five large companies, and move towards industrial democracy. It was *Labour's Programme 1973* which contained the phrase that the party intended "to bring about a fundamental and irreversible shift in the balance of power and wealth in favour of working people and their families".[32] One wonders whether left-wing members of the party's national executive thought that former ministers like Wilson, Callaghan, Jenkins and Healey would be willing to be tied to such a programme. But the leaders, now without the prestige of being ministers, knew that they had a party to satisfy or at least to placate. Healey, although he did not promise, as often alleged, to "squeeze the rich until the pips squeak", told the 1973 conference proudly that under a Labour government "the burden of taxation [would be] distributed fairly . . . [T]here are going to be howls of anguish from the 80,000 people, people who are rich enough to pay over 75 per cent on the last slice of their income."[33]

Steeply rising prices tend to have a disastrous effect on the glue binding civil society, and the fact that the Conservatives had pledged to bring price rises under control made their failure to do so particularly contentious. Inflation led to industrial unrest and a miners' strike early in 1974 was the occasion for Edward Heath, the Conservative prime minister, to call a general election for 28 February 1974 in which he hoped that the issue "who governs Britain?" would be decided favourably for his government.

The manifesto for this election reflected the shift to the left which had taken place in the executive and the party at large. Without specifically mentioning the twenty-five companies which Wilson had succeeded in keeping out of the manifesto, it promised to nationalize mineral rights and development land. "We shall also take shipbuilding, ship-repairing and marine engineering, ports, the manufacture of airframes and aeroengines into public ownership and control." Public ownership was also to be extended to sections of pharmaceuticals, road haulage, construction, machine tools, and North Sea oil and gas. Plans for banking and insurance, which the party conference had previously voted to nationalize, and building societies were "still under consideration". Redistribution of income and wealth was also promised with an annual wealth tax and related measures. Steps towards industrial democracy and various measures of social reform, including the elimination of poverty and taking steps towards economic and social equality were among the other proposals. The Conservative Industrial Relations Act of 1971 was to be repealed. The phrase from *Labour's Programme 1973* about "a fundamental and irreversible shift . . . of power and wealth [to] working people and their families" survived and the manifesto declared that the party was proud of its socialism. Wilson, who strongly opposed "more socialism", could not have been pleased by the tone of the manifesto, though he may have felt as, according to Tony Benn, he did about party conference reso-lutions: "We only take notice of Conference resolutions when it suits us, everyone knows that."[34]

In any event the manifesto does not seem to have influenced his behav-iour in the election campaign. Socialism as a theme was almost completely ignored. Ben Pimlott describes Wilson in this campaign as a reassuring figure, "a long-established national leader whom the voters could trust not to get into a flap". Benn, who had now moved sharply to the left, wrote in his diary: "Wilson is really fooling about on the fringes, seen at press conferences and ticket-only meetings; whereas Heath is on the streets in walkabouts, giving a De Gaulle impression."[35] Opinion polls predicted a close result and the outcome was disastrous from the point of view of forming a strong government.

The election of February 1974 was Harold Wilson's third victory, "[b]ut it was an odd kind of win" (Pimlott). "Labour did not win. But the Conservatives lost" (Hattersley). "[The result] was far from being a triumph for the Labour Party" (Jenkins).[36] The party now had four more seats but over 200,000 fewer votes than the Conservatives. Labour won 301 seats in a House of Commons of 635 members. The Liberals finally made a breakthrough with over six million votes, 19.3 per cent of the total and more than half the vote of each of the two main parties, but they were perversely rewarded with only fourteen MPs. A few years later Eric Hobsbawm noted in an influential essay that Labour had polled fewer votes at this election than at any time since 1935 and that it had lost over two million votes since reaching its high-water mark in 1951. The result in percentage terms, 37.1, was even worse; the lowest share of the poll since 1931. In the eight previous elections Labour had won the support of well over 40 per cent of the voting public, but this situation was not to recur until 1997.

There was to be Labour government for the next five years, but its prob-lems were as intractable as in the 1960s. They were partly political, for a second election in October 1974 failed to work the magic of 1966. They were partly economic, as Denis Healey, the new chancellor of the exche-quer, soon found. A Labour government and economic crisis seemed to be permanent companions. The election in October was the occasion for a Labour manifesto similar in many of its proposals to its predecessor. Nationalization proposals remained, Wilson referred to himself and his colleagues as "democratic socialists" in his foreword and the "funda-mental and irreversible shift" appeared at the end of the document. Much emphasis was placed on relations with the trade unions and a "social contract" which would attempt to ensure industrial peace. The social contract had been part of the February manifesto and election campaign, but now it assumed an even more central role; put briefly, it involved wage restraint, a difficult commitment to fulfil during an inflationary period, in return for measures of social welfare, full employment and social justice. In general the tone of this manifesto was more conciliatory and less contentious than its predecessor.

This was the first time since 1910 that two general elections had been held in a calendar year. Unlike 1910 the two elections did not produce almost identical results, but the similarities were greater than the differences. Labour had fewer votes than in February, the result of the fact that the voting percentage of the electorate had dropped considerably, but the party's share rose to 39.2 per cent and it gained 18 more MPs. It now had an overall majority of three in the House of Commons, a majority which it lost in 1976 with the formation of the Scottish Labour Party and by-election defeats. (Labour lost seven of the twenty seats which it defended at by-elections in this parliament and gained none.)

The political history of this parliament was disastrous for Labour. There was a referendum of the electorate on continued British membership of the Common Market in which cabinet members publicly took different sides and Roy Jenkins made a personal attack on Tony Benn. The Labour Party at a special conference voted by nearly two to one against continued membership, but the referendum resulted in a vote in favour by an even greater margin, with the support of most politicians and virtually all the press. There were internal disputes between members of the government on other issues and unsuccessful attempts to secure devolved government in Wales and Scotland. A pact with the Liberals had to be formed in 1977 to keep Labour in power. The chief negotiator on the Labour side was Michael Foot, formerly the leading figure of the back-bench left wing, now as a cabinet member moving towards the centre and making his peace with former opponents. Though the negotiations were successful, however, the pact appeared to be a grubby compromise.

Arguably the two most important leaders of the Labour Party at the start of the October 1974 parliament were Harold Wilson and Roy Jenkins. Two years later neither was a minister. Jenkins, who as seen above had long been antagonistic to Wilson, wrote in his memoirs of the Common Market referendum campaign: "My heart had been much more in those large Britain in Europe meetings than in any Labour Party gathering for some time past." He was careful to indicate that he was referring only to a single issue, though "a big and wide-ranging one", but he added: "I had felt more spontaneous agreement with platform-sharers at [the Britain in Europe meetings] than with Benn or Foot or Wilson."[37] He soon found that this agreement with members of other parties extended to other issues. After failing in the vote to succeed Wilson he opted to accept the presidency of the European Commission from January 1977, a post which had first been offered him nearly a year earlier. It was the end of his time as a Labour leader.

Wilson's resignation in March 1976, wholly unexpected outside his innermost personal and political circle, was the political bombshell of this parliament. He was just sixty and had spoken to several colleagues of leaving at that age. He had told his aides Bernard Donoughue and Joe Haines in early 1974, and his assistant Marcia Williams shortly afterwards, that he would retire in the spring of 1976. Yet despite these warnings his colleagues were as stunned as the press and public. "I was as flabbergasted as nearly all the rest of my colleagues", Denis Healey admitted later. Various other supposed explanations for his departure were put forward, as Ben Pimlott notes: "a medical diagnosis, or hounding by the secret service, or blackmail, or tensions between Wilson and members of his staff", but in the period of nearly thirty years since his departure none of these has been shown to be more than subsidiary. Geoffrey Goodman, who worked for him in 1975–6, wrote in an obituary notice nearly twenty years later that Wilson was a tired man in 1976 who "had had enough".[38] This is plausible. Wilson was the first prime minister for many years to leave office voluntarily and he was probably the youngest who had ever done so, but it is probable that family pressure and his own volition were the reasons for his departure. To the outsider the surprise is that he had wanted to carry on through thirteen years of problems and obloquy.

The Labour Party, though disoriented politically, was rich in talent. Six of its leaders stood for election to replace Wilson: Benn, Callaghan, Crosland, Foot, Healey and Jenkins, then still a minister. All but Callaghan, the non-graduate, were intellectuals who had attended Oxford. Crosland and Jenkins had much in common personally and politically but they both stood, splitting the "Gaitskellite" vote. So did Denis Healey, the three men guided more by "intense rivalry" and personal ambition than by logic in the view of their disciple and biographer Giles Radice. Benn represented the left, Foot the left-centre and Callaghan was seen as the candidate of the moderate centre. Trade unionist MPs supported him but so did others, in general inconspicuous and unglamorous members. In the view of his biographer he was "the natural unifying candidate",[39] a man who combined approachability with weight of character. Foot had most votes, though not a majority, on the first ballot but it was Callaghan who won convincingly on the third and Foot who became leader of the House of Commons. Soon afterwards he became a notably loyal deputy party leader and, in practice, deputy prime minister. Callaghan was to remain leader for only about four and a half years; after three leaders in over forty years, the next four were to last collectively less than half as long.

As already suggested, these were difficult years for the British economy and for the politicians who administered it. In the by no means impartial view of Roy Jenkins this "last scene of 'Labourism' . . . was played out by one of the most experienced and intelligent Cabinets of recent British history . . . with an amazing lack of imagination combined with a dogged but unconvinced determination."[40] Callaghan himself was, in the view of Bernard Donoughue, who saw them both at close quarters, tougher, more determined, more willing to stand up for his views and more authoritarian than Wilson.

Denis Healey did what he could to control raging inflation without antagonizing the trade unions, introducing and administering an incomes policy which took, he wrote, half his time and combating the old enemy, the balance of payments, though the floating pound introduced by the Conservatives in 1972 should in theory have ameliorated the problem. Oil prices had soared and Healey in response produced deflationary budgets which were contrary to traditional Labour Party policy. The continuing decline in the value of the pound caused deep alarm and there was also constant worry over the level of the public sector borrowing requirement. Healey not unnaturally found his period at the treasury "exceptionally hard and frustrating work".[41] It would have been difficult for any chancellor to be popular with the rank and file in these circumstances. Healey's record as a leading member of the party's right wing and his abrasive personality did nothing to persuade the left to support him. In July 1976 he announced cuts in spending together with a higher levy on employers' national insurance contribution. These policies neither saved him from having to apply to the International Monetary Fund for a loan after arduous battles in cabinet nor having a rough reception when he tried to justify his actions in a brief contribution from the floor at the Labour Party conference in the autumn. He rounded on his critics ("There are some people who would like to stop the world and get off") and was both cheered and booed, but the hostile Tony Benn, while condemning in his diary a "vulgar and abusive" speech, admitted that it was "bold and vigorous . . . Tonight the media presented it as Denis having won over the Conference to these tough new measures, and so on."[42] Healey, who proceeded to introduce further spending cuts, later pointed out that from 1977 to 1979 economic conditions improved. In his last year as chancellor price rises slackened, unemployment fell and the balance of payments moved into surplus. Personal incomes, which fell in the aftermath of the 1976 measures, rose again subsequently.

The economic problem which caused the worst heartache to the party was the fact that the policies to which Labour had been loyal since the days of Stafford Cripps and which followed Keynesian lines, seemed to have failed. The ugly word and the ugly reality of "stagflation" appeared on the scene. The party had been loyal to Keynes's prescriptions but now found that inflation and economic stagnation, apparent opposites, had a tendency to be yoked together. Unemployment, which stood at just over 250,000 when Labour left office in 1951, was well over one million in 1976 and rising and inflation, though it had begun to fall, still stood at about 20 per cent per annum. Healey abandoned belief in Keynesian policies after exposure to economic problems at the treasury and wrote later that Keynes had ignored both the trade unions and the outside world. Demand management, he thought, had become unreliable. His less flamboyant colleague Edmund Dell felt even more strongly that demand management had harmed economic policy. He recollected that this view had support from within the treasury and recorded in his diary: "So we are all anti-Keynesians now."[43] Dell was probably less politically sensitive than Callaghan and Healey, but the prime minister and chancellor must have known that the abandonment of Keynesianism as a fundamental belief and the return to the deflationary policies of the 1920s (to which, it should be remembered, later Labour chancellors had periodically resorted) would be a body blow to the self-confidence and intellectual consistency of the party.

Nonetheless, speaking two days before Healey made his pugnacious defence of his economic policies to the party conference of 1976, Callaghan told the conference in the words of his son-in-law the economist Peter Jay:

> We used to think that you could spend your way out of a recession, and increase unemployment by cutting taxes and boosting Government spending. I tell you in all candour that that option no longer exists, and that in so far as it ever did exist, it only worked on each occasion since the war by injecting a bigger dose of inflation into the economy, followed by a higher level of unemployment as the next step. Higher inflation followed by higher unemployment . . . That is the history of the last 20 years.

This passage, his biographer Kenneth Morgan points out, stunned his almost silent audience. Eric Shaw confirms the private view of Edmund Dell: "The Keynesian social democratic era was passing."[44]

Within days of his speech to the party conference Callaghan made another, at Ruskin College Oxford, in which he urged that a "Great Debate" be held on education. His own view was that many working-class children were not being given the support and encouragement which they needed and that informal teaching methods tended to hold back levels of attainment. Children should be taught "basic literacy and numeracy", to prepare them both for a constructive role in society and for employment. It appeared to his critics that he was questioning the desirability of working-class children enjoying a widely-based curriculum designed to broaden their opportunities, and some felt that comprehensive schools themselves, now cherished by most Labour Party members and teachers' organizations, had been called into question. His biographer writes that the speech "struck a powerful chord . . . amongst the general public",[45] but it also increased disquiet and dissent within the Labour Party itself.

Although the economy improved in the later 1970s the Labour Party as a whole was not in a buoyant state as a general election approached. Harold Wilson was no longer leader; George Brown had resigned his membership, Tony Crosland had died suddenly in early 1977 and Roy Jenkins was disaffected. Tony Benn was a focus for the growing left wing and internal strife, and the two most prominent leaders, Callaghan himself and Denis Healey, were unsympathetic to the growth of the left in the party. Callaghan, having rejected the option of holding a general election in autumn 1978, was faced with a strike wave in the winter of 1978–9 which the media presented as "the winter of discontent" and Callaghan as an uncaring figure out of touch with reality at home while he discussed world affairs in the sunny Caribbean. Referenda on Welsh and Scottish devolution were held in March 1979 and failed to win sufficient support from the respective electorates to be carried through. As the government had advocated devolution the public lack of enthusiasm was a defeat for Labour, particularly for Michael Foot who had promoted it. Finally, on 28 March a motion of no confidence in the government was passed by a single vote, the first time a government had been overthrown by the House of Commons since 1924. In Callaghan's later words "one was enough and a general election was inevitable".[46]

The governments of 1974–9, faced with severe difficulties within the Labour Party and prolonged economic crisis, were by no means unmitigated failures. The party manifesto for the 1979 general election, seeking to win the support of the electorate and hence displaying its claimed successes in the best possible light, was able to point to lower inflation, a variety of social reforms, nationalization of aircraft production and shipbuilding, employment protection legislation, measures to reduce the inequality of women and abolition of tied cottages. Callaghan insisted: "It was a miracle that we had governed as long and effectively as we had and carried out so much of our programme." But as Eric Shaw writes, "[o]ne is left with the impression of a Government struggling to do its best in extremely bleak conditions, where the familiar landmarks were vanishing, and where few of the levers used in the past to control events seemed to work." A Labour leadership whose actions seemed to many activists to be characterised by a "wizened conservatism"[47] could only have avoided major internal problems by a convincing general election victory. What occurred instead was a convincing defeat.

The election manifesto made some concessions to the left. The "fundamental ["irreversible" had disappeared, Tony Benn noted sadly] shift . . . of wealth and power" made another appearance and the party was proclaimed to consist of "democratic socialists". Extensive measures of social reform were promised. But the tone lacked fire. Callaghan intervened to ensure that radical proposals which he disapproved were defeated, notably the abolition of the House of Lords. In a foreword he declared: "Our purpose is to deepen the sense of unity and kinship and community feeling that has always marked out our fellow countrymen and women." His biographer feels that "[h]is message [was] one of moderation and reason", and the view of the authors of the Nuffield College study of the election was that Callaghan "could be seen as the most conservative Prime Minister since Baldwin".[48] (As seen above the same comment had been made about Wilson in 1970.) Tony Benn complained bitterly that Callaghan had fought a one-man election, ignoring both the Labour Party and its manifesto.

Labour moderation was of no avail against the Conservatives and their aggressive leader Margaret Thatcher, who had replaced Heath in 1975. Labour had more votes than in October 1974 and nearly as high a percentage of the poll as in February 1974, but the major change was in the position of the Conservative Party. Its percentage rose from under 36 to nearly 44, its votes by well over three million. It gained over sixty MPs to give it an adequate majority of over forty; Labour lost fifty and now had 70 fewer members than the Conservatives. The outlook was bleak and was to become bleaker.

7 STRIFE AND AFTER

1979–1994

The years 1979–94 were a gloomy period for Labour, and if the Conservative governments that were in power uninterruptedly during the period had their problems an effective opposition was not generally one of them, at least before 1990. Margaret Thatcher proved to be the most successful politician in modern British history, not only remaining prime minister for longer than any predecessor since 1827 but carrying through an ambitious programme which brought important changes to the country, transforming her own party and ultimately the Labour Party as well. She moved with the grain of change in British society, something which all politicians hope to do though not all succeed. It was in the later part of this period that individualist values previously identified with Labour's political opponents began to supersede within the party the collectivist principles to which it had been loyal for so long. The long acceptance after 1945 by both main parties of a "middle way" in British politics, a kind of welfare state capitalism with elements of public ownership and financed primarily by direct taxation, receded and in some respects disappeared.

It is not surprising that Labour's election defeat in 1979 after five disappointing years (eleven if the earlier Wilson government is included) led to an initial sharp turn to the left, and indeed as we have seen in previous pages, this process began well before the defeat. Critics within the party concentrated not only on policy but on party structure, convinced that it was necessary to tie inescapably members of parliament and the party leadership to conference decisions and manifesto commitments which had often been ignored by hard-pressed Labour governments. Party conference was not automatically hostile to the leadership but Labour's executive committee had moved to the left and was a constant thorn in the leadership's side. Activists designed a series of constitutional measures which they hoped would ensure that conference and leader spoke with a single voice. A prolonged debate took place within the party over proposals to establish an electoral college comprising trade unions, the parliamentary Labour Party and individual members to elect the leader; to compel sitting MPs to undergo a mandatory reselection procedure; and to give the party executive the right, after consultation with the leader and colleagues, to draw up the election manifesto. It was finally and narrowly decided in 1980 that the first two proposals should be adopted but, again narrowly, that the executive alone should not have decisive power over the manifesto. James Callaghan, still leader until this conference, wrote a few years later about his final year in office: "It was not a happy period . . . I deeply resented the charges of 'betrayal' made by the left and used as an excuse to fetter the Parliamentary Party and to organize factions to replace Members of Parliament with whom they did not agree."[1] It should be added that he was also under strong attack from the right for accepting an electoral college for leadership elections in which MPs formed a minority.

The left had won important victories which were not restricted to internal party matters, since the 1980 conference also voted to end British membership of the Common Market, reduce defence spending and close British and American nuclear bases, preferably by multilateral negotiation. There was danger, however, of forgetting that the right wing of the party retained considerable importance and that it was easier to adopt new policies than to implement them. The left also neglected three important facts of British political life not limited to this period. The first was that it was in a permanent minority within the Labour Party's power structure except for brief periods in the ascendant of which this was one. Second, the British electorate was generally and increasingly uninterested in party politics, a factor which could not benefit the left. Third, much of the press was eager to denounce "extremists" and to use the prominence of the left as a reason to oppose the Labour Party itself.

Eric Hobsbawm expressed persuasively his opposition in 1981 to "the proposition that all that stands between us and the next Labour government is a good left-wing programme for Labour and the proof that the party programme will not be betrayed . . . [B]oth left and right, however embattled, belong to a broad movement and have a right to be there".[2] Hobsbawm, a lifelong communist, was closely associated with the journal *Marxism Today*, which tried to mobilize both moderate and left-wing opinion against the policies of the Thatcher government, but he spoke for a minority of the left. Many years later Perry Anderson expressed the view, also persuasively, that it was the unsuccessful policies of the Wilson and Callaghan governments which had "led to the rise of the [Labour] Left in the first place."[3] It should also be remembered that the party left has consistently claimed that socialist policies put forward by a united Labour Party would appeal to the electorate in practice and that the party has generally not sought to put the claim to the test.

Callaghan finally announced his resignation as party leader in October 1980. The electorate for his successor consisted for the last time of members of parliament alone, and if they had voted according to their political convictions Denis Healey, the candidate of the party right, would have been elected. After pressure from his friends Michael Foot decided to stand. Though 67 and physically frail he remained "the old lion", as Tony Benn called him, uniquely popular with large sections of the party. He enjoyed the support of the unions as the man responsible for reversing Conservative legislation restricting union functions, and in the constituencies among members who remembered his long left-wing history. Support for Foot had the advantages for the parliamentary electorate, his biographer Mervyn Jones points out, of voting to unite the party and placating those constituency members tempted to exercise their new powers of reselection. Jones comments that in Healey's view a victory for Foot would enable potential Labour deserters "to claim that the party was falling into the hands of the extreme left . . . and give them a plausible excuse for deserting it".[4] Two other candidates also stood, but Foot took most of their votes on the second ballot, which he won by 139 to 129.

It was later asserted, notably by Roy Hattersley, that if Healey, a more pugnacious character than Foot, had been elected the long tenure of Conservative governments would have been much reduced. It was true as Healey himself wrote that Foot was not a strong leader: "He was a natural rebel, and found leadership uncongenial; moreover, though a brilliant orator, he had no administrative experience or executive ability."[5] He was, given his own record, to find difficulty as leader in disciplining dissenters, though he strongly opposed attacks on the freedom of action of the parliamentary party. It seems likely, though the evidence is inconclusive, that a Healey leadership would have restrained many of the party right from defecting, at least for a period, but at the price of arousing irreconcilable anger and bitterness amongst the constituency membership. The Labour Party was so divided in 1979–81 that it would probably not have held together much longer whoever led it. Prominent members held firmly opposing views on important issues, and it would have needed a leader of altogether exceptional ability and force of character to have compelled or persuaded them to work together. The active rank and file was also divided, though proportionately many more supported left-wing views than did members of parliament. Neither Foot nor Healey nor any other possible party leader possessed the required unifying powers and Healey, similar to Aneurin Bevan in this respect, had a talent for antagonizing his friends as well as his political enemies.

Foot by 1980 was no longer the rebel he had been. His relations with Tony Benn, who now led a strong opposition faction, were tense. Foot's experience of government, especially under Callaghan, had pushed him towards the centre; he was now, as his old friend Barbara Castle wrote later, "a changed man politically, anxious for compromise". As a leading champion of the rights of parliament, moreover, he could not accept any suggestion that the parliamentary party should be subordinate to the party conference. "[I]t is . . . inconceivable that the Parliamentary Party would finally concede control over what it must do and pledge itself to do in Parliament to a body outside", he wrote.[6] This comment may have been true, but it ignored the normal impotence of the ordinary member of parliament in a system of tightly disciplined political parties. In any case in matters of constitutional change within the party, the crucial issue of the time, Foot was in firm opposition to the Bennite left and to Benn himself, with whom he pleaded not to stand for election as his deputy and whom he later accused of a tendency to "reduce the affairs of the Labour Party to the politics of the kindergarten . . . [T]he responsibility for transmuting every controversy of the time into an internal Labour Party dispute rested directly with Tony Benn", he charged.[7]

Healey was elected deputy leader, first without opposition by his parliamentary colleagues and then under the rules of the new electoral college, which had been finally constituted after a special party conference, in January 1981. The contest with Benn, the hero of the left, was prolonged and bitter. Benn had alienated not only Foot but most of his former cabinet and parliamentary colleagues, though he remained popular with the constituency parties. He was excoriated by academic and media supporters of the traditional Labour Party. Kenneth Morgan, for example, has called him "by instinct a dissident, an individualist, almost an anarchist . . . Benn has magnified or created structural tensions within his party unique in its history". Eric Hobsbawm characterizes him as "a good and honest man who almost brought the party to ruin" and the political commentator Peter Jenkins suggests that his career "became a pilgrimage of self-destruction".[8] Healey had the support of most Labour MPs but relatively few active members of the party rank and file. The unions were divided, though the majority supported Healey. In the second, decisive ballot, Healey won just over 50 per cent of the vote, Benn just under. "I scraped in to victory by a hair of my eyebrow", Healey wrote: "an absolute whisker's difference", Benn confirmed.[9]

The election for deputy leader was arguably more important than the leadership election, and is a further demonstration in Labour Party history of the significance of the individual. If Benn had won, in Roy Hattersley's view, "thousands of moderates would have deserted Labour and the Bennite alliance . . . would have turned the Party into an unhealthy alliance of pressure group and protest movement".[10] Making due allowance for Hattersley's position as a leading moderate and Healey supporter, it is hardly possible to feel that a victory for Benn, who enjoyed relatively little support amongst the public at large and almost total opposition in the press to his personality and policies, would have made the party either more united or more electable. On the other hand, had Benn not stood the party left would have had no popular alternative candidate for the deputy leadership. The left had now reached its high point and its strength began to decline. By the time the election for deputy leader was over at the end of September 1981, the Labour Party faced another grave crisis, the defection of some of its best-known names to the newly formed Social Democratic Party.

The growth of left-wing sentiment in the party had been observed with anger and dismay by considerable numbers of members of the parliamentary party. The three most important opponents of the move to the left were David Owen, who had replaced Tony Crosland as foreign secretary after the latter's sudden death in 1977, Bill Rodgers and Shirley Williams, who had served in the Callaghan cabinet as transport and education secretaries. They joined Roy Jenkins, who had just completed his term as president of the European Commission, to put forward late in January 1981 the document which came to be known as the Limehouse declaration, from the location of Owen's East London home. The signatories were known familiarly from a much-publicized Chinese precedent as the "Gang of Four". There were differences of emphasis among the four, Rodgers and Williams being more hesitant about leaving the Labour Party than the others and Owen and Jenkins each wanting to lead the new grouping, but the four were able to come together at a time which could hardly have been worse for Labour.

The Limehouse declaration, urging "a realignment of British politics" was, in David Owen's words, "in the main an appeal to those who wanted to resist the drift towards extremism in the Labour Party". It was issued immediately after the Labour Party special conference at which the proposed constitutional changes were confirmed. The Social Democratic Party itself was launched amidst enormous publicity two months later: "we found", Rodgers wrote, "that we had placed ourselves in the leadership of an army already formed and waiting".[11] Twenty-eight Labour and one Conservative MP joined the new party in 1981–2, and so did some prominent intellectuals and media personalities. The new party won by-elections sensationally, particularly Williams at Crosby, near Liverpool, and Jenkins at Glasgow Hillhead. Liberal allies won seats at Croydon and Bermondsey in London, all four victories taking place within two years of the establishment of the new party. Amongst the early by-elections it was only in Warrington that Labour managed narrowly to hold onto a seat against the SDP. In this election the SDP was represented by Jenkins, since the Hillhead contest was still in the future. Opinion polls put the SDP–Liberal alliance ahead of both Conservatives and Labour for a few months in 1981–2, and at a dizzy 50 per cent of respondents at the end of 1981. This, it should be remembered, was soon after Benn had been narrowly defeated by Healey for the Labour deputy leadership.

The SDP–Liberal alliance was more dangerous to Labour than has perhaps been appreciated in later years. Roy Hattersley and Denis Healey took credit to themselves for preventing a worse disaster, Healey for his victory in the deputy leadership race, Hattersley for refusing to defect. "For a moment it looked as if Roy Jenkins was right, and that the new centre grouping had broken the mould of British politics", Healey wrote. Hattersley claimed that without hard work and campaigning for moderate policies by himself and others of like mind, "the Party would have disintegrated".[12] They may have claimed too much, but Healey and Hattersley were the most prominent members of the centre-right to remain in the Labour Party in these years, and if they and those they influenced had joined the SDP it would have been at best considerably more difficult for Labour to recover, as it did, its position in British political life before the end of the decade in which the new party was launched. At worst from the Labour point of view the party mould might in fact have been broken.

Foot was trebly unlucky in losing much of his right wing, in leading what remained a turbulent and divided party and in doing so at a time when, contrary to the experience of the Suez conflict of 1956, the Conservative government fought a short and victorious war against Argentina for sovereignty over the South Atlantic Falkland Islands. The deflationary policies of the government had led to unpopularity with voters until the Argentinian occupation of the Falklands at the beginning of April 1982. Neither Labour nor Conservative parties emerged wholly unscathed from the affair, but though Foot made clear his opposition to the Argentinian invasion and his support for the restoration of British sovereignty his party was deeply divided. Healey, whose own initial view was less bellicose than Foot's, recollected not unfairly that "most of the Left saw it as a colonial war in which Britain should have no part". The war, as Healey also noted, led to a huge tide of popular patriotism which was expressed in some of the tabloid press as "mindless jingoism" and established Margaret Thatcher, the prime minister, as "a powerful national leader".[13] General Galtieri the Argentinian leader, on this reading, spelled doom for the Foot–Healey leadership.

Other factors also paved the path to electoral catastrophe in 1983, most importantly the continued inability of the Labour Party to work as a united team on important issues. Foot and his colleagues faced "an endless succession of crises" in the words of Eric Shaw[14] which they were unable to resolve. One was what to do about the candidacy of Peter Tatchell in 1981–3 for the apparently safe Labour seat of London Bermondsey. Tatchell was both a left-winger and a homosexual and was a gift to the media who were presented with opportunity for sensation almost on their doorstep. At first the Labour executive narrowly refused its endorsement and thus supported the somewhat rash public pronouncements which the party leader had made, but when the veteran Labour MP Bob Mellish finally resigned his seat Tatchell was adopted and endorsed with Foot's agreement. The by-election took place in February 1983, the local Labour Party was deeply divided and Tatchell suffered a humiliating defeat, universally regarded as a defeat for Foot as well.

Another problem was the Militant Tendency, a small Trotskyist group which practised "entryism" to the Labour Party while insisting that it was a newspaper rather than a political organization. The question of what course of action to take about Militant was hard fought on the Labour executive and led to further bitterness within the party when five of its leading members were expelled in February 1983 by a large majority of the party executive over the protests of the Bennites. The left had now become a minority on the executive, but they made clear their view that Militant supporters should not be expelled. Foot accused Militant and Benn in turn accused the executive majority of "democratic centralism".[15] He also told the executive that the expulsions were a sop to the Conservative press, which would go on to demand more concessions. As for Militant it survived the attack to cause more problems later in the decade, as will be seen below.

A further difficulty was that the party remained disunited about defence policy and, in particular, what to do about nuclear weapons. It was from 1981 unequivocally committed to unilateral nuclear disarmament despite the fact that important figures like Healey, Hattersley and Callaghan, now an influential elder statesman, opposed it. Healey wrote a few years later that "the majority of the Shadow Cabinet . . . thought like me that it would be politically wrong and electorally disastrous to give up our Polaris force for nothing",[16] and it was widely known that he did not support party policy in this respect. Callaghan publicly rejected unilateralism and later insisted in a letter to Foot that the British people and Labour voters also rejected it. It became the conventional wisdom that the electorate would not vote for such a policy.

Finally, Foot was himself a problem, attacked mercilessly in the media as old (70 in July 1983), infirm (he walked with a stick) and out of touch (a survivor of the Attlee years), a weak leader who could not control his party. He was fully trusted by neither the right, which remained powerful despite the SDP defections and who would still have preferred Healey as leader, nor by the Bennite left. Both wings gave him their qualified support because they thought that he was the only leader who could maintain an uneasy unity within the party and because Labour leaders were not generally subject to open challenge while in office. Kenneth Morgan writes that in the face of these irreconcilable groups "it is hard to see how any leader bent on preserving the unity and mass appeal of a disintegrating coalition could have done much better".[17] This view, which is now hardly controversial, indicates the low point which the party had reached.

In the election of June 1983 Labour was disastrously defeated. The party manifesto for the election, *The New Hope for Britain*, was for the first time printed in large format, its thirty-nine pages being allegedly termed "the longest suicide note in history" by Gerald Kaufman MP, a former Wilson aide. The manifesto was in some respects no more to the left than its predecessors, its nationalization proposals being limited to "a significant public stake" in a relatively small number of industries, though Conservative privatizations were to be renationalized with minimum compensation. There would also be public ownership "in other important sectors" the manifesto wrote in almost Morrisonian language, "as required in the national interest". The promise to ban nuclear arms, in tandem with "securing nuclear disarmament agreements with other countries and maintaining co-operation with our allies" was, however, new and striking. Andrew Thorpe expresses the view that the commitment to work for "[u]nilateralism and multilateralism . . . hand in hand" was a "nonsensical formula", but Foot himself insisted after the election that "it did *not* mean throwing away all our defences . . . [I]t did *not* mean that advance on all disarmament fronts could be achieved at once . . . A step-by step process was what I favoured and what we actually proposed."[18]

The legislative powers of the House of Lords were to be ended as was hunting with dogs. Labour was to work for the unification of Ireland by consent. Britain would withdraw from the European Common Market. Measures were to be introduced to create greater equality for women and ethnic and sexual minorities. Private schools were to lose their tax advantages and value added tax was to be charged on their fees. Foot spoke in a foreword of Labour's "democratic socialism" and of its "programme of socialist reconstruction", and "the fundamental and irreversible shift . . . of power and wealth" which dated from 1973 was again included. On balance, controversial as it was, the programme appears more radical than socialist, but as Eric Shaw points out, it implied a strong role for government in controlling the economy and, if elected "would have encountered very stiff resistance from extremely powerful forces, both at home and abroad".[19]

Mervyn Jones points out that Labour waged two election campaigns simultaneously. There was, on the one hand, enormous enthusiasm for Foot himself and for other leaders. Foot tended in his many local speeches to appeal to the spirit of 1945 and the party took comfort in gratifying canvassing returns. On the other hand, there was the national campaign which followed quite a different pattern. The Conservatives used modern forms of electioneering, particularly television, while Labour clung to traditional methods, including exhausting election tours and public meetings. Labour faced innumerable drawbacks as described above: it had lost a sizeable section of the party and formerly friendly media personalities to the SDP; it remained publicly divided over nuclear defence; its leader was constantly ridiculed; its policies were criticized by its former leaders; it fought an inadequate campaign; it faced a government which had waged a short and successful war; it was bitterly assailed by most of the press. It is hardly surprising that under these circumstances the election result was disastrous.

The Conservatives won 397 seats, four more than Labour in 1945 though with a smaller percentage of the poll. Labour won 209 seats, sixty fewer than in 1979, one less than the Conservatives in 1945 and only 27.6 per cent of the vote, well under its 1931 total. Tony Benn was the most notable casualty, having unsuccessfully fought an adversely redistributed seat in Bristol. He told his diary that his loss in Bristol and defeats in the wider party were ameliorated by the fact that the general election had shifted it "irreversibly . . . towards socialism",[20] but his return for Chesterfield at a by-election nine months later was a more tangible consolation. The Liberal–SDP alliance was scarcely two percentage points behind Labour, but it had neither a traditional electorate to appeal to nor a following amongst a specific social class and returned only 23 MPs, seventeen of whom were Liberals. Shirley Williams, Bill Rodgers and most of their colleagues lost their seats; apart from Jenkins and Owen, only three of the MPs who had defected to the SDP remained in the Commons. Labour had been saved from near annihilation by the eccentricities of the British electoral system. The SDP had, as it intended, made an important impact on British politics but, it appeared, by ensuring permanent Conservative dominance, which it had not intended. Eric Hobsbawm, a sympathetic though controversial critic, urged Labour to take steps to appeal to a broader electorate:

> Millions of people who might have been expected to vote Labour, abandoned the party in 1983, not because they suddenly ceased to see themselves as workers, but because they felt the party did not represent their interests and aspirations adequately or effectively . . . The working class has changed. The country has changed. The situation has changed. And, let us not forget, the party too has changed.[21]

The sweeping character of the Labour defeat obviously meant that a new leader would be elected sooner rather than later. Indeed, the vultures circled without delay. Labour had been led for over forty years from 1935 by Oxford graduates. Callaghan ended that ascendancy, but what was by this time more important was that the party leaders since 1955 had been MPs who had first been elected in 1945 and had now reached old age or were approaching it. Denis Healey was nearly 66 and even Tony Benn, first elected in 1950, was within two years of his sixtieth birthday. Now arose an opportunity to choose a younger leader. Such an opportunity was presented in the form of Neil Kinnock, born in 1942 and hence considerably younger than Margaret Thatcher as well as his Labour predecessors and rivals. He came from a family of Welsh miners. His father on leaving the pit had become a labourer so that Kinnock was born into an unambiguously working-class family, alone among Labour Party leaders since the 1930s. He had attended University College Cardiff and was, as he pointed out, the first member of his family to attend university. He was elected to parliament in 1970 as a left-wing firebrand determined to keep alive the memory of Aneurin Bevan, but he was not in sympathy with the Bennites. He supported John Silkin, a minor candidate, as deputy leader in the 1981 contest, attacking Benn's decision to stand for the post as "tactically mistaken" and supporting Foot and his policies. He was shadow education spokesman in Callaghan's last year and then under Foot and established himself as an orator, notably in an acclaimed speech delivered at the end of in the 1983 campaign when he hoarsely told his audience: "If Margaret Thatcher wins on Thursday, I warn you not to be ordinary. I warn you not to be young. I warn you not to fall ill. I warn you not to get old."[22]

Kinnock was elected to the party leadership on the first ballot, Healey having decided not to stand (though he was to become shadow foreign secretary) and Benn who was not then an MP being in consequence ineligible. In the event Kinnock was the only one of the four leaders between Harold Wilson and Tony Blair who was other than a stopgap. Roy Hattersley, who was nearly ten years older than Kinnock and had first been elected to parliament in 1964, was elected deputy leader, the "dream ticket" of the supposed left-wing Kinnock and right-wing Hattersley now being in place. Peter Shore, who was badly beaten by Kinnock in the leadership contest, later wrote that the new leader had "two huge handicaps", lack of experience in government and his youth and political immaturity. "He had a complete kit of then-fashionable left-wing viewpoints but, as events were to show, no settled convictions on any of them."[23] It would be easy, though perhaps mistaken, to dismiss these harsh words as the sour grapes of the bad loser. Events after 1997, however, demonstrated that previous experience of government was not essential to success in government, and time was to show that Kinnock was not as much on the left nor Hattersley as much on the right as had been supposed, or perhaps as they were in 1983. As to the handicap of age, it may be guessed that Kinnock's youth, confidence and energy, "the sharpest available personal contrast to Michael Foot"[24] who was nearly thirty years his senior, attracted at least as many voters as they repelled. Politics after all is not only about governing but also about the perceptions and prejudices of the electorate.

Kinnock was more successful than Foot, but he remains the only Labour leader to have lost two elections while winning none. Like Foot he had internal party difficulties and for most of his leadership the problem of facing Margaret Thatcher, a formidable opponent. Like Foot he was unlucky in the time of his leadership. The challenge of the left was by no means at an end and Kinnock remained at odds with many of his left-wing colleagues. In January 1984 Tony Benn wrote that an informant had been told by "an unimpeachable source" that Kinnock opposed his candidacy at Chesterfield and, by his parliamentary colleague Austin Mitchell, "'like all Labour Leaders [Kinnock] talks left and walks right'". Distrust of the new leader shines out of the Benn diary. Kenneth Morgan, like Peter Shore, says that in terms of ideology, "Kinnock has travelled fairly light. He is anything but a doctrinaire." It is probably more significant, as Morgan also notes somewhat blandly, that Kinnock wanted electoral success for the Labour Party and sought to shape it with this aim in view: "At key moments in the period 1977–83, Kinnock emerged as a mainstream socialist, realistic though never right-wing, committed above all to the unity and coherence of a broad-based party."[25] Events moved him along the road to the centre ground, almost inevitably for a Labour Party leader hoping to form a government within a measurable timespan and in the process inescapably alienating his own left wing.

Kinnock himself understood well enough that he lived in a changed world in which belief in individualism appealed to many voters and in particular to the press which helped to shape their thinking. Perception followed reality; heavy industry and the trade union movement were shrinking and jobs in the white collar, non-unionized sector of the economy were fast increasing. It was not accurate, in Britain at least, to suggest that "[t]he traditional working class [was] now no more than a privileged minority" as the influential French writer André Gorz commented in 1980,[26] but a major change in society and class relations was underway. Trade unions were increasingly unable to assert convincingly that they represented the bulk of the employed population. Influenced by the rhetoric of Margaret Thatcher, public and private discourse alike began to eschew the language of social class. Thatcher herself believed, David Cannadine points out, that "class" was a misleading Marxist concept and that the growing middle class was in any case the essence of the nation. Privatization of nationalized industries, though alleged by critics to be bribing the voters with their own money, was a huge, over-subscribed success. The subsidized sale of council houses was popular and endorsed by Kinnock in 1985. He also urged the Labour Party in 1986 to accept certain restrictions on trade union activity. He told its conference in 1987 that the party was compelled to accept realities:

> They are the realities of a changing economy, a changing society, and they are the realities of a changing electorate too. They present their own fresh challenges, they make their own demands on our candour. If this movement pretends, for instance, that a few million more people owning a few shares

each will not make any difference to their perception of their economic welfare then this movement will be fooling itself . . . [T]hey do make a difference to their owners' personal economic perceptions. This is a matter of fact. And the result of it is that our policies are going to have to take account of that reality, and of a number of others.

It was in this passage of his speech that Kinnock posed the question of how the docker with his own house, car, microwave, video and "a small place near Marbella" was to be attracted to Labour. One does not say in such a case, he pointed out, mimicking and claiming to quote Ron Todd of the Transport Workers, "'let me take you out of your misery, brother'".[27]

Kinnock, like all party leaders, had faults. He could be abrasive, it was easy to accuse him of being an opportunist who abandoned principles for his own ends, he was Welsh, a fact which counted against him with some English journalists and voters. Perhaps the most damaging charge was that he was prolix, a "Welsh windbag". Peter Kellner wrote in a generally friendly introduction to a collection of his speeches: "[E]ven his closest friends wince at his tendency to stretch a succinct statement into an elasticated tangle." Tony Benn, who was not friendly, complained in his diary of Kinnock's wordiness. After a meeting of a sub-committee of the Labour Party national executive in 1981 before Kinnock became leader for example, he recorded: "He went on interminably as he always does . . . Kinnock droned on."[28]

The period before the next general election was more centred on structural reform within the party than on reshaping policy. Kinnock's determination to rebuild the party met an early hurdle in the form of how to control the Militant Tendency, a thorn in the side of the leadership in spite of the expulsion of five of its members early in 1983 as described above. For the first two years of the Kinnock leadership pressure on Militant was internal, trying to reduce its influence and prevent constituency parties from nominating Militant members for parliamentary seats. In 1985, however, the battle became spectacularly public, with Kinnock attacking directly the Militant-dominated Liverpool city council which had publicly challenged both the government's tight spending targets and the Labour Party leadership. Kinnock told his party conference that autumn:

The people will not, cannot, abide posturing. They cannot respect the gesture-generals or the tendency-tacticians . . . I see the casualties; we all see the casualties. They are not to be found amongst the leaders and some of the enthusiasts; they are to be found amongst the people whose jobs are destroyed, whose services are crushed, whose living standards are pushed down to deeper depths of insecurity and misery.[29]

The attack was hotly opposed by Militant, its sympathizers and others on the left and apprehensively received by other party members, specially those in local government who felt no friendship for Militant but were subject to strict financial controls by the government. There was uproar in the conference but Kinnock became the hero of the press and much of the party. Roy Hattersley, a close colleague though not on personally intimate terms with his leader, recalled the speech subsequently as "the best speech of his life . . . brave and brilliant", one which "began to nudge the Labour Party back into the mainstream of politics".[30] Like Benn's defeat in the deputy leadership race in 1981 it was a seminal event in the restoration of centre-right domination of the party. As for Militant, after an internal party inquiry into the situation in Liverpool eight members (and later a ninth) were expelled by the national executive, an action which was overwhelmingly endorsed at the party conference of 1986. A number of members from other places, not all identified with Militant, were also expelled. Kinnock had emerged the clear victor, but at the price of permanently antagonizing the left. It was a price he was willing, perhaps eager to pay.

Eric Shaw, who has closely studied the history of Labour Party administration, shows in detail how the party gradually became more subject to central control in these years. Some of Tony Benn's supporters began to drop away and coalesce with others as the "soft left" in support of Kinnock. By the mid-eighties there was a strong desire to end internal party quarrels and restore a semblance of unity. Popular election of leader and deputy leader enforced their legitimacy and authority. Militant was widely opposed for its "revolutionary posturing and arid dogma", though its efforts on behalf of the people of Liverpool were acknowledged by many within the party. In consequence of all these developments, the party's disciplinary code was tightened. By the time that Shaw's book was published in 1988 there had been "a steady drift towards tighter discipline and firmer central control . . . Both Kinnock and the NEC [the National Executive Committee] are clearly keen to strengthen their grip in [sic] the Party machine". Shaw's prediction that defeat in the general election of 1987 was "likely to accelerate this drift"[31] was to prove accurate.

The most important domestic political development in the mid-eighties was the strike of the coal miners, which lasted for a full year in 1984–5. This issue excited more passion within the labour movement than any such controversy for many years, due to its longevity, the hatred felt within the party for the Thatcher government, the massive police presence and violence which took place between police and strikers, and the fact that the miners for many people symbolized the working class and labour movement. The miners were fighting for their jobs, not higher wages, and this too aroused sympathy, but they had not held a ballot before striking, a factor which antagonized not only the press but sections of the Labour Party itself. The failure to hold a ballot was, as Roy Hattersley pointed out, their "crucial error".[32] The miners were led by Arthur Scargill, a man of many qualities, but emollience and moderation were not among them.

Kinnock tried to have the best of both worlds by supporting the striking miners but distancing himself from their leaders and from violence on both sides. It is doubtful whether this discriminating approach did him much good. Although Kinnock came from a mining family he feared that the strike would anger voters and lead to electoral loss for the Labour Party, thus being guilty in the view of the writer David Howell of "disabling capitulation before a particular brand of electoral politics . . . Hostages are given to prevailing sentiments about strikes, about pickets and police, about the proper scope of political agitation." If by "prevailing sentiments" Howell meant the majority view of the public he illustrated the acute dilemma facing all Labour Party leaders, now in the most dramatic fashion, attempting to respond to his members' deepest emotions without alienating other voters. Kinnock's ambivalent support for the miners was the obvious course of action open to him as an ambitious party leader. Speaking to the Labour Party conference in 1985 after the strike had been defeated he unsuccessfully opposed a resolution which would have restored to the miners all the funds which they had lost from fines, sequestration and receivership:

> It is a fact that if we were ever to endorse the idea of retrospective reimbursement we would harm our chances because people would be very confused about our attitude towards the rule of law and we would give heavy calibre ammunition to our enemies to misrepresent us, to defame us and to demolish the hope that the miners have got of getting support from a Labour government.[33]

The message was not heroic but it was inevitable in the context of contemporary British politics.

The general election, the first under Kinnock's leadership, took place in June 1987. The Labour manifesto, entitled *Britain Will Win*, was glossier than the 1983 version and considerably shorter. In his leader's introduction Kinnock attacked the Conservative record and the prospect of a third term. He wrote briefly of the need for improved investment, about pressures on the environment and the dangers of crime and unemployment. The country should face these problems together. This, he wrote, borrowing a phrase from both Michael Foot and Hugh Gaitskell, was "democratic socialism in action." This was the last time that socialism, democratic or other, was to find a place in a Labour Party manifesto.

As for the body of the document, there were promises of social reform including an attack on poverty, improvements in education, housing, health and jobs; unemployment was to be reduced by a million within two years. Women and ethnic minorities were to have "a fair deal", including a new ministry for women, and industrial democracy was to be expanded. Trade unions were to have greater rights though Conservative-instituted strike ballots were to remain. Gas and telephones, privatized in whole or part by the Conservatives since 1983, would be restored to public control or ownership, but there were no other promises of the kind. There would, however, be "a socially owned stake in high-tech industries and other concerns where public funds are used to strengthen investment". Taxation was to be designed to assist "the most needy" and a special tax would apply to "the wealthiest one per cent of the population". The commitment to leave the Common Market was replaced by a promise "to work constructively with our EEC partners" while defending British interests.

The final section of the manifesto was devoted to foreign policy and defence. By 1987 Kinnock may already have been privately persuaded that a defence policy of unilateralism would not appeal to the electorate as a whole, but both he and the party were firmly committed to abandoning nuclear weapons by the decision made by the conference in 1981, confirmed in subsequent years. The manifesto did what it could to square the circle, promising that the country would abandon its nuclear weapons while remaining a loyal member of NATO, laying emphasis on conventional arms and encouraging talks between the United States and the Soviet Union about the mutual reduction of their own nuclear forces. Removing American cruise missiles from Britain would in the first instance depend on these negotiations, but if they failed "we shall, after consultation, inform the Americans that we wish them to remove their cruise missiles and other nuclear weapons from Britain". The policy was thus similar in its essentials to that of 1983, with the important exception that whereas in 1983 the party promised specifically to reduce overall defence spending, in 1987 as Eric Shaw points out, the money saved from nuclear weapons was to be used to provide conventional arms.

Electoral defeat in 1987 was probably inevitable. Mrs Thatcher remained a commanding figure and enjoyed support from the American government which extended to what seemed insultingly dismissive treatment by Ronald Reagan when Kinnock and Healey visited Washington in March 1987. Much of Kinnock's period in the leadership had been preoccupied with the long miners' strike and the fight against Militant. Reformist aides who later became prominent in Tony Blair's "New" Labour Party, including Charles Clarke, Philip Gould, Peter Mandelson and Patricia Hewitt, were brought into the party machine and Kinnock introduced the gentler red rose to replace the red flag as the party's emblem. The party recruited the film director Hugh Hudson to make a highly praised election television broadcast. The campaign as a whole was far more successful than in 1983. But these changes were insufficient to bring election victory, and disputes and indecision within the party over taxation and defence policy were harmful.

In the event, despite the failure of the Conservatives to win a greater share of the vote than in 1979 or 1983, Labour won barely 3 per cent more than it had done in the previous election and the Liberal–Social Democrat alliance, which had done well in recent by-elections, maintained most of its vote. (Although the alliance as a whole returned only one less MP, the SDP which had won two by-elections since 1983 lost three, one of whom was Roy Jenkins. Its demise as a separate party followed in 1990.) The number of Labour MPs rose by twenty to 229 and the Conservative tally fell by 21 to 376. This progress was insufficient; after four years Kinnock and his colleagues would have to start again. Their domestic policy was condemned by opponents as collectivist in an age of individualism and their defence policy as signifying surrender to any prospective enemy who was furnished with nuclear arms. The party's very existence seemed threatened by the increased numbers of the middle class, owner occupation, mass shareholding and the decline of the unions. With no ageing leader to blame, no short and popular war and a weakened Labour left, it could be argued that 1987, not 1983, represented the nadir of Labour fortunes. Peter Jenkins commented succinctly soon after the election: "Thatcher had won almost as well as in 1983 without the 'Falklands Factor'; Labour had lost almost as badly without the 'Foot Factor'".[34]

It was fortunate for the leader that he was young and resilient enough to make a new start, though the path to election victory now seemed endless, and in fact more years in opposition lay ahead than behind the Labour Party. A review of policies was instituted and pursued vigorously. Kinnock was to be attacked from the left for a "counsel of defeat and retreat" and hailed from the party right as "a giant of a man . . . a modernizing hero", but the attacks and praise both oversimplified the nature of the political process. Labour Party figures have often insisted that they could no nothing without political power, though the assertion perhaps underestimates the influence of a strong opposition. In any event, winning elections is the strongest passion of the ambitious politician and it is inevitable that if defeat follows defeat, policies will be changed. Tom Sawyer, a left-wing trade union leader and former Bennite who later became Labour Party general secretary, put forward this view in a speech in 1988: "I say that to put Labour into Government, into a position where we can put our principles into practice, is the most sophisticated and principled aim that the party could have."[35]

It was evident to the younger generation of Labour leaders and advisers that the policy review would have to be sweeping. Peter Mandelson, the party's director of campaigns and communications, reflected soon after the election that "the climate of me-ism, self-enterprise and greed" was

widely thought to be "too entrenched for the Labour Party to overcome
. . . How Thatcherite must Labour become in order to appeal to the new
working class?" How could the party appeal to middle-class professionals
and appear not to be simply the party of the "have nots"? Tony Blair,
who had sat as MP for Sedgefield since 1983, wrote in an article a few
months after the election:

> The real question for the Labour Party is why it is not achieving sufficient
> electoral support . . . Some of the Labour Party conference resolutions
> betray a comforting view that . . . we can become a true socialist movement
> without the need, as Colne Valley Labour Party puts it, "to appeal to the
> wavering middle ground". In practical terms, this is the most dangerous
> delusion of all.[36]

Traditional Labour policies had obviously become unpopular with
important sections of the electorate. Privatization, for example, had
created millions of new shareholders, who feared that under a Labour
government their gains would be lost. This was the background to the
policy review. In the years 1988–91, David Owen later noted approvingly,
Labour reversed "almost every policy that was losing them votes" and
consequently, in his view, making them "wholly unfit to govern".
Naturally and plausibly he attributed much of the credit for the transformation to the activities of the SDP. Similarly, Bill Rodgers wrote that
Kinnock's policy review "eventually made Labour an electable party
again by shifting it on to SDP territory".[37]

The most important policy shift concerned defence. Kinnock had long
been identified with nuclear disarmament but under the pressure of electoral defeat he decided that the policy should now be abandoned. After a
motion at the Labour Party conference of 1988 advocating steps towards
multilateralism was narrowly defeated, Gerald Kaufman, the party's
foreign affairs spokesman, took the lead in returning the party to a multilateral position, pointing out that before a Labour government could
return to office the Trident missile programme of the Conservative
government would be largely complete. But it was Kinnock who told the
party's national executive in May 1989 that Labour had to renounce the
policy of abandoning nuclear arms "without getting anything in return".
At the party conference the following autumn a motion in favour of
unilateral nuclear disarmament was defeated by a majority of three to two
and Kinnock took the opportunity of the impending break-up of the
Soviet Union and its allies to present his new defence policy as Labour's
peace programme for a changing world. "In fact", writes Peter Kellner,
"Labour's switch to multilateralism represented an unambiguous victory
for those who had believed that unilateralism had been a wrong-headed
policy all along."[38] The anti-nuclear policy, which Kinnock had come to
regard as an albatross around his neck, was now definitively abandoned.

Other policies were easier to change, partly because they aroused less passion within the party, partly because steps had already been taken to modify them before 1987 and partly because the left wing, which had suffered numerous defeats in the 1980s, had steadily lost power and influence. In 1990 a policy statement entitled *Looking to the Future* promised that income tax would start at a rate of below 20 per cent and rise to a maximum of 50 per cent, a plan which had already been suggested to the Labour Party conference. Public ownership was played down in favour of regulation of private industry, full employment in favour of the control of inflation. Private capital was a source of partnership, not an enemy. As Martin Smith pointed out in 1992: "The goal is not to abolish capitalism but to run it in a humanitarian way without an unquestioning faith in either the market or state intervention."[39] Traditional Labour policies were being reinstated after the temporary shift to the left in the 1980s.

Kinnock and Hattersley both took opportunities to insist firmly that individualism and socialism were not only compatible but inseparable. Thus Kinnock told the party conference in 1988: "The great inspiration, the great distinction of democratic socialism is that it does not just desire the ends of individual liberty, individual identity, individual choice, it actually commits itself to collectively providing the means for the people to exercise their rights in practice." Labour's collectivism, he went on, aimed to reward the individual. "[I]t is individualism without the Tory grub of greed."[40]

It could not be expected that Kinnock could modify so many policies without notice or criticism. He injudiciously called Robert Adley, a Conservative MP who mocked him for abandoning past policies, "a jerk".[41] The word smacks of the American school playground rather than British political discourse, and he was criticized for unparliamentary language; other Labour leaders would probably have spoken with greater dignity. Potentially more seriously Tony Benn and Eric Heffer stood in the elections for leader and deputy leader in 1988, and John Prescott also stood as deputy leader, more for organizational reasons than through dissatisfaction with party policy. In the event Kinnock beat Benn overwhelmingly, and though Prescott won nearly a quarter of the vote Hattersley was also comfortably confirmed in his post. As the 1987 parliament drew to a close internal opposition was divided and weakened, and Kinnock's position was unshakable. As with the Bevanites prominent left-wingers found that to be a constant rebel was an unrewarding role, though as in the case of the leader himself a left-wing past was career-enhancing.

Kinnock had had his share of the problems presented to the party leadership by a determined minority ever since Attlee's later years, and he understood the harm which a disunited party did to its standing with the uncommitted electorate. The party leadership must have envied the triumphant smoothness with which the Conservatives conducted their affairs, even while ridiculing them for their concentration on presentation, propaganda and public relations. If it was not yet possible to persuade the bulk of the press to abandon its hostility to Labour, it seemed practicable at least to try to prevent the party from speaking with more than one voice.

By 1992 Labour had done much to revamp its policy and to reduce to a minimum internal dissent about the changes which had been made. It had also done much to centralize decision-making in the hands of the leadership. The leader's office became larger and more important, "a major seat of power . . . whose staff played key roles in overseeing policy-making, mustering support for the leader and isolating critics".[42] The friendly media were briefed and where possible managed by the party leadership. By-election candidates were carefully vetted from 1988 to reduce the risk of selecting individuals who could be damned as extremist by the Conservative press. A policy of one member one vote was adopted at local level so as to reduce the influence of local activists and trade unions on the selection of candidates. (This policy aroused strong opposition and was not finally resolved during Kinnock's time as leader.) Steps were taken to reduce the importance of trade union bloc votes at the party conference, a former left-wing concern now moving to the political right thanks to the force of events. In 1990 it was decided to increase the share of constituency Labour Parties in conference votes from 9 to 30 per cent.

The parliamentary shadow cabinet, more amenable to the party leader than the national executive, was given a more important share in policy making, and its members allowed to explain their policy statements from the platform at the party conference. They were, however, compelled to abide by party policy or resign, a sanction which was not available to use against non-parliamentary members of the executive. A national policy forum was set up late in the Kinnock period to share policy making with the annual conference. Thus the party's structure was transformed and its power base followed the same path. As Eric Shaw notes: "The highly pluralistic, deeply polarized Party characterized by the institutional dispersal of powers and weak central authority had been replaced by a powerful central authority exercising tight supervision over all aspects of organizational life."[43] As we shall see, these changes were to survive the Kinnock leadership and to be further refined in the 1990s. They had been introduced not only because party managers viewed the controls used in Herbert Morrison's day as inadequate but because increased dissent within the party had made new measures seem necessary. The growth of the left had made tighter discipline necessary; its decline had made it possible.

By 1992 Margaret Thatcher had been replaced by John Major, a more emollient personality who called a general election for 9 April. The changes made over nine years in the Labour Party now reached their culminating point. The party manifesto, entitled *It's Time to Get Britain*

Working Again, was glossy and, for the first time, illustrated. Kinnock prudently and inevitably declared near the start of his foreword: "At the core of our convictions is belief in individual liberty." At the heart of the manifesto was the determination to rebuild the economy, whose decline since 1990 had pushed up unemployment and, it was hoped, made the Conservatives vulnerable. A sub-heading proclaimed Labour's desire to form "a government which business can do business with" and the text asserted: "It is the government's responsibility to create the conditions for enterprise to thrive." Income tax was to be reformed by increased exemptions for low incomes and a higher rate for the wealthy, and the ceiling on national insurance contributions was to be removed. Old age pensions were to be substantially increased and linked with prices or earnings, whichever was higher. A statutory national minimum wage was promised but the only act of nationalization or near-nationalization proposed was restoration of "public control of the National [electricity] Grid", privatized by the Conservatives. Trade unions were, like employers and others, termed "social partners", a term borrowed without acknowledgement from continental socialists. Ballots before strikes and for the election of union officials were to remain, though employees were to be granted the right to union membership. "There will be no mass or flying pickets." As for defence policy, a Labour government would join the United States in negotiating a reduction in nuclear arms in what was now a post-Soviet Union world. "Until elimination of those stocks is achieved, Labour will retain Britain's nuclear capability, with the number of warheads no greater than the present total."

Labour lost the election, its fourth successive defeat and a result particularly disappointing in the absence of Margaret Thatcher, though some felt that John Major presented a more difficult target than his domineering predecessor. The principal reasons often given for the Labour defeat can be summed up in two words: taxes and Kinnock, though it should be noted that left-wingers blamed the abandonment of socialist policies and failure to appeal to manual workers and the poor, and castigated the party for, in Gregory Elliott's words. "[o]ozing respectability and competence".[44]

Labour insisted in its manifesto that most taxpayers would be better off under its financial proposals. John Smith, who had been shadow chancellor since 1987, calculated that the large majority of taxpayers, especially the low paid, would retain more income after his proposed changes, but the Conservatives laid enormous emphasis on Labour's tax plans before and during the campaign. Michael Heseltine, the Conservative cabinet minister and later deputy prime minister, proclaimed: "Taxes to the left of them, taxes to the right of them – into the valley of taxes rode the Labour Party."[45] David Hare, who was given a privileged position to observe the Labour election campaign before writing a play about it, mentioned the widespread belief after the election that "Labour had lost the initiative way back in January when they failed to meet the challenge of [the Conservative] 'TAX BOMBSHELL' posters which convinced voters they would each be £1,000 [or more] worse off under Labour." Hare was doubtful about this view and tended to blame the Labour Party itself for defeatism. Writing of a Labour strategy meeting on 25 March addressed by the Kinnock aide Philip Gould, he noted:

> The underlying message he brings today is that, although John Smith's shadow budget has done something to convince the electorate that Labour will not put taxes up immoderately, nevertheless the Tories start with such a huge in-built advantage on the question of tax that Labour does well to get off it as fast as possible . . . Labour strategists regard tax and the economy as issues on which Labour simply *cannot win*. They start from too far behind.[46]

Tony Blair and Gordon Brown, as well as academic students of the election, concluded that it was not only those on high incomes but those who hoped that they would enjoy such incomes in the future who were alienated by Smith's tax plans. In any event, there seems little doubt that Smith's national insurance and income tax proposals antagonized many otherwise sympathetic voters.

If the other main factor in the defeat of Kinnock was Kinnock himself, the Conservative press took to itself much of the credit for its relentless pursuit of the Labour leader. The tabloid papers attacked at length and without mercy the supposed "nightmare on Kinnock Street". *The Sun* sarcastically requested on election day "if Kinnock wins today will the last person to leave Britain please turn out the lights" and subsequently claimed to be the paper "wot won it" for the Conservatives. "As voting day drew near, poisonous misrepresentations poured out of almost every tabloid newspaper", Barbara Castle recalled.[47] Conservative politicians too concentrated on the leader of the opposition. Kinnock's verbosity, his Welshness, his lack of ministerial experience, his inexpertise in economic matters, his changed policies were all subjected to obloquy and ridicule. There was also a feeling in some quarters of what was supposed to be the new classless Britain that the Labour leader was "not quite a gentleman". This attitude was demonstrated in reactions to a huge rally held in Sheffield late in the campaign when Kinnock was charged with behaving like a Welsh "boyo" rather than a serious politician. Roy Hattersley doubted whether the leader's "incomprehensible greeting" (usually rendered "well all right" or a variant and shouted three times from the platform) had lost the party as many as one hundred votes. Others disagreed, however, and from the unforgiving left Richard Heffernan and Mike Marqusee termed the rally "a public relations disaster" which "convinced many that

Kinnock's Labour Party was indeed the massive confidence trick the Tory tabloids said it was".[48]

The election loss was the harder to bear because opinion polls had suggested that a Labour victory was likely. In the event the Conservative vote was close to the share which the party had won in 1987 and 1983 and not far below their percentage in 1979. They won more votes than any political party in the whole of British electoral history but still lost forty seats, giving them 336 and an overall majority of 21. Labour had 271 seats, an improvement of 42, but it should be noted that the party's share of the vote rose to only 34.4 per cent. The Liberal Democrats, the new incarnation of the Liberals and Social Democrats, won 20 seats but their share of the vote continued to slip. Soon afterwards Kinnock announced his resignation as party leader.

He was succeeded by his colleague John Smith, the shadow chancellor who had first been elected to parliament in 1970, the same year as Kinnock. Smith's only opponent for the leadership was Bryan Gould, a fellow member of the shadow cabinet, since the election rules effectively prevented challenge from all but influential parliamentarians. Gould was supposed to be a member of the centre left and Smith of the centre right, but by this time such labels had largely lost their meaning; it would have been difficult to have fitted Kinnock into a meaningful category in 1992. Smith was now the only surviving member of a Labour cabinet still active in the higher reaches of the party hierarchy, for Hattersley, who had also been a Callaghan cabinet member, decided to resign with his leader. It was not a surprise that Smith won an overwhelming victory. Margaret Beckett, formerly identified with Bennite politics, but now no longer a member of the irreconcilable left, was elected to the deputy leadership. Gould, beaten for both the top two posts and omitted from the front opposition bench, soon returned to his native New Zealand.

Smith had several advantages, being widely respected, unchallenged by a powerful left wing (the first new party leader to enjoy such a situation for many years) and possessing, unlike Kinnock, acknowledged economic expertise. He was not as young as Kinnock when first elected, being already aged 53 in April 1992. He had two principal disadvantages. He was a Scot, leading the party at a time when Labour needed desperately to appeal to the voters of south-east England, where it had won only three parliamentary seats outside greater London. There appears to have been in the English press and public less prejudice against Scots than against the Welsh, but a Smith leadership did nothing on geographical grounds to appeal to undecided southerners. More ominous but less obvious at the time was the fact that he had had a serious heart attack in 1988 from which he appeared to have made a full recovery. Smith was born into a Labour family and was, as Hugo Young wrote in *The Guardian* after his death, "[s]teeped in Labourism". Roy Hattersley, to whom he was close, insisted that Smith was "the best House of Commons performer of his generation" and if it was true as his biographer Andy McSmith commented, also in *The Guardian*, that he "achieved a personal ascendancy unmatched by any Labour leader since Clement Attlee", this says as much about the decline of the Labour left from the later 1980s as it does about Smith. (Even Tony Benn, then aged 68, lost his seat on the Labour Party executive in 1993.) On the other hand, Smith was careful to praise "a politics that springs from the roots of democratic socialism" and "the values of democratic socialism", to address conference delegates in 1993 as "comrades and friends" and, while praising freedom and ambition, to make clear his opposition to "[p]overty, unemployment, low wages and low skills".[49]

Smith had in the event less than two years to serve as leader before his death. One of his principal concerns was with the party bureaucracy, which had been transformed since 1983 and was, as might be expected, full of Kinnock supporters. Although Smith was neither a throwback to the Foot years nor a saint he hoped to achieve civil relations within the party. In addition, he was less concerned than his predecessor with relations with the media, a subject which had become almost an obsession under Kinnock. He was not attracted to Peter Mandelson, whose biographer terms the Smith leadership period "the wilderness years". Smith commented in 1993: "I don't like the black art of public relations that's taken over politics. We're talking about the government of the country – not the entertainment industry."[50]

The cause with which Smith was most strongly identified during his brief period of leadership was the continuation of the Kinnock drive for the internal election system usually termed one member one vote. Securing this reform meant reaching an agreement with the trade unions, who were at best suspicious of change. To make matters worse it was well known that the Labour "modernizers" were generally unsympathetic to the unions who were a potential alternative power base and in their view obstructed the emergence of a party which would appeal to the southern middle class. It would not have been easy, however, to replace their massive financial support. After concessions and debate including an impassioned appeal from John Prescott at the party conference in 1993 and Smith's determination (known to his close colleagues) to resign if he failed to secure reform, he won a narrow victory, ensuring that the electoral college for electing the leader was revamped and that the union bloc vote which left minorities unrepresented was reformed. Both union and constituency members would vote for the party leader by ballot and selection of parliamentary candidates would be made by the one member one vote system in the constituencies. This was a tricky situation for Smith, who found his natural allies amongst trade unionists, but he recognized that the union bloc vote was an electoral liability and that to reduce it would appeal to potentially sympathetic voters and journalists.

Smith also chaired the joint policy committee within the party made up largely of members of the national executive and the shadow cabinet. His parliamentary colleague Peter Shore commented in 1993: "No previous Leader has enjoyed such personal and institutionalized control over party policy." It was unlikely that he would find himself at odds with the decisions of the executive or the party conference, "the unhappy, sometimes traumatic experience that had beset so many of his predecessors", Shore wrote. With institutional reform effected and the party riding high in the opinion polls, Smith was in no hurry to introduce further policy reforms. In any event, as the modernizer Philip Gould points out: "His instinct was for consolidation, not modernization."[51] He re-emphasized full employment as a major Labour goal and he established a commission on social justice which included several non-Labour members and reported at book length after his death.

Smith's sudden death took place after a heart attack on 12 May 1994. He was, after Aneurin Bevan, Hugh Gaitskell and Tony Crosland, the fourth leading Labour figure who had died in middle age and in full political vigour since 1960. As previously observed, politicians are not noted for allowing sentiment to inhibit their behaviour and in any case the party would have suffered seriously if it had not taken steps to replace Smith with minimal delay. After a campaign in which party members appeared to appreciate fully the role given to the membership under the new system of election, Tony Blair was elected party leader on 21 July with majorities in all three constituent parts of Labour's electoral college: members of parliament, trade unions, individual members. He won 57 per cent of the combined vote. John Prescott beat Margaret Beckett, who had been acting leader in the weeks after Smith's death, for the position of deputy leader by thirteen percentage points. The day of New Labour had arrived. To it we now turn.

8 NEW LABOUR

1994–2005

The transformation of the Labour Party in the mid-1990s was the product of three important developments. The first and most significant was that Britain was a changed country in which the old social signposts had either undergone heavy modification or disappeared altogether. Second, the Conservatives had by 1992 won four consecutive elections and Labour felt compelled to institute changes which would make victory likely at the next election. Third, a new leader was elected who had the determination and authority and, it should be stressed, the enthusiastic support of most of his party, to effect important changes in policy.

The Labour Party had been created primarily to represent the large and largely poor working class, particularly by increasing its parliamentary representation. By the 1990s the working class had shrunk and was no longer, in the main, poor. It is difficult to assess social class accurately but the trends are clear. The postwar years saw a steady growth of middle-class occupations and a sharp decline in the percentage and number of those who belonged to the manual working class. In 1945 two-thirds of the labour force belonged to the working class according to an authoritative study by Anthony Heath and colleagues. By 1979 the working-class percentage had fallen to about half, then to 37 per cent in 1992 and 34 in 1997. Employees in service industries, generally regarded as doubtfully supportive of Labour, rose from just under 45 per cent to over 60 per cent of the workforce between 1959 and 1981, while in the following ten years workers in manufacturing dropped from over six million to under five million. Steven Fielding notes that between 1979 and 1997 employees in manufacturing declined from 32 to 18 per cent, while workers in service industries rose from 58 to 75 per cent. Trade union membership fell from 53 per cent of the civilian workforce in 1980 to 32 per cent in 1994 and, like the Labour Party itself, was decreasingly composed of manual workers. If a largely working-class electorate had failed to provide reliable election victories for the Labour Party, it was highly unlikely that a more middle-class electorate would do so unless the party could claim plausibly to have made significant changes in its policies.

The consequence of economic, technological and social change was that a new society began to emerge in the 1960s and gather pace in later years. The psychological gap between social classes was greatly reduced. A nation of producers had by the end of the 1980s become a nation of consumers, a phenomenon observable throughout western Europe, together with the abandonment or transformation of older programmes by socialist or social-democratic political parties. By the early 1990s over two-thirds of dwellings in the United Kingdom were owner-occupied, about the same percentage of British households owned at least one car, colour television was all but universal and other forms of consumer durable were also widespread. These factors were highly influential in shaping a new society in Britain; the deference and divisions of the past were much reduced. The term "working class" was no longer in common use by the 1990s though the vaguer "working people" was still heard, and some commentators claimed that social classes had virtually disappeared.

This is not to say that poverty and inequality, which bore a close relation to each other, had disappeared. Surveys showed that inequality of income had increased and that Britain was one of the most unequal of industrial or post-industrial societies. The commission on social justice established by John Smith as leader of the Labour Party concluded in 1994 that the lower half of income recipients, who received a third of national income in 1979, had seen their share drop to a quarter by 1992. In the same year, 1992, infant mortality was over 50 per cent higher among the families of unskilled workers than in the professional classes and the latter group could expect at birth to live seven years longer than the former. Differential longevity among occupational groups had increased rather than diminished.

The incomes of poor people, however, had increased, if more slowly than that of other groups. Their possession of consumer durables formerly regarded as luxuries had risen sharply and the nation as a whole was increasingly affluent and better educated despite the restriction of some social benefits and the introduction of increased charges for others. Foreign holidays became accepted as a norm among groups which had previously lacked the opportunity to enjoy them. People felt more equal and behaved as if they were. The use of titles and surnames declined, a small point which like the reduction of class difference in spoken English had important repercussions on social life. Informality of dress became common. The media and advertisers encouraged these trends and the drive for greater equality through political means, previously identified with the Labour Party, lost much of its urgency. The statistics of change were not immediately available but new forms of social mores anticipated their publication.

As repeatedly observed throughout this book, serious political parties aim above all things to win elections. If elections are lost programmes are changed. The left-wing cartoonist Vicky represented Hugh Gaitskell asking after the lost election of 1959, "Which party would you like Labour to resemble?".[1] Revision of party policies took place under Gaitskell and continued under Wilson and Callaghan, a process which, as previously discussed, intensified under the leadership of Neil Kinnock from the later 1980s. Kinnock may thus be regarded as the John the Baptist of what was to become New Labour. "I did not begin new Labour; Neil did",[2] Tony Blair told the Labour Party conference in 1996.

Had John Smith lived there would probably have been no explicitly "New" Labour Party. There would have been no glamorous young leader and the style of the party would have been less innovative, but it is unlikely that policies would have been substantially different. The Callaghan government in which Smith had served had been dedicated to consensus and Smith as prime minister would have been likely to follow the same road. There would have been the same rejection of central planning and state control demanded by the Blairite modernizers. As Peter Mandelson and Roger Liddle, two of the most important publicists of New Labour pointed out, "every past Labour government has wanted to see a thriving private sector within a mixed economy". But the changes sought by New Labour went beyond a return to the politics of Callaghan, they insisted. "[T]he party constantly has to identify ways of reconnecting itself with ordinary voters", they asserted, "speaking their language and voicing their concerns and aspirations".[3] This meant that it should speak to and for the political centre, not for a minority of activists.

Philip Gould argued almost from the inception of his appointment to the staff of the Labour Party in 1985 that it must appeal to "the new middle classes". Writing soon after the general election of 1997 he commented: "The middle class can no longer be viewed as a small, privileged sub-sector of society. Mass politics is becoming middle-class politics. Winning the [twenty-first] century means winning middle-class support." Tony Blair observed in a speech delivered in 1993 that Labour had lost the election the previous year because the party had changed less than British society had done. "The changes in class composition, the breakup of the old class structure, mean that to form a new electoral majority the Left has to reach out beyond its traditional base."[4] The solution was to appeal to the ever-growing middle class; the implication was that high taxation and the powerful state should no longer be identified with the Labour Party. Thus Blair claimed in 1995: "the objective of any government is to lower rather than increase the tax burden on ordinary families".[5] As we shall see, taxation policy was to become one of the party's most important concerns.

This brings us to the personality of Tony Blair himself. At the time of writing he has been leader of the Labour Party for eleven years, longer than any other leader except Clement Attlee and Harold Wilson. Born in May 1953, Blair had been a member of parliament for the same period, eleven years, when he was elected party leader after the unexpected death of John Smith. Neil Kinnock, the predecessor with whom he can be most appropriately compared, had been an MP for thirteen years when he succeeded Michael Foot in 1983. Kinnock entered parliament aged 28, Blair was 30. Both became party leader at the age of 41. Blair, however, the son of a self-made law lecturer and barrister, attended Fettes, a public school in Edinburgh, and Oxford, before becoming a barrister and an MP and subsequently the youngest prime minister since the early nineteenth century only three years after becoming party leader. This privileged upbringing was in stark contrast to Kinnock's working-class origins in South Wales. Blair had no Labour background on which to draw. This was probably an advantage in the eyes of much of the press which had conducted an unrelenting vendetta against Kinnock. As Blair's recent biographer Anthony Seldon writes, he "knew relatively little of the history of the Labour Party when he became leader; and what little he did know, he did not like".[6]

Part of the reason for the kinder reception accorded to Blair lay in his sedulous efforts to court proprietors and editors, but an important aspect lay in his own personality. He has been described by aides and others as friendly and charming, informal, conversational in speaking rather than oratorical, relaxed, plausible and successful in "exud[ing] an aura of class-lessness". When in a tight political corner soon after becoming prime minister he commented: "I think most people who have dealt with me think I'm a pretty straight kind of guy and I am".[7] Most past Labour leaders would not have wished or perhaps dared to make such an appeal, but Blair, supported by the prestige of his high office, was able to do so successfully. He was sometimes accused, however, of exaggerated respect for those who had excelled in amassing wealth and power.

By the end of the 1980s Blair was already a leading Labour figure and well known as a modernizer. Although he had included membership of the Campaign for Nuclear Disarmament in the *curriculum vitae* for his successful selection conference in Sedgefield in 1983, unlike Neil Kinnock he had no left-wing past to modify or renounce. In his first years as an MP he referred to himself as a socialist, but with no connotation of class antagonism. "[S]ocialism . . . stands for co-operation, not confrontation; for fellowship, not fear", he proclaimed in his maiden speech in the House of Commons. This kind of definition was far from new but it was signif-icant in view of Blair's later career. A press profile in 1991 referred to "[t]he suspicion that he has no bottom, that he doesn't believe in anything very much",[8] an allegation which he denied but which in any case seems to have done him little harm in the political world.

Blair's adherence to what may be termed "collective individualism", the claim that the community should assist its members to realize their full potential, was not new in the Labour Party. Herbert Morrison, Aneurin Bevan and Harold Wilson had all emphasized the aim of enhancing individual well-being by collective policies. The same view was expressed frequently under the Kinnock–Hattersley leadership in which Blair was a shadow cabinet member from 1988. The tone changed, however, with Blair. Before he became leader the Labour Party had espoused collectivist policies intended to benefit individuals. Now collectivist policies would be followed only where self-provision was impracticable or where established practice was popular and there was little demand for change. Belief in individualism extended to ownership of industry. Anthony Seldon traces Blair's scepticism about public ownership as far back as 1987, though this sentiment was not yet expressed publicly.

Like his predecessors Blair wanted to speak for all sections of society. Like most of them but with fewer reservations he sought to disarm potential opposition from groups which had traditionally been wary of or hostile to a Labour government. "He does not like confrontation", his former aide Derek Scott wrote recently, "preferring the 'big tent' politics in which as many people and groups as possible are brought within his political tepee. In pursuit of this, he attempts to reconcile the irreconcilable and the hard edges of policies are blurred."[9] Blair was not so much a different kind of leader as a leader in a different age, one in which social change, eighteen years of the Conservatives, the decline of the left in the Labour Party as well his own character gave him unprecedented opportunities to amend or abandon past policies.

He worked cordially with Paddy Ashdown as leader of the Liberal Democrats until 1999 and seems to have hoped, though unsuccessfully, to continue the warm relationship with the new Liberal Democrat leader, Charles Kennedy. He did not address his conference delegates as "comrades" and his references to socialism disappeared after he became prime minister. Both terms, he probably believed, would have been inimical to the policy of the big tent. The middle class was attracted to Labour in unprecedented numbers. Robin Cook, who was foreign secretary in the first Blair government and later a persistent critic, observed to a colleague late in 2002: "Tony's great historic achievement for the Labour Party is to enable it to break out of electoral dependency on dwindling numbers of the manual working class, and to colonize the expanding middle classes as Labour's natural territory."[10]

As we have seen Blair used the word "left" in speeches in his period as leader of the opposition, though he preferred "left-of-centre", "centre and centre-left" or, as Stephen Driver and Luke Martell have pointed out, "radical centre". Later he used the term "third way" to illustrate his belief that the division between left and right was outmoded. That New Labour politics supersede the older categories is a favoured theme of Anthony Giddens, the leading theorist of the third way and an influential associate of Blair: "The division between left and right reflected a world where it was widely believed that capitalism could be transcended, and where class conflict shaped a good deal of political life. Neither of these conditions pertains today."[11] "Third way", like other previously common New Labour phrases, has lost its popularity but its essence lives on.

The belief in the centre ground, politics based neither on social class nor on sharp division between right and left helps to explain Blair's admiration for the United States, where political parties have been less ideological and less class-based than those in western Europe. The insistence that equality of opportunity, much prized by Blair, is greater in the United States than elsewhere is an important part of the American claim to democratic leadership throughout the world and a significant component of the "deep empathy"[12] which Blair and Gordon Brown, his leading colleague, have long felt for that country.

In the period between the leadership contest in 1994 and the general election of 1997 much attention was devoted to reshaping the party. The most important change was the replacement of the famous Clause Four, section 4 of the party constitution of 1918 as amended in 1929, which committed it to belief in "common ownership of the means of production, distribution and exchange". Hugh Gaitskell, it will be recalled, had wanted to jettison this commitment after the general election of 1959 and had lacked sufficient support to do so. Harold Wilson and James Callaghan, the only subsequent Labour prime ministers before Blair, had no intention of carrying out the clause but did not seek a clash on the subject. They had sufficient trouble in curbing their left wing without initiating a fight, and John Smith too avoided confrontation over what he regarded as an "academic"[13] issue.

Blair's determination to succeed where Gaitskell had failed had little relevance to any likely Labour programme but much to do with persuading party members and the public that the theoretical commitment to large-scale public ownership had been abandoned. Having trailed his coat at the party conference of 1994, soon after his election as party leader, Blair agreed a new version of the clause with his advisers and, after discussion, with his deputy John Prescott. The new version was longer and more discursive than its predecessor. It began straightforwardly enough: "The Labour Party [in one version, "New Labour"] is a democratic socialist party", but it was clear that socialism had taken on a new meaning. It asserted that "by the strength of our common endeavour, we achieve more than we achieve alone". The party believed in "a community in which power, wealth and opportunity, are in the hands of the many not the few . . . the enterprise of the market and the rigour of competition . . . a thriving private sector and high quality public services, where those undertakings essential to the common good are either owned by the public or accountable to them." It also expressed faith in equality of opportunity and a society which "delivers people from the tyranny of poverty, prejudice and the abuse of power".[14] This was a statement of aims by a progressive political party which did not intend to confiscate property or restrict the growth of high incomes.

An overwhelming majority of the individual membership supported the new version of the clause at a special party conference held in April 1995. Later in the same year the union share of the vote at the party conference was reduced from 70 to 50 per cent, a decline from over 90 per cent in only five years. This could genuinely be presented as evidence of a new Labour Party. It should be noted, however, that it was not institutional change which enabled the new leader to stamp his will on the party but his popularity and the absence of strong opposition to his plans. If there had been a strong left wing as in Callaghan's day institutional innovation would have been difficult or impossible to carry through. Successful leaders are those who work with the grain of their times and Blair was the right personality at the right time.

The draft Labour programme for the general election of 1997 was put to the individual members of the party, an exercise in Napoleonic plebiscitary democracy, in November 1996. John Rentoul, one of Blair's biographers, points out that "the question on the ballot paper might as well have been, 'Do you want to win the election?'"[15] The rank and file was eager to show its support for the new leadership. The surprising feature, Rentoul points out, was not the 95 per cent support given to Blair but the fact that as many as 60 per cent of members, a high turnout for this kind of exercise, took part.

The draft was followed by the general election manifesto, which, though doubtless ignored by the great mass of the electorate, entered the public consciousness through journalistic repetition and interpretation and was the most authentic statement of party aims in 1997. It differed from earlier manifestos in several respects. It was more generally available than previous policy statements for purchase by the public. It was more profusely illustrated than ever before and in full colour. It was no novelty that socialism was not mentioned, but it was significant that class conflict was firmly rejected in the leader's foreword as having "no relevance whatsoever to the modern world".

The manifesto was based on the draft programme but there were changes and additions. The most important of these, following a statement by the shadow chancellor Gordon Brown in January 1997, was the assertion that there would be "no return to the penal tax rates that existed under both Labour and Conservative governments in the 1970s . . . [W]e are pledged not to raise the basic or top rates of income tax throughout the next Parliament." This passage ignored the fact that there had been

Conservative income tax reductions in 1971 and 1979 and that the sweeping cuts in the Thatcher and Major years had been resisted by Labour in the House of Commons, but it served an important purpose. Though criticized as unnecessarily limiting an incoming Labour government's freedom of action the pledge must have played a part in convincing voters and financial opinion that the party had turned its back on the past policy of high income tax rates, specially on the wealthy, in favour of continuing the Conservative emphasis on flat taxes on consumption which were less noticed or less unpopular. It will be remembered that Hugh Gaitskell had been blamed for promising not to raise income tax in the 1959 election, but economic conditions had changed and the promise could be made more plausibly in 1997. The historian Steven Fielding points out that many voters had done well out of the Conservative policies of privatization and reduced income tax, while Labour was "linked to massive industrial discontent and unprecedented economic failure".[16] "New Labour", the manifesto stated unequivocally, "is not about high taxes on ordinary families. It is about social justice and a fair deal." The pledge not to raise income tax rates was reinforced by the promise, also made previously by Gordon Brown, not to exceed current Conservative spending targets for the first two years of a Labour government.

Brown was already the dominant voice of Labour in the field of economics and his importance, discussed below, was to grow in his years as chancellor of the exchequer. He had a more left-wing past than Blair and deeper roots in the Labour Party, and his perhaps reluctant agreement not to raise income tax for a full parliament or exceed the planned Conservative spending limits for two years is therefore of particular interest. The theme of Labour as the party which held a fair balance between different interests was stressed in the manifesto. It praised business enterprise, "healthy profits", a market economy and competitiveness. Higher productivity was strongly advocated. The manifesto supported "partnership" in industry between unions, employees and employers and made clear that "[t]he key elements of the trade union legislation of the 1980s will stay". On the other hand, workers would be free to join a union if they wished, and if a given workforce voted in favour of union membership "the union should be recognized". A Labour government would introduce a national minimum wage and the manifesto promised to tackle social divisions, inequality and poverty, which was to be combated chiefly by the provision of employment for those out of work.

The manifesto offered something to almost everybody but assiduously guarded the Labour flank against attack by the Conservative Party and its supporters in the press, who were now fewer and less vociferous than in the past. Persistent Labour courting of press proprietors, particularly Rupert Murdoch, whose *Sun* was assumed to have had such a devastating effect on Neil Kinnock's hopes in the election of 1992, had been rewarded by majority press support for Labour for the first time in its history. Philip Gould, the Blair insider, pointed out that the manifesto contained few new ideas, but "the ideas it had were what the voters wanted and what New Labour stood for".[17]

The election campaign was followed by a landslide Labour victory. It is true that Labour won only 43.2 per cent of the vote, a percentage little higher than that of the Conservatives in the previous three general elections and below their level in 1979. Labour had nearly two million more votes, however, than in 1992 and its share of the poll rose by over a quarter from the 34.4 per cent of 1992 to a higher level than at any election since 1966. The Conservatives with only 30.7 per cent, on the other hand, had their lowest share in any general election in the twentieth century. Labour won 418 seats, an increase of 147 over 1992, the Conservatives 165, a catastrophic loss of over half their previous total. Nearly a quarter of the successful Labour candidates were women, an increase since 1992 from 37 to 101. This result followed a long and sometimes contentious campaign within the party to raise the number of women candidates. The Liberal Democrat vote declined as it had done in 1992 and 1987 but the party's supporters used their votes well and there were now 46 Liberal Democrat MPs, twice as many as in any election since 1931. The only drawback from the Labour perspective was that the percentage of the registered electorate who voted fell from 77.7 in 1992 to 71.5 in 1997, but politicians' ritual regret over the size of the poll may be regarded sceptically.

Tony Blair called the next general election in June 2001, following the Thatcher precedent of picking a moment which gave room for manoeuvre rather than, as Callaghan and Major had done, serving full terms with disastrous results. On this occasion the manifesto, which again referred to the party as "New Labour", covered 44 pages, the bulkiest manifesto the party had ever published. Like its predecessor it was lavishly illustrated in colour and Tony Blair's image was on the cover as in 1997 and as Harold Wilson's and Neil Kinnock's had been in earlier years. At this election Labour could boast of the progress it had made and the promises it had kept since 1997. As in 1997 socialism was not mentioned. The pledge was again made not to raise the basic or higher rate of income tax.

The opportunity was taken to strike once again the authentic New Labour note. Partnership between government, employers, employees and the voluntary sector was praised and the "nanny state" condemned. Labour promised light regulation of industry, more doctors and nurses and improved schools. The tone of the manifesto was summed up in the fourth paragraph of Blair's introduction: "My passion is to continue the modernization of Britain in favour of hard-working families, so that all our children, wherever they live, whatever their background, have an equal chance to benefit from the opportunities our country has to offer and to share in its wealth."

Labour had never previously won two consecutive elections with working majorities. Now it won two consecutive landslides. Its share of the vote declined to 40.7 per cent, a lower percentage than the Conservatives had won in any election between 1979 and 1992, and it returned six fewer MPs than in 1997, but the Conservatives gained only one per cent of the vote and one additional MP. The largest gains were recorded by the Liberal Democrats, who gained six more seats than in 1997 with a share of the poll which rose from 16.8 to 18.3 per cent. The percentage of the electorate who voted fell from 71.5 to 59.4, the lowest level since 1918 when the election held shortly after the end of the Great War took place in conditions of economic, political and personal dislocation.

A Labour victory in 1997 was not unexpected and its repetition in 2001 was also anticipated. The scale of the Labour landslides, however, was remarkable. The British single-member constituency system exaggerates electoral success and failure. Labour was fortunate to find its principal enemy in disarray. The Conservative Party was disunited after the widely resented fall of Margaret Thatcher from power in 1990. Her successor John Major was regarded by many as amiable but weak, and after eighteen years in power the party would have been extraordinarily fortunate to win a fifth consecutive election. Financial crisis in 1992 and a series of scandals created difficulties for the Conservatives, and the leadership problem continued after Major's resignation in 1997. The movement of press opinion, previously mentioned, was also significant. The Conservatives were confused by Labour's move towards the political centre and uncertain how to respond.

The most obvious conclusion to draw from Labour's election victories, however, is that a significant fraction of the electorate found New Labour policies congenial. A centrist party appealed to an electorate without strong ideological convictions. For the largest section of the voting public the Blairite consensus was the most attractive option on offer. Labour's advocacy of policies designed to be uncontroversial to most sectors of opinion, rejecting new measures of public ownership and higher direct taxes, co-operating with business leaders and holding trade unions at arm's length were not simply acts of expediency. There is every reason to conclude that Blair's Labour Party was motivated by the conviction that these were the correct policies for a new political landscape.

The main responsibility for putting the Labour programme into effect on the home front lay with the chancellor of the exchequer, Gordon Brown, who served for the full eight years of the first two Blair governments and was again confirmed in the post after the general election of 2005. Both the length of his tenure of office and his ministerial importance are unprecedented. Brown was well prepared for the post, holding an important position in the party and having worked closely with Blair for many years. His intellect was impressive and he was well versed in economics. As chancellor he enjoyed exceptional power not only in economic affairs but across the entire field of domestic politics. Blair's economic adviser Derek Scott, whose activities were evidently resented by Brown and his staff, wrote recently:

> Tony Blair delegated an unprecedented amount of prime-ministerial authority to the Chancellor that went well beyond the normal and inevitably central position played by the Treasury in all administrations . . . Cabinet colleagues [caught] Gordon trying to settle matters affecting their departments behind their back, but he was only able to do this because the Prime Minister had allowed his own authority to be diluted.[18]

As chancellor Brown has enjoyed conspicuous success, whether through good judgment, good fortune or both. One of his first acts was to give the Bank of England responsibility for setting interest rates, a task already undertaken by the central bank in most comparable countries. Brown and his team of ministers and advisers set the broad framework of policy for inflation within which the Bank of England was to work, the chancellor retaining ultimate authority but freed from responsibility for detailed economic management. The apparent loss of power involved was in fact illusory. He had now, in Robert Peston's words, "greater independence from Downing Street . . . [pressure] to cut interest rates or not raise them for political reasons . . . and far greater authority over other departments". His reputation for economic competence also rose. As William Keegan points out, handing the responsibility for interest rates to the Bank of England "has been widely regarded as an outstanding success, contributing to the stability and reputation for prudence that Gordon Brown and his colleagues desperately sought".[19]

Since 1997 the British economy has been characterized by stability and growth, a factor which has encouraged the Labour Party to place the claim of economic competence at the forefront of its election strategy. Growth had been achieved under the previous Conservative administration following the forced exit of sterling from the European Exchange Rate Mechanism in 1992, but there had been too many preceding difficulties for the government to be able to claim responsibility when economic success arrived. How much Labour in power has done to maintain a growing economy is a matter of dispute. *The Economist* wrote early in 2005 that there had been much longer unbroken growth in earlier postwar years, that a fall in the rate of inflation had taken place all over the world and that official unemployment rates disguised the true extent of economic inactivity. Brown's critic Derek Scott wrote that Brown and Blair had enjoyed "generally benign economic circumstances", not "a small or non-existent majority, a political party that was running off the rails, a clapped-out economy, an unreformed trade union movement and an international economy falling apart with oil prices doubling twice in a decade"[20] which their predecessors had faced. If the Labour government had taken no other action after granting interest rate independence to the Bank of England in 1997, he suggested, the subsequent performance of the economy would probably have been similar to its actual behaviour.

This analysis may be correct, but as both authors would no doubt acknowledge, apparent economic success or failure always depend on outside circumstances. Politicians and journalists alike are quick to distribute credit or blame to the behaviour of individuals rather than to more fundamental economic forces. Brown's tenure of the chancellorship has in any case not been marked by self-inflicted difficulties. In consequence he and his supporters claim that he has been the most successful chancellor of modern times in terms of steady growth, low inflation and increased employment.

Brown's aim was to do as much as he could for the low paid, those on benefits and the public services without alienating the financial markets and the economically powerful, or losing his reputation for prudence. The result has been a series of eventful budgets. Once the two-year adherence to the planned Conservative spending limits ended the amount of money spent on public services rose steadily. Significantly increased resources were devoted to the target areas of education and health. Parents of dependent children, poorly paid wage earners and state pensioners without private means did particularly well. New Labour not being ostensibly redistributionist most of the measures to help the poor were modest in themselves, but taken together they added up to a considerable fillip for many of those on low incomes. On the other hand, the determination not to raise income tax contributed to the fact that after seven years of Labour government incomes were at least as unequal as they had been in 1997.

All the necessary finance, however, could not be raised by growth in the economy and the continued reduction of unemployment. At the beginning of the 2001–5 parliament Brown predicted that he would need to borrow about £16 billion during the lifetime of the parliament. The true figure appeared in spring 2005 to be much higher and the Conservative leader Michael Howard asserted that the 2005 budget was a device to ensure that the electorate would "vote now, pay later".[21] The assumption that taxes would be raised after a general election if a Labour government was returned was supported by respected independent bodies, including the Institute for Fiscal Studies and the International Monetary Fund, and opinion in the City of London supported them. Brown, however, had previously confounded his critics by accurately predicting improved tax receipts and delaying or avoiding predicted increases in taxes, and he strongly denied the validity of these warnings.

Conservatives and others complained about the financing of public expenditure by so-called "stealth taxes", levied on expenditure or on business and, it was hoped, unnoticed by the general public. Higher council tax charges which were the subject of strenuous and repeated complaint by pensioners and other groups, abolition of tax credits for pension schemes and companies, frozen income tax allowances, taxes on petrol, tobacco and fuel used in business enterprises, increased stamp duty on house purchase, abolition of mortgage tax relief and the ending of tax allowance for most married couples were prominent among increases. In April 2002 a one per cent rise in the national insurance charge was levied, specifically intended to raise money for the National Health Service. This increase, though apparently accepted by the public, was the subject of much protest, especially strong since critics insisted that it was a rise in income tax by another name. Brown was increasingly the subject of complaints by business leaders but he made important tax concessions as well as increases. A study by the Organization for Economic Cooperation and Development in 2003 found that taxes on business in Britain were lower than in other major European Union economies and that the overall tax burden in Britain was also comparatively low. Taxation policy remained controversial, but with unemployment and inflation both low and economic growth, employment, business profits and employee incomes all continuing to rise, a starting tax rate of 10 per cent introduced in 1999 and a reduction of the standard rate of income tax by 1 per cent to 22 per cent in 2000, it was not easy for the Conservatives to make their charges of financial profligacy and higher taxes stick.

The fiscal policy of the government has been complemented by its efforts to form an enduring partnership with business and finance. Here the prime minister has played an important role. Speaking to the Confederation of British Industry in November 2001 Tony Blair asserted that there would be "no new ramp of employment legislation taking us back to the 1970s". Partnership between government and business was "a founding principle of new Labour and it will not change".[22] It is clear that this kind of statement was the product both of conviction and of the reduced power of trade unions in Britain. We have seen that in 1980 union membership, then about 13 million, covered over half the civilian workforce. In autumn 2003 there were 7.4 million trade unionists, under 30 per cent of employees; membership numbers, though by then stable, had fallen even since the first Blair government was formed in 1997. The difficulties faced by unions was underlined by the fact that employment in manufacturing industry fell by a further million between 1997 and 2005. A party which wanted to retain power had little choice but to try to enlist support from the business community.

The theorists of New Labour were sceptical about the desirability and efficiency of public enterprise, whether national or local. Peter Mandelson and Roger Liddle, for example, wrote in 1996:

> New Labour does not regard public ownership of industry as necessary in order to manage the economy . . . The truth is that the record of the old nationalized industries was at best patchy . . . They employed more people than could conceivably be justified on grounds of efficiency . . . [T]here are circumstances in which local councils are much better at planning, financing and regulating public services than they generally are at owning, managing and directly providing them.[23]

The experience of government undoubtedly reinforced this view.

It was important to New Labour that it should not be seen as advocating centralized public ownership as an ideological aim. Relying on private industry for finance also provided a pragmatic means of raising capital from extra-government sources and reduced the potential level of the public sector borrowing requirement. William Keegan comments that advocacy of the private finance initiative (PFI) and the public–private partnership was used in the early phase of New Labour as a means of showing that the party was not going to adopt "tax and spend" policies, increase the scope of the public sector or antagonize middle-class taxpayers. In Anthony Seldon's words, this means of financing public capital expenditure owed "more to the philosophy of Thatcherism than socialism [and] sent a deep shiver through the party",[24] but the fact that it was a Conservative invention was probably not a disadvantage in New Labour eyes.

PFI has proved extremely controversial. Gordon Brown, though an early opponent, was to become its most prominent advocate. Writing in *The Times* in September 2002 he asserted: "No responsible Labour government could maintain trust in fiscal responsibility while lurching back to the bad old days of reckless borrowing." PFI was helping to build "40 new hospitals, 150 new schools and scores of road and rail projects".[25] This was in addition to increased expenditure by the government itself on capital projects. Ken Livingstone, the mayor of London, was forced against his wishes to accept private capital and to part-privatize the London Underground. This move was said to be at the insistence of Brown, who had little sympathy for Livingstone.

Critics complained that public assets were handed for a lengthy period to private companies and that despite the use of private capital the state was compelled to bear the ultimate risk of projects which were too important to be allowed to fail. It was also insisted that PFI-built projects, notably hospitals, were sometimes inadequate or too expensive for their purpose. London Underground was a special target, with alleged excessive profits for the private sector. William Keegan, in his generally sympathetic account of Gordon Brown's policies, asks: "[D]id Brown, and Prescott with him, jump too far from an ideological belief in the powers of the state to a naïve belief in the wonders of the private sector? . . . A Chancellor who believed in 'what works' became hung-up on what often patently didn't work."[26]

Privatization continued though on a smaller scale, the major government-owned industries having been transferred to private hands under the Conservatives. Majority stakes in air traffic control and the Commonwealth Development Corporation were sold, the number of private prisons increased, the refitting of warships was allocated to private companies and the post office was increasingly subject to competition. Some members of the government were reported to support the full privatization of the post office but greater competition and closure of branch post offices were decided upon as a preferable option; the 2005 manifesto confirmed that privatization was not intended. Transfer of the remaining council homes to private, non-profit making social landlords, who enjoyed access to funding for repairs and improvements denied to local government, was encouraged . The government also supported the trend towards economic "globalization" and generally refrained from financial support for failing industries.

Labour insisted, however, that it dealt fairly by both sides of industry. A national minimum wage of £3.60 an hour for adults was introduced in April 1999. It rose by over 7 per cent per annum to £4.85 in September 2004 and is scheduled to rise to £5.05 in October 2005. The rates were criticized as being set at a low level acceptable to the Confederation of British Industry but a national minimum wage was a significant innovation. The Employment Relations Act of 1999 gave workers the right to union recognition if a majority which included at least 40 per cent of the workforce in a given establishment voted in favour. Hundreds of recognition agreements were reached in ensuing years, though they have done no more than halt the long-term decline in union membership. A further concession to the unions was the agreement reached by ministers and union leaders at Warwick University in July 2004 which covered important aspects of employment. The Labour Party manifesto the following year promised: "we will deliver [the agreed policies] in full".

Social policy was a major preoccupation of the government. Gordon Brown, whose influence was dominant in this field, aimed to improve the condition of the poor by providing employment and improving social benefits for vulnerable groups. The belief in employment was repeated in the Labour manifesto in 2005: "Work is the best anti-poverty strategy." The "New Deal", financed by a tax on the windfall profits of privatized firms, provided assistance towards finding work for the young unemployed and by August 2001, 300,000 jobs had been created. How many of them would have existed in any case is a matter of controversy. The distribution of benefits, specially pensions, was also controversial. Labour's traditional policy had been to provide equal benefits to all those eligible and in 1992 John Smith had promised to restore the link between old age pensions and earnings broken by the Thatcher government. New Labour adopted a different policy, shifting from universalism to targeting assistance on the poorest pensioners. Brown aimed to end the greatest extremes of poverty without setting taxes at a level which it was assumed the electorate was not prepared to pay. As Howard Glennerster points out:

> Labour governments have always dreamed of providing adequate basic pensions and never did so . . . [T]he universal flat rate pension could have been made far more generous so that it produced a livable income well above the means test level. But that would have taken much of the available funds Brown had to spend for this and the next Parliament.[27]

Pensions were increased generously for the poorest but most recipients were restricted to increases commensurate with the rate of inflation after an injudicious increase of only 75 pence in the weekly basic rate in 2000 was amended by larger rises in following years. The principal problems with targeted or means-tested payments were that retired people who had small occupational pensions or savings were penalized and that over a million eligible people failed to apply for benefits to which they were entitled. Research published by the Joseph Rowntree Foundation in late 2003 concluded that nearly 30 per cent of pensioner households did not take up the minimum income guarantee to which they were entitled and a year later this situation had worsened. Despite these problems, however, the researchers concluded in 2003 that pensioners as a group "enjoy better incomes than they have in the past".[28]

Brown had less influence on education and health which, however, were even more controversial within the Labour Party than pensions policy. Money was poured into education which was declared to be Labour's top priority, once the self-imposed two-year spending limit ended though problems were found with its efficient distribution, leading in some cases to reductions of teaching staff. Levels of attainment in the schools rose but fell short of government targets. Changes were made to traditional Labour policies, including invitations to private firms and other agencies to administer schools where local authorities were judged to have failed. Conservative measures including "league tables" modified to attempt to show the "value added" by the schools, enhanced school inspection and the national curriculum, streamlined to make it less burdensome, were continued. The charge was made, though denied by the government, that it was so concerned to raise attainment in the basic subjects that the curriculum was narrowed and creativity inhibited. The increasing use of unqualified teaching assistants was hotly contested by the National Union of Teachers, which accused the government of trying to recruit poorly paid teachers disguised as a measure to reduce the workload of existing staff.

New Labour understood that the remaining grammar schools, which tended to do well in the league tables, retained strong support from parents. The hurdles which it constructed to their absorption into the system of comprehensive schools which covered most of the country were severe, so that most advocates of a unified system of secondary education abandoned efforts to incorporate the grammar schools. Supporters of the common secondary school were less vocal than they had been in the past and ministers were often ambivalent about its qualities. Ruth Kelly, the secretary of state for education, said in March 2005 that comprehensive schools had raised standards but had not been a "universal engine of social mobility".[29] The schools, she asserted, tended to be divided on grounds of social class, had not developed an individual character or sufficiently involved parents and pupils in their administration. This kind of statement had also been made by her predecessors.

Labour educationists sought, as had Hugh Gaitskell and Harold Wilson in the past, to find ways of encouraging diversity in schools without abandoning the comprehensive principle. Kelly's conviction was that the education system should be comprehensive but that the schools should vary in their specialisms. The result was a bewildering array of city technology colleges, city academies, partly selective specialist schools and beacon schools. City academies, which recruited private sector sponsorship and participation in their management, were particularly contentious. The government aimed to create 200 academies by 2010, but the 17 which existed in early 2005 did not enjoy universal support. Teachers' unions opposed them as divisive, expensive and a threat to state education and in March 2005 the House of Commons select committee on education urged that the progress of city academies should be evaluated before more were established. Their results in tests of attainment led to widely differing conclusions, supporters insisting that significant progress had been made, opponents taking the opposite view.

Higher education also presented problems, notably within the Labour Party itself. The party manifesto in 2001 set an "historic commitment": 50 per cent of young people under the age of 30 should have some experience of higher education, though not in all cases to traditional degree level. This raised the question of who would pay for the burgeoning higher education sector. In 1998 fees of £1,100 payable in advance were introduced for all but the poorest students, and the remaining maintenance grant was terminated for most. The student loan scheme previously introduced by the Conservatives was enlarged. In January 2003 Charles Clarke, the then education secretary, announced that there would be an increase of fees in 2006 to a maximum of £3,000, to be paid only once students had left higher education and were earning at least £15,000 per annum. Universities were to be urged to attract more students from working-class homes.

Students and their supporters rejected all fees and demanded that higher education should be financed by increased taxes on the wealthy. What most disturbed Labour backbenchers was the proposal to allow universities to charge differential fees up to the limit of £3,000. The government's desire to create a "market" in higher education, with the most prestigious universities rivalling leading institutions in the United States, was strongly opposed. It was feared that less prestigious universities would suffer from what appeared to be the introduction of a two-tier system of higher education. The government insisted, however, that potential students from working-class homes would have greater opportunity in a larger system of higher education and would benefit both from remission of part of the fees and delaying repayment of the rest until their incomes were adequate. It also made clear that if further money were to be spent on education it would be devoted to early childhood or adult skill training, not to universities. The crucial vote in the House of Commons in January 2004 was won by a margin of only five, however, with about ninety Labour backbenchers either abstaining or voting against the government. Few protagonists were satisfied with the result. The most prestigious universities wanted to be able to raise fees to a much higher level, grassroots opinion in the Labour Party was deeply uneasy if not hostile to the £3,000 fee and the government was poised unhappily in the middle, insisting that the fee would not increase except to take account of inflation before the end of the parliament elected in 2005.

Health policy was also a highly contentious subject. Blair's first health secretary, Frank Dobson, was not an advocate of change in the administration of the National Health Service, but he lasted for less than three years in the job before leaving it in a vain attempt to prevent Ken Livingstone from being elected mayor of London. His successors, Alan Milburn and John Reid, were more enthusiastic about changes which would decentralize the health service, provide a significant role for the private sector and give the patient a greater element of choice of services than had hitherto prevailed. The Labour election manifesto in 2001 declared in words especially applicable to health policy: "Where private-sector providers can support public endeavour, we should use them. A 'spirit of enterprise' should apply as much to public service as to business." Early in 2002 Milburn told *The Times* that the role of government should be to oversee a policy rather than directly to administer it. Local services, he continued, should be provided in diverse ways. "We must redefine the NHS from a centrally run, monopoly provider of services and give people the freedom to provide better standards of care for NHS patients."[30]

Thus was born the policy of self-governing "foundation" hospitals pursued by Milburn and his successor John Reid, though at the price of widespread dissension within both the parliamentary and the wider Labour Party. In November 2003 the policy was approved by the House of Commons by only seventeen votes, despite the huge Labour majority among MPs. Reid himself claimed that foundation hospitals would extend access, increase patient choice and give an important part to the public in their administration. Whitehall's monopoly control of hospitals would be ended, together with the "myth" that the minister of health could direct local hospitals how best to provide health care. His opponents, particularly strong among the trade unions, attacked what they regarded as a two-tier system which threatened to lead to the privatization of hospitals. They were strongly opposed to the policy of expanding health provision by inviting the private sector to share in the work of the NHS, though without charge to individual patients. The government commissioned 460,000 operations from outside the NHS by the time of the general election of 2005, but Reid denied that such treatment would be the norm. In future, he predicted, a maximum of 15 per cent of operations would be conducted by the private sector.

It may be guessed that patients were more concerned with receiving prompt, efficient and free care than with who provided it. It may also be supposed that most patients were less eager for the "choice" promised by the government than with conditions in their own local hospital. What was certain was that the government poured money into the NHS; expenditure doubled between 1997 and 2005, it claimed, waiting times were cut, numbers of doctors and nurses increased. It was also the case that complaints still remained. These included the favourite Conservative charge of alleged inefficient expenditure, continued long waiting lists and cancellation of operations in some cases, lack of cleanliness and the spread of infection within hospitals, and a sharp decline in availability of NHS dentists. Medical staff complained that they were being given too many targets and that their clinical judgment was being subordinated to political expediency. In general, however, Labour felt that health care was one of its greatest successes and strenuously proclaimed it as such.

As we have seen, the aim of New Labour and in particular Gordon Brown was to provide higher pensions for those without private means and employment for the jobless. Poor children remained to be helped. In March 1999 Tony Blair pledged to end child poverty, which had risen markedly during the period of Conservative government and which affected in 1999 nearly one child in three, within twenty years or (somewhat confusingly) "a generation". Seven hundred thousand children were to be removed from poverty "by the end of the Parliament".[31] The party manifesto in 2001 claimed that over a million children had already been rescued from poverty, and in both 2001 and 2005 Labour promised to halve the number by 2010–11, "both in terms of relative low-income and in terms of material deprivation" in the words of the 2005 manifesto.

Measuring poverty is a complicated undertaking. Throughout the European Union the criterion used is not an absolute measurement but the income of the poor relative to others, so that the level required to escape poverty rises as incomes of the entire population grow. To be poor is to fall below 60 per cent of median income, a criterion adopted in the mid-nineties to replace the previous calculation of 50 per cent of mean, or average income. This criterion presents an obvious problem to a government determined not to impose heavier income taxes on the wealthy. It decided in 2003 to adopt a measurement of poverty which includes both "absolute" and "relative" versions of low income. "This is confusing",[32] writes Ruth Lister, one of the leading experts in the field, and the non-expert historian can only agree. Nonetheless, independent assessment of poverty levels using the old criterion has continued.

The report to the Joseph Rowntree Foundation in December 2003 concluded that in 2001–2, twenty-two per cent of the British population, 12.5 million people, lived in homes in which income fell below 60 per cent of the median. Thirty per cent of children, or 3.8 million, fell into this category. Health problems reflected starkly differences of income and showed no sign of relative improvement. The share of income going to the richest levels of households had risen, in contrast to the share of the poorest groups. Nonetheless, there were definite signs that poverty levels had fallen. Compared with 1996 the number of people below a fixed low income threshold had fallen by a third. Children and pensioners, the report concluded, were "still disproportionately affected by poverty but to a lesser extent than before". Halfway through the period to 2004, by which time the aim of the government was to reduce the number of children in poverty by at least a quarter, it was about two-fifths of the way towards its target. The number of people living on a low income was at a lower level than at any time in the 1990s. Hence it was "right to be positive about the progress that is being made in reducing poverty in Britain".[33]

A year later a summary report published by the same foundation found that the number of recipients of low income had continued to decline among children and their parents and among pensioners. The number of children in low-income households was 3.6 million in 2002–3, a fall of 700,000 since 1996–7. "[I]t may well be that the Government achieves it[s] short-term target of reducing child poverty by a quarter by 2004."[34] Tax credits, income support, the minimum wage and the growth of the economy had had a clear effect. In 2003–4, however, further progress was limited and the Institute for Fiscal Studies expressed doubt at the end of March 2005 whether the initial target would be reached.

Other aspects of New Labour's domestic policy can only be mentioned.

The government continued the Conservative policies of restricting the expenditure of local councils and keeping the collection of the local business rate in its own hands. The council tax was maintained, though in 2005 the party promised its reform "[i]n the longer term". Transport policy was originally designed to favour public transport over the private car, but the pressure of motorists was too great to resist and larger road programmes were later announced. Despite Labour's ostensible concern for the environment a plan for a large expansion of British airports was made public in December 2003. It is difficult to see how an elected government can put protection of the environment ahead of the pressure of millions of motorists and holiday makers as well as employees whose jobs depend on maintenance or expansion of the relevant industries.

As previously mentioned local authorities were encouraged to transfer their housing stock to other landlords, chiefly housing associations. Power was devolved to a Scottish parliament, a Welsh assembly and elected mayors in some English cities, though the government was accused of giving the devolved bodies too little power and trying to retain indirect control of their functions. The House of Lords lost most of its hereditary peers and the Labour Party promised in its 2005 manifesto to complete its reform, though there was internal disagreement over how this should be done. In the wake of international terrorism the government introduced measures opposed by much of the legal profession and many civil libertarians. Despite occasional parliamentary rebellions the party itself was firmly controlled by the leadership in a way which would have been envied by Herbert Morrison and George Brown and an effort made to reduce financial dependence on trade unions. This policy, however, has caused embarrassment as some large individual donors to party funds have appeared to request or be granted special favours.

The most important objectives of New Labour in foreign policy have been critical support for the European Union and a close alliance with the United States. There has been a greater desire to co-operate with other European countries, though in moments of crisis old antagonisms are quickly resurrected. The anti-European rhetoric of the tabloid press has changed little and it has probably affected both government and public. Britain has remained aloof from the introduction of the common currency, the Euro. British politicians have urged reform on the union, presumably irritating other European leaders. Gordon Brown, who has often been critical of its policies, wrote in September 2004 that the union should "set a new target for reducing state aids and for reorienting future aid to market-oriented causes . . . Only by rejecting the old trade-bloc Europe – inward-looking, inflexible and sclerotic – and wholeheartedly embracing a global Europe – reforming, flexible, outward-looking and competitive – will the EU respond to the new challenges of globalization."[35]

Labour, like the Conservatives in earlier years, has tried to limit the power of the European Commission and to prevent the growth of a more centralized union. The government has opposed EU social initiatives in the interests of business firms, and in its 2005 manifesto the party made clear that "key national interests like foreign policy, taxation, social security and defence" would remain in British hands. Tony Blair has made friendly gestures towards his European colleagues but he, like the Conservatives, has sought a larger, looser grouping of European countries. The recent expansion of the union suggests that this aim will be realized.

As for the United States, the government has maintained and strengthened the close relationship the desirability of which, in the words of the writer and broadcaster James Naughtie, "has been so obvious in Downing Street . . . [f]or a couple of generations . . . that it has not been seriously questioned".[36] There appears to be a rapport, probably for linguistic and cultural reasons, between British and American politicians missing in EU relations. The rapport extends to the media and, in an age of cheap transport and constant communication, much of the public. Tony Blair like many Americans speaks the language of morality as justification for foreign intervention, a language less frequently heard from other European leaders.

The relationship with the United States was most fully demonstrated by the Iraq war in March 2003 when Britain supported both diplomatically and militarily the American campaign against Saddam Hussein. This action was the subject of strong protest in Britain and many Labour supporters were among its most strenuous opponents. One hundred and thirty-nine Labour MPs voted in the House of Commons against war and huge crowds of anti-war protesters gathered in several cities. Criticism was particularly strong that the American-led coalition went to war without a specific mandate from the United Nations. The government broke ranks with France, Germany and Russia and joined conservative governments in Spain and Italy in supporting the Americans. Subsequently it was criticized because no weapons of mass destruction were found in Iraq, since the elimination of these weapons was the principal reason given for going to war.

There is no doubt that Blair, who worked closely with the American president George Bush, was the principal supporter within the British government of joining the war coalition. The reasons which motivated him have been hotly debated. His biographer Anthony Seldon writes that there were three strands to his thinking, his concern about the weapons of mass destruction widely believed to be in Iraqi hands, his desire to intervene in Iraq from 1998 if not earlier, and "his personal moral revulsion with Saddam Hussein". James Naughtie points to Blair's desire to educate and lead his party and to act as a bridge between the United States and other European countries, though the American connection was paramount. Naughtie quotes from a television interview given by Blair in September 2002, before the war began: "The reason why we are with America in so many of these issues is because it is in our interests. We do think the same, we do feel the same and we have the same – I think – sense of belief that if there is a problem you've got to act on it."[37] In any case there has been no subsequent apology for British participation in the war. The Labour Party manifesto in 2005 stated with pride that "the butchery of Saddam is over" and Blair strongly defended British intervention in Iraq during the election campaign.

The general election was called for May 2005, a four-year term having become by this time accepted practice. The Labour manifesto marked a change with past procedure. Instead of the glossy, colour-illustrated brochures of 1997 and 2001 there was now a sober paper-backed book of 112 small pages. It was printed in black and white and there was a single photograph, inevitably of Tony Blair. He began his preface with the sentence: "New Labour's 2005 manifesto applies the unchanging values of our party to the new priorities of the British people." He stressed the theme of choice: "No going back to one-size-fits-all monolithic services . . . Going forward instead . . . by raising investment and driving innovation through diversity of provision and power in the hands of the patient, the parent and the citizen." The manifesto repeated for the third time the pledge not to raise the basic or higher rates of income tax during the life of the next parliament. Blair stated in writing the undertaking which he had previously given in interviews, that 2005 was to be his last election as prime minister and party leader. He made explicit at the launch of the manifesto, however, his belief that the party had changed permanently: "This manifesto is quintessentially New Labour . . . [W]hen [at the next election] this party is under new leadership it will continue to be the modern progressive New Labour party of the past 10 years."[38]

The election itself produced a Labour government with a majority reduced from 165 to 67. Forty-seven Labour MPs lost their seats and the party won a little over 36 per cent of the vote, a decline from nearly 41 per cent and an unprecedentedly low figure for a governing party. The explanation for the decline seemed to lie partly in the opposition of many voters to the war in Iraq and the prime minister who had prosecuted it, partly in the wear and tear of eight controversial years in office. The party drew comfort from the fact that although the Conservatives gained over thirty seats their share of the vote rose only from 31.7 per cent to just over 33 per cent. Their electoral support remained at a critically low level. The Liberal Democrats gained votes at Labour's expense, but with under 23 per cent and 62 MPs they did not pose an immediate challenge. In an election marked by an exceptionally high level of postal voting, a slightly higher proportion of the electorate voted than in 2001. Labour remained in power and was probably both relieved that it had secured a victory even if narrower than hoped, and convinced that despite the distortions of the single-member electoral system it would be suicidal to abandon it for proportional representation. The press pointed out that the government faced a new situation which it would have to manage with care. A leading article in *The Independent,* for example, commented: "Labour's loss of almost 50 seats . . . diminishes Mr Blair's authority, restricts his room for manoeuvre and leaves the Commons with the best approximation to a three-party system that Britain has had for decades."[39]

How new is New Labour? Many academics, journalists and others have attempted to answer this question since 1994. I am one and I take this opportunity to repudiate my former view that New Labour is the old Labour Party in modern dress. There are important similarities between the old party and the new, not least that the left wing, now much weakened, denounces the leadership in similar terms to the past as gradualist, cowardly and muddled. There are significant respects in which continuity has been maintained. But the differences are greater.

Labour had been a working-class party; now it aimed to be the party of the middle classes. It had been the party of producers and now devoted itself to consumer interests. It had represented the trade unions. In its new version it proclaimed itself the party of enterprise and competition, and held the unions at arm's length. It had been, if not a socialist party, sympathetic to state control of industry and, ostensibly, to socialist aims. It became the party of the "market economy", regarding public ownership as both undesirable and unnecessary. It had been the party of universal social benefits. In office it "targeted" recipients by the use of what it formerly denounced as a means test. It had supported progressive direct taxes and, in principle, redistribution of wealth. Now it fought three successive elections on the promise not to raise income tax for an entire parliament and redistribution, though not forgotten, was confined to unspectacular tax changes. Tony Blair himself recently told a Labour journal that he wanted to "lift" the disadvantaged and the poor, "but we don't necessarily do that by hammering the people who are successful".[40] These changes amount to a transformation of the party. A return to the Labour Party of the past seems unthinkable in a society so different from that which prevailed until the 1960s.

The intention of New Labour has been to achieve a new consensus in Britain, one which will keep the party in power for many years. It has sought to govern from the political centre. Spending on education, health and social welfare has greatly increased but the government has largely avoided new direct taxation. In a predominantly middle-class society this mixture of fiscal conservatism and social compassion is not surprising. The state is now seen by much of the electorate as of reduced importance to its welfare. The Labour Party has both encouraged this process and responded to it. It has obeyed the law that a political party's most important task is to be elected. The pragmatic character of the party throughout its history and the grip on policy enjoyed by the leadership have facilitated the move towards the political centre. The primary reason for the move, however, lies beyond politics. Society has changed. There is still acute poverty in Britain, but it is now a nation in which the bulk of the population live in comfort and in which the social conscience is consequently blunted. Leaders will come and go, but whenever the post-Blair era begins the party of Bevin and Dalton, even of Gaitskell and Wilson, will not return.

NOTES

PREFACE

1 See p. 116 below.
2 Sidney Webb, "Historic", p. 50.
3 Kingsley Martin in *New Statesman*, 3 April 1948, reprinted in Martin, *Critic's London Diary*, p. 138.

I THE BACKGROUND 1880–1900

1 St Helier, *Memories of Fifty Years,* p. 182.
2 Rowntree, *Poverty,* p. 179.
3 Mathias, *The First Industrial Nation*, p. 346; Fraser, *The Coming of the Mass Market,* p. 133.
4 Pollard, *History of Labour in Sheffield*, pp. 132, 226.
5 Briggs, *Mass Entertainment,* p. 9.
6 Quoted in Mason, *Association Football and English Society*, p. 143.
7 Bell, *At the Works*, p. 126; Shadwell, *Industrial Efficiency,* p. 491.
8 Hamilton, *Arthur Henderson*, p. 16; Rogers, *Labour, Life and Literature*, p. 25.
9 Snell, *Men, Movements, and Myself,* p. 139.
10 Rae, *Contemporary Socialism,* p. 83; Phillips, *Rise of the Labour Party*, p. 1.
11 B. Webb, *My Apprenticeship*, vol. 1, p. 206.
12 Quoted in G. K. Chesterton, *Autobiography,* p. 167.
13 Quoted in Hobsbawm (ed.), *Labour's Turning Point,* p. 47 and Tsuzuki. *H.M. Hyndman*, p. 50.
14 Shaw, *Morris as I Knew Him*, pp. 15–16.
15 Morris, *News from Nowhere,* p. 1.
16 Cole, *British Working Class Politics,* p. 92; Rae, *Contemporary Socialism*, p. 87.
17 Quoted in Burgess, *John Burns*, pp. 82–3.
18 Shaw, *The Fabian Society,* p. 10.
19 Quotation from Margaret Cole, *The Story of Fabian Socialism*, p. 337; Rae, *Contemporary Socialism*, p. 88.
20 Pugh, *Educate, Agitate, Organize,* p. 7.

21 *Diary of Beatrice Webb*, vol. 2, p. 60, quoted in M. Cole, *Fabian Socialism*, p. 83.
22 S. Webb, "Historic", p. 60; S. Webb quoted in Hobsbawm (ed.), *Labour's Turning Point*, p. 45; Shaw, "Transition", p. 183.
23 Quoted in Prynn, "The Clarion Clubs", p. 68.
24 Blatchford, *Merrie England*, p. 200.
25 Reid, *Keir Hardie*, p. 113.
26 Morgan, *Keir Hardie*, pp. 36, 43.
27 Quoted in Powell, *Keir Hardie in West Ham*, p. 17.
28 E. P. Thompson, "Homage to Tom Maguire", p. 279.
29 Snowden, *An Autobiography*, vol. 1, p. 67; David Howell, *British Workers and the Independent Labour Party*, p. 358.
30 Morgan, *Keir Hardie*, p. 63.
31 Quoted in Rubinstein, "The Independent Labour Party and the Yorkshire Miners", p. 127.
32 Mann, *Tom Mann's Memoirs*, p. 101; Morgan, *Keir Hardie*, p. 89; Johnson, "Social Democracy and Labour Politics in Britain", p. 77.
33 *Diary of Beatrice Webb*, vol. 2, pp. 66, 79; Shaw quoted in Cole, *Fabian Socialism*, p. 50n.
34 Quoted in Rubinstein, *School Attendance in London*, p. 13.
35 Quoted in Johnson, *Social Democratic Politics in Britain*, pp. 158–9.
36 G. Howell, *Trade Unionism New and Old*, pp. 136–7, 163; Thorne, *My Life's Battles*, p. 135.
37 Quoted in Hammond, *C.P. Scott*, p. 74.
38 Webb, *Industrial Democracy*, p. 861; quoted in part in Halévy, *History of the English People, epilogue vol. 1*, book 2, p. 229.
39 Bealey and Pelling, *Labour and Politics*, p. 14; Labour Representation Committee, *Foundation Conference Report*, p. 10.
40 *Annual Register*, 1894, p. 89; 1895, p 10.
41 Lansbury, *My Life*, p. 73.
42 *TUC Report 1899*, p. 65.
43 *Ibid.*, p. 66.
44 Quoted in Bagwell, *The Railwaymen*, p. 206.
45 LRC, *Foundation Conference Report*, pp. 11–12.
46 Marquand, *Ramsay MacDonald*, p. 69.

2   LABOUR IN PEACE AND WAR, 1900–1918

1 Barker (ed.), *Ramsay MacDonald's Political Writings*, p. 93.
2 *H/C Deb.*, 14 May 1907, col. 282; Bagwell, *The Railwaymen*, p. 233.
3 Pease, *History of the Fabian Society*, p. 151.
4 Halévy, *History of the English People: epilogue vol. 1*, book 2, p. 235.
5 *Annual Reports of the Labour Representation Committee*, 1903, p. 36; 1904, p. 48.
6 *The Times*, 31 January 1906.
7 Hyndman, *Further Reminiscences*, p. 273.
8 Quoted in Bealey and Pelling, *Labour and Politics*, p. 278.
9 Halévy, *History of the English People: epilogue vol. 2*, pp. 91–2.

10   Lloyd George, *Better Times*, p. 36.
11   Gwynn and Tuckwell, *Life of Sir Charles Dilke*, vol. 2, p. 367.
12   Quoted in Caroline Benn, *Keir Hardie*, p. 250.
13   Pelling, *Short History of the Labour Party*, p. 21; *Punch*, 13 October 1909, p. 265.
14   Davies, *To Build a New Jerusalem*, p. 38.
15   Quoted in W. Thompson, *Victor Grayson*, p. 18.
16   Martin, "'The Instruments of the People'?", p. 133.
17   Blewett, *The Peers, the Parties and the People*, p. 297.
18   Quoted in Tanner, *Political Change and the Labour Party*, p. 142.
19   *H/C Deb.*, 31 January 1913, col. 1646; 30 May 1911, col. 1018.
20   MacDonald, *The Social Unrest*, p. 86; Snowden, *Socialism and Syndicalism*, pp. 214, 242.
21   Pelling, *Popular Politics and Society*, p. 118.
22   *Ibid.*, p. 118; Phillips, *Rise of the Labour Party*, p. 23.
23   Marquand, *Ramsay MacDonald*, p. 151.
24   Quoted in Rubinstein, *A Different World for Women*, p. 191.
25   McKibbin, *Evolution of the Labour Party*, p. 82; *Diary of Beatrice Webb*, vol. 3, p.195.
26   Tanner, *Political Change and the Labour Party*, pp. 318, 345, 347.
27   Harris, *Private Lives, Public Spirit*, p. 195.
28   Meacham, *A Life Apart*, p. 202.
29   Marquand, *Ramsay MacDonald*, p. 169; Snowden, *An Autobiography*, vol. 1, pp. 358–9; *Diary of Beatrice Webb*, vol. 3, p. 214.
30   Quoted in Marquand, *Ramsay MacDonald*, p. 189.
31   *H/C Deb.*, 12 January 1916, cols 1726–7, 18 April 1916, col. 2261.
32   Bullock, *Ernest Bevin*, vol. 1, p. 44
33   Morgan, *Labour People*, p. 82.
34   Leventhal, *Arthur Henderson*, p. 79.
35   Beer, *Modern British Politics*, p. 149.
36   Tudor Jones, "Labour's Constitution and Public Ownership", pp. 295, 300; Tomlinson, "Labour and the Economy", p. 52.
37   Tanner, *Political Change and the Labour Party*, p. 357.
38   McKibbin, Matthew, Kay, "The Franchise Factor in the Rise of the Labour Party", p. 88.
39   Craig (ed.), *British General Election Manifestos*, pp. 31–2. Quotations from election manifestos before 1955 are drawn from this source; in and after 1955 from the manifestos themselves.
40   *Diary of Beatrice Webb*, vol. 3, p. 329; MacDonald quoted in Marquand, *Ramsay MacDonald*, p. 236.
41   *The Times*, 11 December 1918.

3   LABOUR BETWEEN TWO WARS, 1918–1939

1   MacDonald, *Socialism: critical and constructive*, pp. 275, 280–1.
2   Williamson, *National Crisis and National Government*, p. 523.
3   Hamilton, *Arthur Henderson*, p. 180; Henderson, *Labour's Way to Peace*, p. 102.

4 *Diary of Beatrice Webb*, vol. 3, pp. 352–3.
5 Shinwell, *Conflict without Malice*, p. 84; *Diary of Beatrice Webb*, vol. 3, p. 408.
6 Griffiths (ed.), *What is Socialism?*, pp. 48, 55, 77.
7 Quoted in Cline, *Recruits to Labour* pp. 32, 50.
8 Lewis, *Private Life of a Country House*, pp. 86–7.
9 Woolf, "Mr. Bennett and Mrs. Brown", p. 320.
10 *Labour Party Annual Conference Report*, June 1918, p. 35; 1919, p. 136.
11 *Labour Party Annual Conference Report*, June 1918, p. 35.
12 Shinwell, *Conflict without Malice*, p. 80.
13 Kirkwood, *My Life of Revolt*, p. 268.
14 Forester, *Labour Party and the Working Class*, p. 64.
15 *Diary of Beatrice Webb*, vol. 3, p. 437.
16 McKibbin, *Ideologies of Class*, p. 285.
17 Gilbert, *British Social Policy 1914–1939*, p. 200.
18 *Labour Party Annual Conference Report*, 1928, pp. 236, 202–3, 216.
19 Wertheimer, *Portrait of the Labour Party*, pp. 175–7.
20 Wilkinson, *Peeps at Politicians*, p. 8.
21 Howell, *MacDonald's Party*, p. 4.
22 Low, *Low's Autobiography*, p. 285; G. D. H. Cole, "The Striker Stricken", p. 71.
23 McKibbin, *Ideologies of Class*, p. 208.
24 Bassett, *Nineteen Thirty-One*, p. 347; Wilson, "Ramsay MacDonald", *Tribune*, 21 October 1966; Marquand, *MacDonald*, p. 639; Morgan, *Labour People*, p. 48; Williamson, *National Crisis and National Government*, p. 523.
25 Laybourn, *Rise of Labour*, p. 81; Howell, *MacDonald's Party*, p. 9.
26 G. Thomas, *Autobiography*, p. 189; Martin in *New Statesman*, 13 November 1937, reprinted in Martin, *Critic's London* Diary, p. 58; Mary Agnes Hamilton, *Remembering my Good Friends*, pp. 130, 123; Lawrence, "Labour – the myths it has lived by", p. 351.
27 Williamson, *National Crisis and National Government*, p. 103.
28 Quoted in Dalton, *Call Back Yesterday*, p. 298. The comment has also been attributed to Thomas Johnston , another former minister.
29 Thorpe, *British General Election of 1931*, pp. 214, 231; Snowden, *An Autobiography*, vol. 2, p. 995.
30 Thorpe, *British General Election of 1931*, p. 254.
31 *Holmes-Laski Letters*, vol. 2, pp. 1334–5.
32 Martin, *Editor*, p. 49.
33 Citrine, *Men and Work* , p. 300.
34 H. Thomas, *John Strachey*, p. 145; Margaret Cole, *Life of G. D. H. Cole*, pp. 172–3; Susan Lowry, *International Herald Tribune*, 26 November 1987; Mitchison, *You May Well Ask*, p. 182.
35 *Labour Party Annual Conference Report*, 1937, p. 160 and quoted in secondary sources.
36 Foote, *Labour Party's Political Thought*, ch. 8.
37 Wrigley, *Arthur Henderson*, p. 185.
38 *Labour Party Annual Conference Report*, 1933, p. 159.
39 Pollard, *Development of the British Economy*, p. 152.

40 Quoted in Barry, *Nationalization in British Politics*, pp. 332, 349.
41 Lyman, "The British Labour Party", p. 147.
42 Martin in *New Statesman*, 5 October 1935, reprinted in Martin, *Critic's London Diary*, p. 23.
43 *Diary of Beatrice Webb*, vol. 4, p. 359.
44 G. D. H. and Margaret Cole, *Condition of Britain*, pp. 419, 449; Laski, "The General Election, 1935", p. 4.
45 G. D. H. Cole, *The People's Front*, pp. 65, 87; Cole and Cole, *Condition of Britain*, p. 411.
46 Attlee, *The Labour Party in Perspective*, p. 136.
47 Dalton, *Practical Socialism for Britain* , p. 140.
48 Wilkinson, *The Town that was Murdered*, pp. 205–6.
49 Dalton, *The Fateful Years*, p. 100.
50 Cole, *The People's Front*, p. 275; Thorpe, *British General Election of 1931*, p. 273.

4   LABOUR IN WAR AND PEACE, 1939–1951

1 Nicolson, *Diaries and Letters 1930–1939*, p. 415.
2 Addison, *Road to 1945*, p. 188; Mass-Observation, "Social Security and Parliament", p. 245; newspaper advertisement for clothes rationing starting 1 June 1941, author's collection.
3 Griffiths, *Pages from Memory*, p. 70; J. Beveridge, *Beveridge and his Plan*, p. 119.
4 Ede, *Labour and the Wartime Coalition*, p. 126.
5 *Ibid.*, p. 111.
6 *Labour Party Annual Conference Report*, 1944, p. 163; Donoughue and Jones, *Herbert Morrison*, p. 331.
7 *Labour Party Annual Conference Report*, 1945, p. 90.
8 Thorpe, *History of the British Labour Party*, p. 112.
9 Nicolson, *Diaries and Letters 1939–1945*, p. 479.
10 Jefferys, *The Churchill Coalition and Wartime Politics*, pp. 201, 202, 204.
11 Eatwell, *The 1945–1951 Labour Governments*, p. 43; McKibbin, *Classes and Cultures*, p. 533.
12 Davenport, *Memoirs of a City Radical*, p. 145; Brooke, *Labour's War*, p. 244.
13 Davenport, *Memoirs of a City Radical*, p. 179.
14 Nicolson in *The Spectator*, 17 August 1945, reprinted in Nicolson, *Comments*, p. 112.
15 Morrison, *Herbert Morrison*, p. 251.
16 Henry Williams in *New Statesman*, 6 September 1947, quoted in D. Martin and Rubinstein (eds), *Ideology and the Labour Movement*, p. 13.
17 Tiratsoo, "Labour and the Electorate", p. 289.
18 Fielding, Thompson, Tiratsoo, *"England Arise!"*, p 121.
19 Cairncross, *Years of Recovery*, p. 509.
20 Cronin, *Labour and Society*, p. 131.
21 Brady, *Crisis in Britain*, p. 338.
22 Dell, *A Strange Eventful History*, p. 162.

23 Hinton, *Labour and Socialism*, p. 169.
24 Dalton, *High Tide and After*, p. 85.
25 Nehru, *Discovery of India*, p. 293.
26 Tharoor, *Nehru*, p. 161.
27 *Labour Party Annual Conference Report*, 1947, p. 137.
28 Nicolson, *Diaries and Letters 1945–1962*, p. 103; quoted in Clarke, *The Cripps Version*, p. 503.
29 Labour Party, *Labour Believes in Britain*, pp. 5, 10 13, 30; *Labour Party Annual Conference Report*, 1949, pp. 155, 211.
30 Dalton, *High Tide and After*, pp. 297, 299.
31 Crossman, "The Lessons of 1945", p. 151.
32 Dalton, *High Tide and After*, p. 339.
33 Cairncross, *Years of Recovery*, p. 504.
34 Quoted in Williams, *Hugh Gaitskell*, p. 268.
35 Quoted in Harris, *Attlee*, p. 485.
36 Quoted in Zweiniger-Bargielowska, *Austerity in Britain*, p. 229.
37 Dell, *A Strange Eventful History*, p. 210.
38 Morgan, *The People's Peace*, p. 105.
39 Foot, *Bevan 1945–1960*, p. 347.
40 Beckett, *Clem Attlee*, p. 265; Attlee, *As It Happened*, p. 166.

5   YEARS OF STRIFE, 1951–1964

1 Gaitskell, *Recent Developments*, p. 39; Haseler, *The Gaitskellites*, p. 214.
2 R. Jenkins, "Leader of the Opposition", p. 119.
3 Bevan, *In Place of Fear*, p. 168.
4 R. Jenkins, *A Life at the Centre*, p. 88; Foote, *Labour Party's Political Thought*, p. 273; Crossman, *Backbench Diaries*, p. 52.
5 Campbell, *Nye Bevan*, p. 273.
6 Wyatt, *Confessions of an Optimist*, p. 210.
7 Mikardo, *Back-Bencher*, p. 151.
8 Campbell, *Nye Bevan*, pp. 264, 213.
9 Perkins, *Red Queen*, p. 115.
10 Duff, *Left, Left, Left*, p. 43; Mikardo, *Back-Bencher*, p. 123.
11 M. Jenkins, *Bevanism*, p. 295.
12 Healey, *Time of My Life*, pp. 151–2.
13 Cronin, *Labour and Society*, p. 176; Bevan, *In Place of Fear*, pp. 31, 32, 115, 118.
14 Griffiths, *Pages from Memory*, p. 123.
15 Morrison, *Herbert Morrison*, p. 306; Dalton, *Political Diary*, p. 599; Jay, *Change and Fortune*, p. 223; Griffiths, *Pages from Memory*, p. 123.
16 Mikardo, *Back-Bencher*, p. 129; Summerskill, *A Woman's World*, p. 154.
17 M. Foot, *Aneurin Bevan 1945–1960*, p. 361.
18 Crossman, *Backbench Diaries*, pp. 348–50; *Labour Party Annual Conference Report*, 1954, p. 94.
19 Mikardo, *Back-Bencher*, p. 152; Wigg, *George Wigg*, p. 123.
20 Hunter, *Road to Brighton Pier*, p. 109.
21 Quoted in Harris, *Attlee*, p. 532.

22 Dalton, *Political Diary*, p. 671; Harris, *Attlee*, p. 534; Hopkins, *The New Look*, p. 358.
23 M. Foot, *Aneurin Bevan 1945–1960*, p. 491.
24 Howell, *Made in Birmingham*, p. 103.
25 Crossman, *Backbench Diaries*, p. 458.
26 Dalton, *High Tide and After*, p. 267.
27 *The Guardian*, 21 February 1977; Gordon Brown, "Equality – Then and Now", p. 35.
28 *Labour Party Annual Conference Report*, 1957, pp. 128, 157.
29 Williams, *Hugh Gaitskell*, p. 507.
30 *Labour Party Annual Conference Report*, 1957, p. 181.
31 Quoted in Hollis, *Jennie Lee*, p. 193.
32 Crossman, *Backbench Diaries*, p. 614,
33 Labour Party, *The Future Labour Offers You*, unpaginated.
34 Bédarida, *Social History of England*, p. 281.
35 R. Jenkins, *Labour Case*, pp. 11–12; R. Jenkins, "Leader of the Opposition", p. 119.
36 Quoted in Brivati, *Hugh Gaitskell*, p. 325.
37 Gordon Walker, *Patrick Gordon Walker*, p. 258.
38 Williams, *Hugh Gaitskell*, p. 549; Stewart, *Life and Labour*, p. 110.
39 Campbell, *Nye Bevan*, p. 361.
40 *Labour Party Annual Conference Report*, 1959, p. 152.
41 Campbell, *Nye Bevan*, p. 377; Butler, *Art of Memory*, p. 79.
42 *Labour Party Annual Conference Report*, 1960. p. 201; Williams, *Hugh Gaitskell*, p. 929.
43 Brivati, *Hugh Gaitskell*, p. 413.
44 Brown, *In My Way, p.* 218.
45 *The Times, Daily Telegraph, The Guardian*, 19 January 1963; *The Listener* (quoting Harold Macmillan), 24 January 1963; *Tribune, New Statesman*, 25 January 1963; Douglas Jay, "Civil Servant and Minister", p. 103.
46 R. Jenkins, *A Life at the Centre*, p. 148; M. Foot, *Loyalists and Loners*, p. 85; Callaghan, *Time and Chance*, p. 150; Brown, *In My Way*, p. 83.
47 *The Times*, 13 March 2001.
48 Quoted in Pimlott, *Harold Wilson*, p. 267.
49 *Ibid.*, p. 299; Haseler, *The Gaitskellites*, p. 244.
50 *Labour Party Annual Conference Report*, 1963, pp. 139–40; P. Foot, *Politics of Harold Wilson*, p. 152.

6   PROGRESS AND DECLINE, 1964–1979

1 Brivati, *Hugh Gaitskell*, p. 13.
2 Pimlott, *Harold Wilson*, p. 266.
3 Jenkins, *A Life at the Centre*; p. 155.
4 Brown, *In My Way*, p. 99.
5 Jay, *Change and Fortune*, pp. 297–8.
6 Gordon Walker, *Political Diaries*, pp. 43–4.
7 Crossman, *Diaries of a Cabinet Minister* 1, p. 134; Benn, *Out of the Wilderness*, p. 207.

8 Ponting, *Breach of Promise*, p. 26.
9 Wilson, *Labour Government*, p. 18. "A hundred days" was a well-worn term originally associated with Napoleon.
10 Crossman, *Diaries*, 1, p. 289.
11 *Ibid.*, p. 159.
12 Heath, *Course of My Life*, p. 278.
13 Pimlott, *Harold Wilson*, p. 399.
14 Crossman, *Diaries*, 1, pp. 488–9.
15 Morgan, *Labour People*, p. 257.
16 Wilson, *Labour Government*, p. 790.
17 Morgan, *Labour People*, p. 257; Benn, *Out of the Wilderness*, pp. 397, 399.
18 Crossman, *Diaries*, 3, p. 459; Shore, *Leading the Left*, pp. 110–11; Ziegler (quoting Rusk), *Wilson*, p. 221.
19 Crossman, *Diaries*, 2, p. 714. See also vol. 3, p. 458.
20 Wilson quoted in Pimlott, *Harold Wilson*, p. 377; Healey, *Time of My Life*, p. 332.
21 *Labour Party Annual Conference Report*, 1967, p. 223; Wilson, *Labour Government*, p. 445; Shore, *Leading the Left*, p. 95.
22 Wilson, *Labour Government*, pp. 199, 236.
23 Castle, *Fighting All the Way*, p. 416; Callaghan, *Time and Chance*, p. 274.
24 *Ibid.*, p. 277.
25 *Ibid.*, pp. 218–19.
26 Pimlott, *Harold Wilson*, p. 483; Wilson, *Labour Government*, pp. 464.
27 Ponting, *Breach of Promise*, p. 309; Cairncross, *Managing the British Economy in the 1960s*, pp. 202, 238.
28 McKibbin, "Homage to Wilson and Callaghan", p. 5; Jefferys, *Labour Party since 1945*, p. 78; Pimlott, *Harold Wilson*, p. 554; Healey, *Time of My Life*, p. 345; Ponting, *Breach of Promise*, p. 400.
29 Brown, *In My Way*, p. 261; Pimlott, *Harold Wilson*, p. 555.
30 Ponting, *Breach of Promise*, p. 404.
31 Hattersley, *Who Goes Home?*, p. 109.
32 Quoted in Foote, *Labour Party's Political Thought*, p. 307.
33 *Labour Party Annual Conference Report*, 1973, p. 129; Healey, *Time of My Life*, p. 369.
34 Benn (quoting Wilson), *Against the Tide*, p. 38.
35 Pimlott, *Harold Wilson*, p. 610; Benn, *Against the Tide*, p. 107.
36 Pimlott, *Harold Wilson*, p. 613; Hattersley, *Who Goes Home?*, p. 126; Jenkins, *A Life at the Centre*, p. 364.
37 *Ibid.*, p. 424.
38 Healey, *Time of My Life* p. 446; Pimlott, *Harold Wilson*, p, 652; *The Guardian*, 25 May 1995.
39 Radice, *Friends and Rivals*, p. 239; Morgan, *Callaghan*, p. 475.
40 Jenkins, *A Life at the Centre*, p. 427.
41 Healey, *Time of My Life*, p. 373.
42 *Labour Party Annual Conference Report*, 1976, p. 319; Benn, *Against the Tide*, p. 616.
43 Dell, *A Hard Pounding*, p. 79.

44 *Labour Party Annual Conference Report*, 1976, p.188; Shaw, *Labour Party since 1945*, p. 134.
45 Callaghan, *Time and Chance*, pp. 410–11; Morgan, *Callaghan*, p. 541.
46 Callaghan, *Time and Chance*, p. 563.
47 Ibid., p. 564; Shaw, *Labour Party since 1945*, p. 158; Elliott, *Labourism and the English Genius*, p. 93.
48 Morgan, *Callaghan*, p. 691; Butler and Kavanagh, *British General Election of 1979*, p. 5.

7 STRIFE AND AFTER, 1979–1994

1 Callaghan, *Time and Chance*, p. 565.
2 Hobsbawm, "The Debate on 'The Forward March of Labour Halted?'", pp. 37–8.
3 Anderson, "The Age of EJH", p. 7.
4 Benn, *End of an Era*, p. 32; M. Jones, *Michael Foot*, p. 453.
5 Healey, *Time of My Life*, p. 481.
6 Castle, *Fighting All the Way*, p. 528; Foot, *My Kind of Socialism*, unpaginated.
7 Foot, *Loyalists and Loners*, pp. 122–3.
8 Morgan, *Labour People*, pp. 311–12; Hobsbawm, *Interesting Times*, p. 271; P. Jenkins, *Mrs Thatcher's Revolution*, p. 125.
9 Healey, *Time of My Life*, p. 483; Benn, *End of an Era*, p.154.
10 Hattersley, *Who Goes Home?*, p. 232.
11 Owen, *Time to Declare*, pp. 481–2; Bill Rodgers, *Fourth among Equals*, p. 210.
12 Healey, *Time of My Life*, p. 484; Hattersley, *Who Goes Home?*, p. 236.
13 Healey, *Time of My Life*, pp. 495–6, 499.
14 Shaw, "Michael Foot 1980–83", p. 167.
15 Benn, *End of an Era*, p. 233.
16 Healey, *Time of My Life*, p. 500.
17 Morgan, *Labour People*, p. 283.
18 Thorpe, *History of the British Labour Party*, pp. 211–12; Foot, *Another Heart*, p. 69.
19 Shaw, *Labour Party since 1979*, p. 14.
20 Benn, *End of an Era*, p. 296.
21 Hobsbawm, "Labour's Lost Millions", pp. 69–70.
22 Quoted in E. Jones, *Neil Kinnock*, pp. 44, 52.
23 Shore, *Leading the Left*, p. 155.
24 Hughes and Wintour, *Labour Rebuilt*, p. 6.
25 Benn, *End of an Era*, pp. 330–1; Morgan, *Labour People*, pp. 337, 339.
26 Gorz, *Farewell to the Working Class*, p. 69; quoted in P. Jenkins, *Mrs Thatcher's Revolution*, p. 236.
27 Kinnock, *Thorns & Roses*, pp. 129–30.
28 Kellner in Kinnock, *Thorns & Roses*, p. 1; Benn, *End of an Era*, p. 179.
29 Kinnock, *Thorns & Roses*, p. 91.
30 Hattersley, *Who Goes Home?*, pp. 274–5.
31 Shaw, *Discipline and Discord in the Labour Party*, p. 302.

32 Hattersley, *Who Goes Home?*, p. 270.
33 Howell, "'Where's Ramsay McKinnock?'" p. 197; Kinnock, *Thorns & Roses*, p. 98.
34 P. Jenkins, *Mrs Thatcher's Revolution*, p. 343.
35 Heffernan and Marqusee, *Defeat from the Jaws of Victory*, p. 96; Gould, *The Unfinished Revolution*, pp. 142, 148; Hughes and Wintour (quoting Sawyer), *Labour Rebuilt*, p. 103.
36 Mandelson quoted in Macintyre, *Mandelson*, p. 152; Blair quoted in Rentoul, *Tony Blair*, p. 140.
37 Owen, *Time to Declare*, p, 765; Rodgers, *Fourth among Equals*, p. 266.
38 E. Jones, *Neil Kinnock*, p. 127; Kellner in Kinnock, *Thorns & Roses*, p. 164.
39 Smith, "Continuity and Change in Labour Party Policy", p. 218.
40 Kinnock, *Thorns & Roses*, pp. 156–7.
41 *H/C. Deb.*, 20 November 1991, col. 283.
42 Shaw, *Labour Party since 1979*, pp. 41, 203.
43 *Ibid.*, pp. 122–3.
44 Elliott, *Labourism and the English Genius*, p. 162.
45 Quoted in McSmith, *John Smith*, p. 252.
46 Hare, *Asking Around*, pp. 162–3, 183.
47 E. Jones, *Neil Kinnock*, pp. 178, 190; Castle, *Fighting All the Way*, p. 590.
48 Hattersley, *Who Goes Home?*, pp. 307; Heffernan and Marqusee, *Defeat from the Jaws of Victory*, p. 319.
49 *The Guardian*, 13 May 1994; *Labour Party Annual Conference Report*, 1993, pp. 94, 100; Brivati (ed.), *Guiding Light*, pp. 168, 170.
50 Macintyre, *Mandelson*, title of ch. 14; Smith quoted in ibid., p. 241.
51 Shore, *Leading the Left*, p. 180; Gould, *The Unfinished Revolution*, p. 161.

8 NEW LABOUR, 1994–2005

1 Quoted in Williams, *Hugh Gaitskell*, p. 562.
2 *Labour Party Annual Conference Report*, 1996, p. 80.
3 Mandelson and Liddle, *The Blair Revolution*, pp. 21, 215.
4 Gould, *The Unfinished Revolution*, pp. 84, 396; Blair, *New Britain*, p. 221.
5 Quoted in Gould, *The Unfinished Revolution*, p. 284.
6 Seldon, *Blair*, p. 216.
7 *The Guardian*, 29 June 1991; quotation from Rentoul, *Tony Blair*, p. 369.
8 Quoted in Rentoul, *Tony Blair*, p. 115; *The Guardian*, 29 June 1991.
9 Scott, *Off Whitehall*, p. 244.
10 Cook, *Point of Departure*, p. 249.
11 Blair, *New Britain*, pp. 211, 293; Driver and Martell, *New Labour*, p. 174; Giddens, *The Third Way and its Critics*, p. 39.
12 Seldon, *Blair*, p. 119.
13 Rentoul, *Tony Blair*, p. 254.
14 Quoted in Sopel, *Tony Blair*, pp. 294–5.
15 Rentoul, *Tony Blair*, p. 286.
16 Fielding, *The Labour Party*, p. 8.
17 Gould, *The Unfinished Revolution*, p. 360.
18 Scott, *Off Whitehall*, p. 20.

19 Peston, *Brown's Britain*, p. 76; Keegan, *The Prudence of Mr Gordon Brown*, p. 234.
20 Scott, *Off Whitehall*, p. 30.
21 *H/C Deb.*, 16 March 2005, col. 270.
22 *The Times*, 6 November 2001.
23 Mandelson and Liddle, *The Blair Revolution*, pp. 23, 24, 153.
24 Seldon, *Blair*, p. 636.
25 *The Times*, 26 September 2002.
26 Keegan, *The Prudence of Mr Gordon Brown*, pp. 275–6.
27 Glennerster, "Social Policy", p. 388.
28 Palmer, North, Carr, Kenway, *Monitoring Poverty and Social Exclusion 2003*, p. 79.
29 *The Guardian*, 30 March 2005.
30 *The Times*, 15 January 2002.
31 Blair, "Beveridge Revisited", p. 17.
32 Lister, *Poverty*, p. 42.
33 Palmer, North, Carr, Kenway, *Monitoring Poverty and Social Exclusion 2003*, p. 10.
34 Joseph Rowntree Foundation, *Findings*, unpaginated.
35 *Financial Times*, 10 September 2004.
36 Naughtie, *The Accidental American*, p. 49.
37 Seldon, *Blair*, p. 571; Blair quoted in Naughtie, *The Accidental American*, p. 136.
38 *The Guardian*, 14 April 2005.
39 *The Independent*, 7 May 2005.
40 Quoted in *The Guardian*, 24 March 2005.

BIBLIOGRAPHY

Addison, Paul, *The Road to 1945: British politics and the second world war* (London: Cape, 1975).

Anderson, Perry, "The Age of EJH", *London Review of Books*, 3 October 2002.

Attlee, Clement, *The Labour Party in Perspective* (London: Gollancz, 1937).

——, *As It Happened* (London: Heinemann, 1954).

Bagwell, Philip, *The Railwaymen: the history of the National Union of Railwaymen* (London: Allen & Unwin, 1963).

Barker, Bernard (ed.), *Ramsay MacDonald's Political Writings* (London: Allen Lane the Penguin Press, 1972).

Barnett, Correlli, *The Audit of War: the illusion and reality of Britain as a great nation*, 3rd edn (London: Pan, 1996).

——, *The Lost Victory: British dreams, British realities 1945–1950*, 2nd edn (London: Pan, 1996).

Barry, E. Eldon, *Nationalization in British Politics: the historical background* (London: Cape, 1965).

Bassett, Reginald, *Nineteen Thirty-One: political crisis* (London: Macmillan, 1958).

Bealey, Frank and Pelling, Henry, *Labour and Politics 1900–1906: a history of the Labour Representation Committee* (London: Macmillan, 1958).

Beckett, Francis, *Clem Attlee*, 2nd edn (London: Politico's, 2000).

Bédarida, François, *A Social History of England 1851–1975*, English edn (London: Methuen, 1979).

Beer, Samuel H., *Modern British Politics: a study of parties and pressure groups*, 2nd edn (London: Faber & Faber, 1969).

Bell, Florence, *At the Works: a study of a manufacturing town*, new edn (Newton Abbot: David & Charles, 1969).

Benn, Caroline, *Keir Hardie* (London: Hutchinson, 1992).

Benn, Tony, *Out of the Wilderness: diaries 1963–1967*, 2nd edn (London: Arrow, 1988).

——, *Against the Tide: diaries 1973–1976* (London: Hutchinson, 1989).

——, *Conflicts of Interest: diaries 1977–1980*, ed. Ruth Winstone (London: Hutchinson, 1990).

——, *The End of an Era: diaries 1980–1990*. 2nd edn, ed. Ruth Winstone (London: Arrow, 1994).

Bevan, Aneurin, *In Place of Fear* (London: Heinemann, 1952).

Beveridge, Janet, *Beveridge and his Plan* (London: Hodder and Stoughton, 1954).

Beveridge, William, *Social Insurance and Allied Services* (London: HMSO, 1942).

Blair, Tony, *New Britain: my vision of a young country*, 2nd edn (Boulder, Colorado: Westview Press, 1997).

——, "Beveridge Revisited: a welfare state for the 21st century" in Robert Walker (ed.), *Ending Child Poverty: popular welfare for the 21st century* (Bristol: Policy Press, 1999).

Blatchford, Robert, *Merrie England* (London: Clarion, 1894).

Blewett, Neal, *The Peers, the Parties and the People: the general elections of 1910* (London and Basingstoke: Macmillan, 1972).

Booth, Charles, *Life and Labour. volume 1: East London* (London: Williams & Norgate, 1889).

Brady, Robert A., *Crisis in Britain: plans and achievements of the Labour Government* (Berkeley and Los Angeles: University of California Press, 1950).

Briggs, Asa, *Mass Entertainment: the origins of a modern industry* (Adelaide: Griffin Press, 1960).

Brivati, Brian, *Hugh Gaitskell*, 2nd edn (London: Cohen, 1997).

—— (ed.), *Guiding Light: the collected speeches of John Smith* (London: Politico's, 2000).

Brooke, Stephen, *Labour's War: the Labour Party during the second world war* (Oxford: Clarendon Press, 1992).

Brown, George, *In My Way: the political memoirs of Lord George-Brown* (London: Gollancz, 1971).

Brown, Gordon, "Equality – Then and Now", in Dick Leonard (ed.), *Crosland and New Labour* (Basingstoke: Macmillan, 1999).

Bullock, Alan, *The Life and Times of Ernest Bevin: vol. 1, trade union leader 1881–1940* (London: Heinemann, 1960).

Burgess, Joseph, *John Burns: the rise and progress of a right honourable*, 3rd edn (Glasgow: Reformers' Bookstall, 1911).

Butler, David and Kavanagh, Dennis, *The British General Election of 1979* (London: Macmillan, 1980).

Butler, Richard Austen, *The Art of Memory: friends in perspective* (London: Hodder & Stoughton, 1982).

Cairncross, Alec, *Years of Recovery: British economic policy 1945–51* (London: Methuen, 1985).

——, *Managing the British Economy in the 1960s: a treasury perspective* (Basingstoke: Macmillan and St Antony's College, Oxford, 1996).

Callaghan, James, *Time and Chance*, 2nd edn (London: Fontana, 1988).

Campbell, John, *Nye Bevan and the Mirage of British Socialism* (London: Weidenfeld & Nicolson, 1987).

Cannadine, David, *Class in Britain* (New Haven and London: Yale University Press, 1998).

Castle, Barbara, *Fighting All the Way* (London: Macmillan, 1993).

Chesterton, G. K., *Autobiography* (London: Hutchinson, 1936).

Citrine, Walter, *Men and Work: an autobiography* (London: Hutchinson, 1964).

Clarke, Peter, *The Cripps Version: the life of Sir Stafford Cripps 1889–1952* (London: Allen Lane, 2002).

Cline, Catherine Ann, *Recruits to Labour: the British Labour Party 1914–1931* (Syracuse, New York: Syracuse University Press, 1963).

Cole, G. D. H., *The People's Front* (London: Gollancz, 1937).

——, *British Working Class Politics 1832–1914* (London: Routledge & Kegan Paul, 1941).

——, "The Striker Stricken: an operetta", in Asa Briggs and John Saville (eds), *Essays in Labour History 1918–1939* (London: Croom Helm, 1977).

Cole, G. D. H. and Margaret, *The Condition of Britain* (London: Gollancz, 1937).

Cole, Margaret, *The Story of Fabian Socialism* (London: Heinemann, 1961).

——, *The Life of G.D.H. Cole* (London and Basingstoke: Macmillan, 1971).

Commission on Social Justice, *Social Justice: strategies for national renewal* (London: Vintage, 1994).

Cook, Robin, *The Point of Departure: diaries from the front bench*, 2nd edn (London: Pocket Books, 2004).

Craig, F. W. S. (compiler and editor), *British General Election Manifestos 1900–1974*, 2nd edn (London and Basingstoke: Macmillan, 1975).

Cronin, James, *Labour and Society in Britain 1918–1979* (London: Batsford, 1984).

Crosland, Anthony, *The Future of Socialism* (London: Cape, 1956).

Crossman, Richard (ed.), *New Fabian Essays* (London: Turnstile Press, 1952).

—— (author), "The Lessons of 1945", in Perry Anderson and Robin Blackburn (eds), *Towards Socialism* ([London]: Fontana, 1965).

——, *The Diaries of a Cabinet Minister 1, 1964–1966* (London: Hamilton and Cape, 1975).

——, *The Diaries of a Cabinet Minister 2, 1966–1968*, ed. Janet Morgan (London: Hamilton and Cape, 1976).

——, *The Diaries of a Cabinet Minister 3, 1968–1970*, ed. Janet Morgan (London: Hamilton and Cape, 1977).

——, *The Backbench Diaries of Richard Crossman*, ed. Janet Morgan (London: Hamilton and Cape, 1981).

Dalton, Hugh, *Practical Socialism for Britain* (London: Routledge & Sons, 1935).

——, *Call Back Yesterday: memoirs 1887–1931* (London: Muller, 1953).

——, *The Fateful Years: memoirs 1931–1945* (London: Muller, 1957).

——, *High Tide and After: memoirs 1945–1960* (London: Muller,1962).

——, *The Political Diary of Hugh Dalton, 1918–40, 1945–60*, ed. Ben Pimlott (London: Cape and London School of Economics, 1986).

Dangerfield, George, *The Strange Death of Liberal England* (New York: Smith & Haas, 1935).

Davenport, Nicholas, *Memoirs of a City Radical* (London: Weidenfeld & Nicolson, 1974).

Davies, A. J., *To Build a New Jerusalem: the British Labour Party from Keir Hardie to Tony Blair*, 2nd edn (London: Abacus, 1996).

Dell, Edmund, *A Hard Pounding: politics and economic crisis 1974–1976* (Oxford: Oxford University Press, 1991).

——, *A Strange Eventful History: democratic socialism in Britain* (London: HarperCollins, 2000).

Donoughue, Bernard, *Prime Minister: the conduct of policy under Harold Wilson and James Callaghan* (London: Cape, 1987).

Donoughue, Bernard and Jones, G. W., *Herbert Morrison: portrait of a politician* (London: Weidenfeld & Nicolson, 1973).

Driver, Stephen and Martell, Luke, *New Labour: politics after Thatcherism* (Cambridge: Polity Press, 1998).

Duff, Peggy, *Left, Left, Left: a personal account of six protest campaigns 1945–1965* (London: Alison & Busby, 1971).

Durbin, Evan, *The Politics of Democratic Socialism: an essay on social policy* (London: Routledge, 1940).

Eatwell, Roger, *The 1945–1951 Labour Governments* (London: Batsford, 1979).

Economist, The, "Labour's Economic Claims: Boasters", 15 January 2005.

Ede, James Chuter, *Labour and the Wartime Coalition: from the diary of James Chuter Ede 1941–1945*, ed. Kevin Jefferys (London: Historians' Press, 1987).

Elliott, Gregory, *Labourism and the English Genius: the strange death of Labour England?* (London: Verso, 1993).

Fielding, Steven, "Don't Know and Don't Care: popular political attitudes in Labour's Britain, 1945–51", in Nick Tiratsoo (ed.). *The Attlee Years* (London: Pinter, 1991).

——, *The Labour Party: continuity and change in the making of "New" Labour* (Basingstoke: Palgrave Macmillan, 2003).

Fielding, Steven; Thompson, Peter; Tiratsoo, Nick, *"England Arise!": the Labour Party and popular politics in 1940s Britain* (Manchester: Manchester University Press, 1995).

Foot, Michael, *Aneurin Bevan 1945–1960*, 2nd edn (St Albans: Paladin, 1975).

——, *My Kind of Socialism* (London: *The Observer*, 1982).

——, *Loyalists and Loners* (London: Collins, 1986).

——, *Another Heart and other Pulses: the alternative to the Thatcher society* (London: Collins, 1994).

Foot, Paul, *The Politics of Harold Wilson* (Harmondsworth: Penguin, 1968).

Foote, Geoffrey, *The Labour Party's Political Thought: a history*, 3rd edn (Basingstoke and London: Macmillan, 1997).

Forester, Tom, *The Labour Party and the Working Class* (London: Heinemann, 1976).

Francis, Martin, *Ideas and Policies under Labour, 1945–1951: building a new Britain* (Manchester: Manchester University Press, 1997).

Fraser, W. Hamish, *The Coming of the Mass Market, 1850–1914* (London and Basingstoke: Macmillan, 1981).

Gaitskell, Hugh, *Recent Developments in British Socialist Thinking* (London: Co-operative Union [1956]).

Giddens, Anthony, *The Third Way and its Critics* (Cambridge: Polity Press, 2000).

Gilbert, Bentley B., *British Social Policy 1914–1939* (London: Batsford, 1970).

Glennerster, Howard, "Social Policy" in Anthony Seldon (ed.), *The Blair Effect: the Blair government 1997–2001* (London: Little, Brown, 2001).

Gordon Walker, Patrick, *Patrick Gordon Walker: political diaries 1932–1971*, ed. Robert Pearce (London: Historians' Press, 1991).

Gorz, André, *Farewell to the Working Class*, English edn (London: Pluto, 1982).

Gould, Philip, *The Unfinished Revolution: how the modernizers saved the Labour Party* (London: Little, Brown, 1998).

Griffiths, Dan (ed.), *What is Socialism? a symposium* (London: Richards, 1924).

Griffiths, James, *Pages from Memory* (London: Dent, 1969).

Gwynn, Stephen and Tuckwell, Gertrude, *The Life of the Rt Hon. Sir Charles Dilke, Bart, M.P.*, vol. 2 (London: Murray, 1917).

Halévy, Elie, *A History of the English People: epilogue vol. 1, 1895–1905*, 2nd English edn (Harmondsworth: Penguin, 1939), three volumes.

——, *A History of the English People: epilogue vol. 2, 1905–1915*, English edn (London: Benn, 1934).

Hamilton, Mary Agnes, *Arthur Henderson: a biography* (London: Heinemann, 1938).

——, *Remembering my Good Friends* (London: Cape, 1944).

Hammond, J. L., *C. P. Scott of the Manchester Guardian* (London: Bell & Sons, 1934).

Hare, David, *Asking Around: background to the David Hare trilogy*, ed. Lyn Haill (London: Faber & Faber. 1993).

Harris, Jose, *Private Lives, Public Spirit: Britain 1870–1914*, 2nd edn (London: Penguin, 1994).

Harris, Kenneth, *Attlee* (London: Weidenfeld & Nicolson, 1982).

Harrison, Martin, *Trade Unions and the Labour Party since 1945* (London: Allen & Unwin, 1960).

Haseler, Stephen, *The Gaitskellites: revisionism in the British Labour Party 1951–64* (London: Macmillan, 1969).

Hattersley, Roy, *Who Goes Home? scenes from a political life* (London: Little, Brown, 1995).

H/C Deb. (House of Commons debates) 1900–2005.

Healey, Denis, *The Time of My Life*, 2nd edn (London: Penguin, 1990).

Heath, Anthony F.; Jowell, Roger M.; Curtice, John K., *The Rise of New Labour: party policies and voter choices* (Oxford: Oxford University Press, 2001).

Heath, Edward, *The Course of My Life: my autobiography* (London: Hodder and Stoughton, 1998).

Heffernan, Richard and Marqusee, Mike, *Defeat from the Jaws of Victory: inside Kinnock's Labour Party* (London: Verso, 1992).

Henderson, Arthur, *Labour's Way to Peace* (London: Methuen, 1935).

Hinton, James, *Labour and Socialism: a history of the British labour movement 1867–1974* (Brighton: Wheatsheaf, 1983).

Hobsbawm, Eric (ed.), *Labour's Turning Point 1880–1900*, 2nd ed. (Hassocks: Harvester, 1974).

——, (author) "The Forward March of Labour Halted?" (1978).

——, "The Debate on 'The Forward March of Labour Halted?'" (1981).

——, "Labour's Lost Millions" (1983).

——, All reprinted in *Politics for a Rational Left: political writing 1977–1988* (London: Verso, 1989).

——, *Interesting Times: a twentieth-century life* (London: Allen Lane, 2002).

Hollis, Patricia, *Jennie Lee: a life* (Oxford: Oxford University Press, 1997).

Holmes, Oliver Wendell and Laski, Harold J., *Holmes-Laski Letters: the correspondence of Mr Justice Holmes and Harold J. Laski 1916–1935*, vol. 2, ed.

Mark DeWolfe Howe (Cambridge, Massachusetts: Harvard University Press, 1953).

Hopkins, Harry, *The New Look: a social history of the forties and fifties in Britain* (London: Secker and Warburg, 1963).

Howard, Christopher, "Expectations born to Death: local Labour Party expansion in the 1920s", in Jay Winter (ed.), *The Working Class in Modern British History: essays in honour of Henry Pelling* (Cambridge: Cambridge University Press, 1983).

Howell, David, *British Workers and the Independent Labour Party 1888–1906* (Manchester: Manchester University Press, 1983).

——, "'Where's Ramsay McKinnock?' Labour leadership and the miners", in Hugh Beynon (ed.), *Digging Deeper: issues in the miners' strike* (London: Verso,1985).

——, *MacDonald's Party: Labour identities and crisis 1922–1931* (Oxford: Oxford University Press, 2002).

Howell, Denis, *Made in Birmingham: the memoirs of Denis Howell* (London: Queen Anne Press, 1990).

Howell, George, *Trade Unionism New and Old*, 3rd edn (London: Methuen, 1900).

Hughes, Colin and Wintour, Patrick, *Labour Rebuilt: the new model party* (London: Fourth Estate, 1990).

Hunter, Leslie, *The Road to Brighton Pier* (London: Barker, 1959).

Hyndman, Henry Mayers, *The Record of An Adventurous Life* (London: Macmillan, 1911).

——, *Further Reminiscences* (London: Macmillan, 1912).

Jay, Douglas, "Civil Servant and Minister", in W. T. Rodgers (ed.), *Hugh Gaitskell 1906–1963* (London: Thames & Hudson, 1964).

——, *Change and Fortune: a political record* (London: Hutchinson, 1980).

Jefferys, Kevin, *The Churchill Coalition and Wartime Politics 1940–1945* (Manchester: Manchester University Press, 1991).

——, *The Labour Party since 1945* (Basingstoke: Macmillan, 1993).

Jenkins, Mark, *Bevanism: Labour's high tide* (Nottingham: Spokesman, 1979).

Jenkins, Peter, *Mrs Thatcher's Revolution: the ending of the socialist era* (London: Cape, 1987).

Jenkins, Roy, *The Labour Case* (Harmondsworth: Penguin, 1959).

——, "Leader of the Opposition", in W. T. Rodgers (ed.) *Hugh Gaitskell 1906–1963* (London: Thames & Hudson, 1964).

——, *A Life at the Centre*, 2nd edn (London: Macmillan, 1994).

Johnson, Graham, "Social Democracy and Labour Politics in Britain, 1892–1911", *History*, 85 (2000).

——, *Social Democratic Politics in Britain 1881–1911* (Lewiston, New York: Mellen Press, 2002).

Jones, Eileen, *Neil Kinnock* (London: Hale, 1994).

Jones, Mervyn, *Michael Foot* (London: Gollancz, 1994).

Jones, Tudor, "Labour's Constitution and Public Ownership: from 'old' clause four to 'new' clause four", in Brian Brivati and Richard Heffernan (eds), *The Labour Party: a centenary history* (Basingstoke and London: Macmillan, 2000).

Joseph Rowntree Foundation, *Findings: monitoring poverty and social exclusion 2004* (York: Joseph Rowntree Foundation, 2004).

Keegan, William, *The Prudence of Mr Gordon Brown*, 2nd edn (Chichester: Wiley, 2004).

Kinnock, Neil, *Thorns & Roses: speeches, 1983–1991* (London: Hutchinson, 1992).

Kirkwood, David, *My Life of Revolt* (London: Harrap, 1935).

Labour Party (London):
——, *Annual Conference Reports* (1906 to present).
——, *For Socialism and Peace* (1934).
——, *Labour's Immediate Programme* (1937).
——, *Labour Believes in Britain* (1949).
——, *General Election Manifestos* (1955–2005).
——, *Industry and Society* (1957).
——, *The Future Labour Offers You* (1958).
——, *Labour's Programme 1973* (1973).
——, *Looking to the Future* (1990).

Labour Representation Committee, *Foundation Conference and Annual Conference Reports, 1900–1905* (London: Hammersmith Bookshop edn, 1967).

Lansbury, George, *My Life* (London: Constable, 1928).

Laski, Harold J., "The General Election, 1935", *Political Quarterly*, 7 (1935).

Lawrence, Jon, "Labour – the myths it has lived by", in Duncan Tanner, Pat Thane, Nick Tiratsoo (eds), *Labour's First Century* (Cambridge: Cambridge University Press, 2000).

Laybourn, Keith, *The Rise of Labour: the British Labour Party 1890–1979* (London: Arnold, 1988).

Leventhal, F. M., *Arthur Henderson* (Manchester: Manchester University Press, 1989).

Lewis, Lesley, *The Private Life of a Country House 1912–1939*, 2nd edn (Stroud: Sutton, 1992).

Lister, Ruth, *Poverty* (Cambridge: Polity Press, 2004).

Lloyd George, David, *Better Times: speeches* (London: Hodder & Stoughton, 1910).

Low, David, *Low's Autobiography* (London: Joseph, 1956).

Lyman, Richard, "The British Labour Party: the conflict between socialist ideals and practical politics between the wars", *Journal of British Studies*, 5 (1965).

Lyons, A. Neil, *Robert Blatchford: the sketch of a personality: an estimate of some achievements* (London: Clarion Press, 1910).

McCallum, R. B. and Readman, Alison, *The British General Election of 1945* (London: Oxford University Press, 1947).

MacDonald, J. Ramsay, *Socialism: critical and constructive* (London: Cassell, 1921).

——, *The Social Unrest: its cause and solution*, 2nd edn (Edinburgh and London: Foulis, 1924).

Macintyre, Donald, *Mandelson: the biography* (London: HarperCollins, 1999).

McKibbin, Ross, *The Evolution of the Labour Party 1910–1924* (London: Oxford University Press, 1974).

——, "Homage to Wilson and Callaghan", *London Review of Books*, 24 October 1981.

——, *The Ideologies of Class: social relations in Britain 1880–1950*, 2nd edn (Oxford: Oxford University Press, 1991).

——, *Classes and Cultures: England 1918–1951*, 2nd edn (Oxford: Oxford University Press, 2000).

McKibbin, Ross; Matthew, Colin; Kay, John, "The Franchise Factor in the Rise of the Labour Party"; in Ross McKibbin, *The Ideologies of Class: social relations in Britain 1880–1950*, 2nd edn (Oxford: Oxford University Press, 1991).

McSmith, Andy, *John Smith: a life 1939–1994*, revised edn (London: Mandarin, 1994).

Mandelson, Peter and Liddle, Roger, *The Blair Revolution: can New Labour deliver?* (London: Faber and Faber, 1996).

Mann, Tom, *Tom Mann's Memoirs*, 2nd edn (London: MacGibbon & Kee, 1967).

Marquand, David, *Ramsay MacDonald* (London: Cape, 1977).

Martin, David E., "'The Instruments of the People'?: the parliamentary Labour Party in 1906", in David E. Martin and David Rubinstein (eds), *Ideology and the Labour Movement: essays presented to John Saville* (London: Croom Helm, 1979).

Martin, David E. and Rubinstein David (eds), introduction to *ibid*.

Martin, Kingsley, *Critic's London Diary; from the New Statesman 1931–1956* (London: Secker & Warburg, 1960).

——, *Editor: a second volume of autobiography 1931–45* (London: Hutchinson, 1968).

Mason, Tony, *Association Football and English Society 1863–1915* (Brighton: Harvester Press, 1980).

Mass-Observation, "Social Security and Parliament", *Political Quarterly*, 14 (1943).

Mathias, Peter, *The First Industrial Nation: an economic history of Britain 1700–1914*, 2nd edn (London: Routledge, 1995).

Mayor, Stephen, *The Churches and the Labour Movement* (London: Independent Press, 1967).

Meacham, Standish, *A Life Apart: the English working class 1890–1914* (London: Thames and Hudson, 1977).

Mearns, Andrew, *The Bitter Cry of Outcast London*, in Anthony S. Wohl (ed.), *The Bitter Cry of Outcast London and other selections* (Leicester: Leicester University Press, 1970).

Mikardo, Ian, *Back-Bencher* (London: Weidenfeld & Nicolson, 1988).

Mitchison, Naomi, *You May Well Ask: a memoir 1920–1940*, 2nd edn (London: Fontana, 1986).

Morgan, Kenneth O., *Keir Hardie: radical and socialist* (London: Weidenfeld & Nicolson, 1975).

——, *Labour in Power 1945–1951* (Oxford: Oxford University Press, 1984).

——, *Labour People: Hardie to Kinnock*, 2nd edn (Oxford: Oxford University Press, 1992).

——, *Callaghan: a life* (Oxford: Oxford University Press, 1997).

——, *The People's Peace: British history since 1945*, 3rd edn (Oxford: Oxford University Press, 1999).

Morris, William, *News from Nowhere: or an epoch of rest being some chapters from a utopian romance*, reprint (London: Longmans, Green, 1934).

Morrison, Herbert, *Herbert Morrison: an autobiography* (London: Odhams, 1960).

Naughtie, James, *The Accidental American: Tony Blair and the presidency* (London, Basingstoke, Oxford: Macmillan, 2004).

Nehru, Jawaharlal, *The Discovery of India*, 23rd impression (New Delhi: Nehru Memorial Fund and Oxford University Press, 2003).

Nicolson, Harold, *Comments 1944–1948* (London: Constable, 1948).

——, *Diaries and Letters 1930–1939*, ed. Nigel Nicolson, 2nd edn ([London]: Fontana, 1969).

——, *Diaries and Letters 1939–1945*, ed. Nigel Nicolson (London: Collins, 1967).

——, *Diaries and Letters 1945–1962*, ed. Nigel Nicolson, 2nd edn ([London]: Fontana, 1971).

Owen, David, *Time to Declare* (London: Joseph, 1991).

Palmer, Guy; North, Jenny; Carr, Jane; Kenway, Peter, *Monitoring Poverty and Social Exclusion 2003* (York: Joseph Rowntree Foundation, 2003).

Pease, Edward R., *The History of the Fabian Society*, 3rd edn (London: Cass, 1963).

Pelling, Henry, *A Short History of the Labour Party*, 2nd edn (London: Macmillan, 1965).

——, *Popular Politics and Society in Late Victorian Britain* (London: Macmillan, 1968).

Perkins, Anne, *Red Queen: the authorized biography of Barbara Castle* (London: Macmillan, 2003).

Peston, Robert, *Brown's Britain* (London: Short Books, 2005).

Phillips, Gordon, *The Rise of the Labour Party, 1893–1931* (London: Routledge, 1992).

Pimlott, Ben, *Harold Wilson* (London: HarperCollins, 1992).

Pollard, Sidney, *A History of Labour in Sheffield* (Liverpool: Liverpool University Press, 1959).

——, *The Development of the British Economy 1914–1990*, 4th edn, reprint (London: Arnold, 1997).

Ponting, Clive, *Breach of Promise: Labour in power 1964–1970*, 2nd edn (London: Penguin, 1990).

Powell, W. Raymond, *Keir Hardie in West Ham: "a constituency with a past"* (London: Socialist History Society, 2004).

Prynn, David, "The Clarion Clubs, Rambling and the Holiday Associations in Britain since the 1890s", *Journal of Contemporary History*, 11 (1976).

Pugh, Patricia M., *Educate, Agitate, Organize: 100 years of Fabian Socialism* (London: Methuen, 1984).

Radice, Giles, *Friends and Rivals: Crosland, Jenkins and Healey*, 2nd edn (London: Abacus, 2003).

Rae, John, *Contemporary Socialism*, 2nd edn (London: Swan Sonnenschein, 1891).

Reid, Fred, *Keir Hardie: the making of a socialist* (London: Croom Helm, 1978).

Rentoul, John, *Tony Blair: prime minister*. 2nd edn (London: Time Warner, 2002).

Rodgers, Bill (William T.), *Fourth among Equals* (London: Politico's, 2000).

Rogers, Frederick, *Labour, Life and Literature: some memories of fifty years* (London: Smith, Elder, 1913).

Rowntree, B. Seebohm, *Poverty: a study of town life*, 4th edn (London: Macmillan, 1902).

——, *Poverty and Progress: a second social survey of York* (London: Longmans, Green, 1941).

Rubinstein, David, *School Attendance in London: a social history* (Hull: University of Hull, 1969).

——, "The Independent Labour Party and the Yorkshire Miners: the Barnsley by-election of 1897", *International Review of Social History*, 23 (1978).

——, *A Different World for Women: the life of Millicent Garrett Fawcett* (Hemel Hempstead: Harvester/Wheatsheaf, 1991).

——, "How New is New Labour?" *Political Quarterly*, 68 (1997).

——, "A New Look at New Labour" *Politics*, 20 (2000).

St Helier, Lady (Mary Jeune), *Memories of Fifty Years* (London: Arnold, 1909).

Saville, John, "Trade Unions and Free Labour: the background to the Taff Vale decision", in Asa Briggs and John Saville (eds), *Essays in Labour History: in memory of G. D. H. Cole 25 September 1889–14 January 1959* (London: Macmillan, 1960).

Scott, Derek, *Off Whitehall: a view from Downing Street by Tony Blair's adviser* (London: Tauris, 2004).

Seldon, Anthony, *Blair*, 2nd edn (London: The Free Press, 2005).

Seyd, Patrick, "Factionalism within the Labour Party: the Socialist League 1932–1937", in Asa Briggs and John Saville (eds), *Essays in Labour History 1918–1939* (London: Croom Helm, 1977).

Shadwell, Arthur, *Industrial Efficiency: a comparative study of industrial life in England, Germany and America*, 2nd edn (London: Longmans, Green, 1913).

Shaw, Eric, *Discipline and Discord in the Labour Party: the politics of management control in the Labour Party* (Manchester: Manchester University Press, 1988).

——, *The Labour Party since 1979: crisis and transformation* (London: Routledge, 1994).

——, *The Labour Party since 1945: old Labour, new Labour* (Oxford: Blackwell, 1996).

——, "Michael Foot 1980–83", in Kevin Jefferys (ed.), *Leading Labour: from Keir Hardie to Tony Blair* (London: Tauris, 1999).

Shaw, George Bernard (ed.), *Fabian Essays in Socialism*, reprint (London and Felling-on-Tyne: Walter Scott, 1908).

——, (author) "Transition" in *ibid*.

——, *The Fabian Society: its early history*, Fabian tract 41, reprint (London: Fabian Society, 1899).

——, *Morris as I Knew Him*, reprint (London: William Morris Society, 1966).

[——, and Webb, Sidney], *A Plan of Campaign for Labor* (sic), Fabian tract 49 (London: Fabian Society, 1894).

Shinwell, Emanuel, *Conflict without Malice* (London: Odhams, 1955).

Shore, Peter, *Leading the Left* (London: Weidenfeld & Nicolson, 1993).

Sims, George R., *How the Poor Live* and *Horrible London*, reprint (London: Chatto & Windus, 1889).

Smith, Martin J., "Continuity and Change in Labour Party Policy", in Martin J. Smith and Joanna Spear (eds), *The Changing Labour Party* (London: Routledge, 1992).

Snell, Harry, *Men, Movements, and Myself*, 2nd edn (London: Dent, 1938).

Snowden, Philip, *Socialism and Syndicalism* (London and Glasgow, Collins [1913]).

——, *An Autobiography*, two vols (London: Nicholson & Watson, 1934).

Sopel, John, *Tony Blair: the modernizer*, 2nd edn (London: Bantam, 1995).

Stewart, Michael, *Life and Labour: an autobiography* (London: Sidgwick & Jackson, 1980).

Summerskill, Edith, *A Woman's World* (London: Heinemann, 1967).

Tanner, Duncan, *Political Change and the Labour Party 1900–1918* (Cambridge: Cambridge University Press, 1990).

Taylor, Robert, "Out of the Bowels of the Movement: the trade unions and the origins of the Labour Party 1900–18", in Brian Brivati and Richard Heffernan (eds), *The Labour Party: a centenary history* (Basingstoke and London: Macmillan, 2000).

Tharoor, Shashi, *Nehru: the invention of India* (New Delhi: Penguin Viking, 2003).

Thomas, Gilbert, *Autobiography 1891–1941*(London: Chapman & Hall, 1946).

Thomas, Hugh, *John Strachey* (London: Eyre Methuen, 1973).

Thompson, E. P., "Homage to Tom Maguire", in Asa Briggs and John Saville (eds), *Essays in Labour History: in memory of G. D. H. Cole 25 September 1889–14 January 1959* (London: Macmillan, 1960).

Thompson, Wilfred, *Victor Grayson: his life and work, an appreciation and a criticism* (Sheffield: Bennett, 1910).

Thorne, Will, *My Life's Battles* (London: Newnes, 1925).

Thorpe, Andrew, *The British General Election of 1931* (Oxford: Clarendon Press, 1991).

——, *A History of the British Labour Party* (Basingstoke: Macmillan, 1997).

Tiratsoo, Nick, "Labour and the Electorate", in Duncan Tanner, Pat Thane, Nick Tiratsoo (eds), *Labour's First Century* (Cambridge: Cambridge University Press, 2000).

Tomlinson, Jim, *Democratic Socialism and Economic Policy: the Attlee years 1945–1951* (Cambridge: Cambridge University Press, 1997).

——, "Labour and the Economy", in Duncan Tanner, Pat Thane, Nick Tiratsoo (eds). *Labour's First Century* (Cambridge: Cambridge University Press, 2000).

Trades Union Congress, *Report of the Thirty-Second Annual Trades Union Congress* (Manchester: Co-operative Printing Society Ltd, 1899).

Tsuzuki, Chushichi, *H. M. Hyndman and British Socialism* (London: Oxford University Press, 1961).

Webb, Beatrice, *My Apprenticeship*, 2nd edn, two vols (Harmondsworth: Penguin, 1938).

——, *The Diary of Beatrice Webb*, vol. 2, 1892–1905: "all the good things of *life"*, eds Norman and Jeanne MacKenzie (London: Virago and London School of Economics, 1983.

——, *The Diary of Beatrice Webb*, vol. 3, *1905–1924: "the power to alter things"*, eds Norman and Jeanne MacKenzie (London: Virago and London School of Economics,1984).

——, *The Diary of Beatrice Webb*, vol. 4, *1924–1943: "the wheel of life"*, eds Norman and Jeanne MacKenzie (London: Virago and London School of Economics, 1985).

Webb, Beatrice and Sidney, *Industrial Democracy*, 2nd edn, reprint (London: the authors,1911).

——, *The History of Trade Unionism, 1666–1920* (London: the authors, 1920).

Webb, Sidney, "Historic", in George Bernard Shaw (ed.), *Fabian Essays in Socialism*, reprint (London and Felling on Tyne: Walter Scott, 1908).

Wertheimer, Egon, *Portrait of the Labour Party*, English ed. (London: Putnam, 1929).

Wigg, George, *George Wigg* (London: Joseph, 1992).

Wilkinson, Ellen, *Peeps at Politicians* (London: Allan, 1930).

——, *The Town that was Murdered : the life-story of Jarrow* (London: Gollancz, 1939).

Williams, Philip, *Hugh Gaitskell: a political biography* (London: Cape, 1979).

Williamson, Philip, *National Crisis and National Government: British politics, the economy and empire, 1926–1932* (Cambridge: Cambridge University Press, 1992).

Wilson, Harold, *The Labour Government 1964–1970: a personal record* (London: Weidenfeld & Nicolson, 1971).

Woolf, Virginia, "Mr. Bennett and Mrs. Brown", in V. Woolf, *Collected Essays*, vol. 1 (London: Chatto & Windus, 1966).

Wrigley, Chris, *Arthur Henderson* (Cardiff: GPC Books, 1990).

Wyatt, Woodrow, *Confessions of an Optimist* (London: Collins, 1985).

Ziegler, Philip, *Wilson: the authorized life of Lord Wilson of Rievaulx* (London: Weidenfeld & Nicolson, 1993).

Zweiniger-Bargielowska, Ina, *Austerity in Britain: rationing, controls and consumption 1939–1955* (Oxford: Oxford University Press, 2000).

INDEX